لَبَّیْک

Rafiq-ul-Haramayn

Detailed Method of Hajj & 'Umrah

Shaykh-e-Tariqat, Ameer-e-Ahl-e-Sunnat,
Founder of Dawat-e-Islami, 'Allamah Maulana Abu Bilal

Muhammad Ilyas Attar

Qadiri Razavi دَامَتْ بَرَكَاتُهُمُ الْعَالِيَه

◈

Translated into English by

Majlis-e-Tarajim (Dawat-e-Islami)

An English translation of Rafiq-ul-Haramayn

◆

Edition:	Second
2nd Publication:	Jumādal Ukhrā, 1436 AH (April, 2015)
Publisher:	Maktaba-tul-Madinah
ISBN:	978-969-631-012-9
Quantity:	4000

Maktaba-tul-Madinah

Aalami Madani Markaz, Faizan-e-Madinah Mahallah Saudagran,
Purani Sabzi Mandi, Bab-ul-Madinah, Karachi, Pakistan

Email: maktabaglobal@dawateislami.net – maktaba@dawateislami.net

Phone: +92-21-34921389-93 – 34126999

Web: www.dawateislami.net

اَلۡحَمۡدُ لِلّٰہِ رَبِّ الۡعٰلَمِیۡنَ وَ الصَّلٰوۃُ وَ السَّلَامُ عَلٰی سَیِّدِ الۡمُرۡسَلِیۡنَ

اَمَّا بَعۡدُ فَاَعُوۡذُ بِاللّٰہِ مِنَ الشَّیۡطٰنِ الرَّجِیۡمِ ؕ بِسۡمِ اللّٰہِ الرَّحۡمٰنِ الرَّحِیۡمِ ؕ

Du'ā for Reading the Book

Read the following Du'ā (supplication) before you study a religious book or an Islamic lesson, you will remember whatever you study, اِنۡ شَآءَاللّٰہ عَزَّوَجَلَّ:

اَللّٰھُمَّ افۡتَحۡ عَلَیۡنَا حِکۡمَتَکَ وَانۡشُرۡ

عَلَیۡنَا رَحۡمَتَکَ یَـا ذَا الۡجَلَالِ وَالۡاِکۡرَام

Translation

Yā Allah عَزَّوَجَلَّ! Open the doors of knowledge and wisdom for us, and have mercy on us! O the One who is the most Honourable and Glorious!

(Al-Mustaṭraf, vol. 1, pp. 40)

Note: Recite Ṣalāt-'Alan-Nabī ﷺ once before and after the Du'ā.

Transliteration Chart

ء	A/a	ڑ	Ř/ř	ل	L/l
ا	A/a	ز	Z/z	م	M/m
ب	B/b	ژ	X/x	ن	N/n
پ	P/p	س	S/s	و	V/v, W/w
ت	T/t	ش	Sh/sh		
ٹ	Ṫ/ṫ	ص	Ṣ/ṣ	ھ/ ہ /ۃ	Ĥ/ĥ
ث	Š/š	ض	Ḍ/ḍ	ی	Y/y
ج	J/j	ط	Ṭ/ṭ	ے	Y/y
چ	Ch	ظ	Ẓ/ẓ	◌َ	A/a
ح	Ḥ/ḥ	ع	ʻ	◌ُ	U/u
خ	Kh/kh	غ	Gh/gh	◌ِ	I/i
د	D/d	ف	F/f	و مدّہ	Ū/ū
ڈ	Ḋ/ḋ	ق	Q/q	ی مدّہ	Ī/ī
ذ	Ż/ż	ك	K/k	ا مدّہ	Ā/ā
ر	R/r	گ	G/g		

اَلْحَمْدُ لِلّٰهِ رَبِّ الْعٰلَمِيْنَ وَالصَّلٰوةُ وَالسَّلَامُ عَلٰى سَيِّدِ الْمُرْسَلِيْنَ

اَمَّا بَعْدُ فَاَعُوْذُ بِاللّٰهِ مِنَ الشَّيْطٰنِ الرَّجِيْمِ ط بِسْمِ اللّٰهِ الرَّحْمٰنِ الرَّحِيْمِ ط

Translator's Notes

Dear Islamic brothers! Dawat-e-Islami's Majlis-e-Tarājim, a department responsible for reproducing the books and booklets of Amīr-e-Aĥl-e-Sunnat, the founder of Dawat-e-Islami 'Allāmaĥ Maulānā Abu Bilal Muhammad Ilyas Attar Qadiri Razavi دَامَتْ بَرَكَاتُهُمُ الْعَالِيَه into various languages of the world, is pleased to present the book '*Rafīq-ul-Ḥaramayn*' in English under the title of '*Rafīq-ul-Ḥaramayn*.' Although any translation is inevitably a form of interpretation, we have tried our level best to convey the thought of the author in its true sense. To facilitate the pronunciation of Arabic letters, a transliteration chart has been added. Terms of Islamic Jurisprudence have not been translated as a caution because in most cases, an English word cannot be a full substitute of an Islamic term. However, a glossary has been given at the end of the book, elaborating Islamic terms. Further, an index and a bibliography have also been given.

This translation has been accomplished by the grace of Almighty Allah عَزَّوَجَلَّ, by the favour of His Noble Prophet صَلَّى اللّٰهُ تَعَالٰى عَلَيْهِ وَاٰلِهٖ وَسَلَّم and the spiritual support of our great Shaykh, the founder of Dawat-e-Islami, 'Allāmaĥ Maulānā Abu Bilal Muhammad Ilyas Attar Qadiri Razavi دَامَتْ بَرَكَاتُهُمُ الْعَالِيَه. If there is any shortcoming in this work, it may be a human error on the part of the *Translation Majlis*, not that of the author of the original book. Therefore, if you find any mistake in it, kindly notify us of it in writing at the following postal or email address with the intention of earning reward (Šawāb).

Majlis-e-Tarājim (Translation Department)

Aalami Madani Markaz, Faizan-e-Madinah Mahallah Saudagran,
Purani Sabzi Mandi, Bab-ul-Madinah, Karachi, Pakistan

UAN: ☎ +92-21-111-25-26-92 – Ext. 1262

Email: translation@dawateislami.net

اَلۡحَمۡدُ لِلّٰهِ رَبِّ الۡعٰلَمِيۡنَ وَ الصَّلٰوةُ وَالسَّلَامُ عَلٰى سَيِّدِ الۡمُرۡسَلِيۡنَ
اَمَّا بَعۡدُ فَاَعُوۡذُ بِاللّٰهِ مِنَ الشَّيۡطٰنِ الرَّجِيۡمِ ؕ بِسۡمِ اللّٰهِ الرَّحۡمٰنِ الرَّحِيۡمِ ؕ

56 INTENTIONS

For Pilgrims of Hajj and 'Umraĥ

(Including narrations, parables and Madanī pearls)

(Those going to perform Hajj and 'Umraĥ should make only those intentions which are practicable for them and which they really intend to act upon.)

1. I will perform Hajj solely for the attainment of the pleasure of Allah عَزَّوَجَلَّ.

   (Sincerity is a condition for Hajj being accepted. In order to attain sincerity, it is essential to avoid ostentation and fame. The Holy Prophet صَلَّى اللهُ تَعَالٰى عَلَيْهِ وَاٰلِهٖ وَسَلَّم has stated, 'An era will come upon people when the rich people of my Ummaĥ will perform Hajj for sightseeing, the middle-class for trading, Qurrā[1] for show-off and for reciting (the Holy Quran) to others, and beggars for begging'.) *(Tārīkh Baghdad, vol. 10, pp. 295)*

2. I will act upon this verse:

وَ اَتِمُّوا الۡحَجَّ وَ الۡعُمۡرَةَ لِلّٰهِ ؕ

And complete the Hajj and the 'Umraĥ for the sake of Allah (عَزَّوَجَلَّ).

[Kanz-ul-Īmān (Translation of Quran)] (Part 2, Sūraĥ Al-Baqaraĥ, verse 196)

---

[1] Qurrā are those who are expert in eloquent recitation of the Holy Quran.

3. (Only those performing Farḍ Hajj should make this intention.) With the intention of obeying Allah عَزَّوَجَلَّ, I will get the privilege of acting upon the following Quranic commandment:

وَلِلّٰهِ عَلَى النَّاسِ حِجُّ الْبَيْتِ مَنِ اسْتَطَاعَ اِلَيْهِ سَبِيْلًا ؕ

And for the sake of Allah it is (obligatory) upon the people to perform the Hajj of this House, who are able to reach there.

[Kanz-ul-Īmān (Translation of Quran)] (Part 4, Sūraĥ Āl-e-'Imrān, verse 97)

4. I will perform Hajj following the example of the Beloved and Blessed Prophet صَلَّى اللّٰهُ تَعَالٰى عَلَيْهِ وَاٰلِهٖ وَسَلَّم.

5. I will seek my parents' prior consent. (The wife should get her husband's consent. The debtor who is unable to pay debt should take permission from the creditor. However, if Hajj has been Farḍ, he will have to perform it even if the creditor has not given permission. *(Derived from Bahār-e-Sharī'at, vol. 1, pp. 1051)* One should not travel to perform Nafl Hajj or 'Umraĥ without parents' consent. There is a general misconception that the offspring cannot perform Hajj unless their parents have performed it.)

6. I will meet Hajj-expenses with Ḥalāl earnings. (Otherwise, there is no hope of Hajj being accepted, though Farḍ will get offered. If someone has doubt about his earnings being Ḥalāl, he should borrow money from anyone else and meet Hajj-expenses from the borrowed money and payback the debt by his own earnings. *(ibid)* It is stated in a Ḥadīš, 'When the one who leaves for Hajj with Ḥarām earnings utters Labbayk, a voice from Ghayb replies, 'Neither your Labbayk is accepted nor is your effort acknowledged, and your Hajj is thrown onto your face, unless

you return the Ḥarām earnings that are in your possession to the deserving people'.) *(Fatāwā Razawiyyaĥ, vol. 23, pp. 541)*

7. I will avoid asking for a discount whilst purchasing things for the Hajj pilgrimage. (A'lā Ḥaḍrat Imām Aḥmad Razā Khān عَلَيْهِ رَحْمَةُ الرَّحْمٰن has stated, 'It is better as well as a Sunnaĥ to argue for discount whilst purchasing things except the ones purchased for Hajj-pilgrimage. It is better to pay what the seller demands whilst making purchases for this pilgrimage.)

   (Fatāwā Razawiyyaĥ, vol. 17, pp. 128)

8. At the time of departure, I will seek forgiveness from my family members, relatives and friends regarding their rights I have violated. I will make them pray for me. {One attains blessings when others pray for him. The prayer made by others for a person is more likely to be answered.

   On page 111 of '*Blessings of Du'ā*' [the 326-page publication of Maktaba-tul-Madīnaĥ, the publishing department of Dawat-e-Islami], it is stated: Sayyidunā Mūsā عَلٰى نَبِيِّنَا وَعَلَيْهِ الصَّلٰوةُ وَالسَّلَام was told, 'O Mūsā! Make Du'ā to Me with the tongue with which you have not committed any sin.' Sayyidunā Mūsā عَلٰى نَبِيِّنَا وَعَلَيْهِ الصَّلٰوةُ وَالسَّلَام said, 'Almighty! Where should I bring such a tongue from?' (Note that this is the humbleness of Sayyidunā Mūsā عَلٰى نَبِيِّنَا وَعَلَيْهِ الصَّلٰوةُ وَالسَّلَام because every Prophet عَلَيْهِ السَّلَام is absolutely secured from committing any sin.) Allah عَزَّوَجَلَّ said, 'Make others pray for you as you have not committed any sin with their tongue.'}

   (Derived from Mašnawī Maulānā Rūm, Duftar Sawm, pp. 31)

9. I will take extra provisions and earn reward by spending them on my companions and by donating them to deserving beggars as charity. (To do so is a sign of Hajj Mabrūr.) A Mabrūr Hajj and 'Umraĥ are the ones that contain righteousness and goodness,

and are free from sin and show-off. The things that make a Hajj Mabrūr include doing people favour, serving them with meals, talking to them softly, saying Salām to them and treating them politely. Therefore, one should take extra provisions so that he could assist his companions and give charity to beggars. In fact, the word 'مَبْرُوْر (Mabrūr)' is derived from the word 'بِر (Bir)' which means righteousness and favour by which one attains the closeness of Allah عَزَّوَجَلَّ. *(Kitāb-ul-Hajj, pp. 98)*

10. I will protect my tongue and eyes etc. from using them unlawfully. (A Ḥadīš is stated on pages 29 and 30 of the book '*Naṣīḥataun kay Madanī Pĥūl*'. Allah عَزَّوَجَلَّ has said: O son of Ādam! Your Dīn (religion) cannot be perfect unless your tongue is straight, and your tongue cannot be straight unless you have shyness from your Rab عَزَّوَجَلَّ. Another Ḥadīš states: The one who lowers his eyes from the things declared Ḥarām by Me (i.e. the one who avoided seeing them), I will bless him with shelter from Hell.)

11. During the journey, I will remain busy remembering Allah عَزَّوَجَلَّ and reciting Ṣalāt-'Alan-Nabī. (An angel accompanies the one who does so, whereas a satan accompanies the one who listens to songs or indulges in useless gossip.)

12. I will make Du'ā for myself and for all Muslims. (The Du'ā made by a traveller is accepted. It is also stated on page 220 of the book '*Blessings of Du'ā*': The Du'ā made by a Muslim for his fellow Muslim in his absence is accepted. It is stated in a Ḥadīš, 'This Du'ā (made for a Muslim in his absence) is accepted very quickly. Angels say, 'The Du'ā you have made for him will be accepted and you will also get a similar favour.')

13. I will talk politely to everyone, and will serve Muslims with meals as much as I can afford. {The Beloved Prophet صَلَّى اللهُ تَعَالٰى عَلَيْهِ وَاٰلِهٖ وَسَلَّم has said: Paradise is the reward for Hajj Mabrūr. He was asked, 'Yā Rasūlallāĥ صَلَّى اللهُ تَعَالٰى عَلَيْهِ وَاٰلِهٖ وَسَلَّم! What makes a Hajj Mabrūr?' He صَلَّى اللهُ تَعَالٰى عَلَيْهِ وَاٰلِهٖ وَسَلَّم replied, 'Polite talking and serving meal (to others).'} *(Shu'ab-ul-Īmān, vol. 3, pp. 479, Ḥadīš 4119)*

14. If I face difficulties, I will show patience. (Ḥujjat-ul-Islam Sayyidunā Imām Abū Ḥāmid Muhammad Bin Muhammad Bin Muhammad Ghazālī عَلَيْهِ رَحْمَةُ اللّٰهِ الْوَالِی has stated: If a Ḥājī suffers a loss or gets into a trouble as regards his wealth or body, he should show patience as it is a sign of Hajj Mabrūr.) *(Iḥyā-ul-'Ulūm, vol. 1, pp. 354)*

15. Behaving in a polite manner, I will serve my companions. I will avoid anger and useless talking. If people said hurtful things, I will tolerate them.

16. I will treat all the orthodox Arab Muslims politely (no matter how harshly they treat me). (On page 1060 of *Bahār-e-Sharī'at*, volume 1, part 6, it is stated: Treat all the Arabs including the Bedouins with extreme politeness. Even if they behave you harshly, endure it with patience. Our Beloved and Blessed Prophet صَلَّى اللهُ تَعَالٰى عَلَيْهِ وَاٰلِهٖ وَسَلَّم has promised to intercede for the one displaying patience in response to the harshness of the Arabs. Do not criticize the acts of the dwellers of Makkaĥ and Madīnaĥ and those of any other Arab. Do not even think ill of them in your heart as this is beneficial in the worldly life as well as in the afterlife.)

17. I will be careful not to cause trouble to people even at crowded places. If anyone causes me trouble, I will have patience and forgive him. {It is stated in a Ḥadīš that if a person holds back his anger, Allah عَزَّوَجَلَّ will prevent torment (from being inflicted

on) him on the Day of Judgement.} *(Shu'ab-ul-Īmān, vol. 6, pp. 315, Ḥadīš 8311)*

18. I will earn reward by inviting the Muslims towards righteousness making individual effort.

19. As long as possible, I will act upon the Sunnaĥs of journey conforming to its rulings and manners.

20. Whilst in the state of Iḥrām, I will frequently recite Labbayk. (Islamic brothers should recite it loudly while Islamic sisters should recite it quietly.)

21. Whilst entering the blessed Masjid-ul-Ḥarām and Masjid-un-Nabawī, I will place right foot first into the Masjid and recite the Du'ā of entering the Masjid. Similarly, whilst exiting the Masjid, I will place my left foot first out and recite the Du'ā of exiting the Masjid. (I will also conform to these manners whilst entering and exiting any Masjid.)

22. Whenever I enter the blessed Masjid-ul-Ḥarām and Masjid-un-Nabawī, I will make the intention of Nafl I'tikāf, earning reward. (Remember that eating something including Saḥarī and Ifṭār, drinking water and even Zam Zam water, and sleeping are all impermissible in Masjid. If you have made the intention of I'tikāf, these acts will become permissible.)

23. As soon as I have my first glance at the Holy Ka'baĥ, I will recite Ṣalāt-'Alan-Nabī and make Du'ā.

24. During Ṭawāf, I will make Du'ā for my forgiveness and that of the entire Ummaĥ at Mustajāb (where 70,000 angels are present to say Āmīn to Du'ā).

25. Whenever I drink Zam Zam water, I will drink it to my full stomach sucking it in three sips having recited بِسْمِ اللّٰه whilst standing facing the Qiblaĥ with the intention of acting upon Sunnaĥ. I will then make Du'ā as it is an occasion of the acceptance of Du'ā. (The Holy Prophet صَلَّى اللهُ تَعَالٰى عَلَيْهِ وَاٰلِهٖ وَسَلَّم has stated, 'The difference between us and the hypocrites is that they do not drink Zam Zam to their full stomach.')

(Ibn Mājaĥ, vol. 3, pp 489, Ḥadīš 3061)

26. Whilst clinging onto Multazam out of love and devotion, I will make the intention of attaining the closeness of Ka'baĥ and its Creator عَزَّوَجَلَّ and gaining blessings from it. (Do this with the hope that every such part of my body that is touching the blessed Ka'baĥ will be freed from Hell, اِنْ شَآءَاللّٰه عَزَّوَجَلَّ.)

27. Whilst clinging onto the cover of the blessed Ka'baĥ, I will make the intention as if I am imploring Allah عَزَّوَجَلَّ for forgiveness and protection like the one who implores a person feeling guilty of his crime and holding that person's dress with extreme humility, and continues to do so unless he is forgiven and granted protection in future. (People apply fragrance onto the cover of the blessed Ka'baĥ; therefore take care in the state of Iḥrām.)

28. Whilst performing Ramī of Jamarāt, I will make the intention of following the example of Sayyidunā Ibrāĥīm Khalīlullāĥ عَلٰى نَبِيِّنَا وَعَلَيْهِ الصَّلٰوةُ وَالسَّلَام, acting upon the Sunnaĥ of Noble Prophet صَلَّى اللهُ تَعَالٰى عَلَيْهِ وَاٰلِهٖ وَسَلَّم, disgracing and driving off satan and that of stoning desires of Nafs.

Parable: Sayyidunā Junayd Baghdādī عَلَيْهِ رَحْمَةُ اللّٰهِ الْهَادِى asked a Ḥājī whether he stoned his desires of Nafs or not whilst performing Ramī. He replied in the negative. Sayyidunā Junayd Baghdādī عَلَيْهِ رَحْمَةُ اللّٰهِ الْهَادِى said, 'You did not perform Ramī.' (That is, you did not perform it as it should be performed.) *(Derived from Kashf-ul-Mahjūb, pp. 363)*

29. The Beloved and Blessed Prophet صَلَّى اللهُ تَعَالٰى عَلَيْهِ وَاٰلِهٖ وَسَلَّم particularly stayed at six places for Du'ā i.e. Ṣafā, Marwah, 'Arafāt, Muzdalifah, Jamra-tul-Aūlā and Jamra-tul-Wusṭā. With the intention of following the example of the Beloved and Blessed Prophet صَلَّى اللهُ تَعَالٰى عَلَيْهِ وَاٰلِهٖ وَسَلَّم, I will also be staying and making Du'ā at these places, wherever possible.

30. During Ṭawāf and Sa'ī, I will avoid pushing and shoving people. (To deliberately shove someone causing discomfort to him is the violation of his rights and a sin. The one who has done so will have to repent of it and seek forgiveness from the one he has caused discomfort to. Islamic saints have narrated, 'To give up even the smallest of deeds disliked by Allah عَزَّوَجَلَّ is dearer to me than to perform 500 Nafl Hajj.')

(Jāmi'-ul-'Ulūm wal-Ḥukm li-Ibn Rajab, pp. 125)

31. I will attain blessings by keeping the company of the scholars and saints of Aĥl-us-Sunnaĥ and by beholding them. I will also request them to make Du'ā for my forgiveness without accountability.

32. I will perform worship in abundance. Particularly I will offer five times daily Ṣalāĥ regularly.

33. I repent of my sins forever and will keep the company of the righteous only. (It is stated in *Iḥyā-ul-'Ulūm* that a sign of Hajj Mabrūr is that the Ḥājī should give up the sins he used to commit, stay away from wicked friends, form friendship with righteous people, give up the gatherings of useless activities and heedlessness and attend the gatherings of the righteous. Imām

Ghazālī عَلَيْهِ رَحْمَةُ اللّٰهِ الْوَالِى has further stated: Another sign of Hajj Mabrūr is that the Ḥājī should lose his interest in the world and focus on the preparations of the afterlife. After he has seen the Ka'baĥ, he should now remain busy making preparation to meet Allah عَزَّوَجَلَّ.) *(Iḥyā-ul-'Ulūm, vol. 1, pp. 349, 354)*

34. After returning from Hajj, I will avoid sins completely, perform good deeds in abundance and act upon Sunnaĥ even more enthusiastically. {A'lā Ḥaḍrat رَحْمَةُ اللّٰهِ تَعَالٰى عَلَيْه has stated: If a Ḥājī who had not fulfilled the rights of Allah عَزَّوَجَلَّ and those of people before Hajj did not fulfill these rights even after Hajj despite being able to fulfill them – (for example, he did not offer missed Ṣalāĥ and fasts, did not pay previously unpaid Zakāĥ and did not fulfill violated rights of people), the burden of all of these sins will be on his back once again as these unfulfilled rights will not be considered fulfilled merely because of Hajj, and delay in their fulfilment would renew these sins. Hajj removes previous sins and is not a letter of freedom to commit sins in future. The sign of Hajj Mabrūr is that the Ḥājī should be more righteous compared to his pre-Hajj state.}

(Fatāwā Razawiyyaĥ, vol. 24, pp. 466)

35. I will visit the holy places of Makka-tul-Mukarramaĥ and Madīna-tul-Munawwaraĥ زَادَهُمَا اللّٰهُ شَرَفًا وَّتَعْظِيْمًا.

36. I will see the holy city of Madīna-tul-Munawwaraĥ زَادَهَا اللّٰهُ شَرَفًا وَّتَعْظِيْمًا with the intention of gaining reward considering it a privilege.

37. Before I humbly make my first visit to the blessed court of the Holy Prophet صَلَّى اللّٰهُ تَعَالٰى عَلَيْهِ وَاٰلِهٖ وَسَلَّم, I will take a bath, wear a new white dress, a new head-cloth, a new cap and a new turban. I will also apply kohl into my eyes and nice fragrance to my dress.

38. I will humbly attend the court of the Prophet of Raḥmaĥ, the Intercessor of Ummaĥ صَلَّى اللهُ تَعَالٰى عَلَيْهِ وَاٰلِهٖ وَسَلَّم acting upon the following commandment of Allah عَزَّوَجَلَّ:

وَلَوْ اَنَّهُمْ اِذْ ظَّلَمُوْٓا اَنْفُسَهُمْ جَآءُوْكَ

فَاسْتَغْفَرُوا اللّٰهَ وَ اسْتَغْفَرَ لَهُمُ الرَّسُوْلُ لَوَجَدُوا اللّٰهَ تَوَّابًا رَّحِيْمًا ﴿۶۴﴾

And if when they do injustice to their souls, then O Beloved! They should come to you and then beg Allah (عَزَّوَجَلَّ) for forgiveness, and the Prophet should intercede for them, then surely, they will find Allah (عَزَّوَجَلَّ) the One who accepts repentance the most, the Merciful.

[Kanz-ul-Īmān (Translation of Quran)] (Part 5, Sūraĥ An-Nisā, verse 64)

39. If possible, I will humbly attend the court of my Beloved Prophet صَلَّى اللهُ تَعَالٰى عَلَيْهِ وَاٰلِهٖ وَسَلَّم like an escaped slave who trembles and sheds tears when returning to the court of his master.

(**Parable:** Whenever Sayyidunā Imām Mālik عَلَيْهِ رَحْمَةُ اللهِ الْخَالِق talked about the Holy Prophet صَلَّى اللهُ تَعَالٰى عَلَيْهِ وَاٰلِهٖ وَسَلَّم the colour of his face would change and he would bow down in respect. **Parable:** Someone asked Sayyidunā Imām Mālik عَلَيْهِ رَحْمَةُ اللهِ الْخَالِق about Sayyidunā Ayyūb Sakhtiyānī قُدِّسَ سِرُّهُ الرَّبَّانِي. Imām Mālik عَلَيْهِ رَحْمَةُ اللهِ الْخَالِق replied, 'He is the best of all narrators I narrate Aḥādīš from. I saw him two times during Hajj-pilgrimage. Whenever someone mentioned the Beloved and Blessed Prophet صَلَّى اللهُ تَعَالٰى عَلَيْهِ وَاٰلِهٖ وَسَلَّم in his presence, he would weep so bitterly that I would feel pity for him. Impressed by his reverence and devotion to the Holy Prophet صَلَّى اللهُ تَعَالٰى عَلَيْهِ وَاٰلِهٖ وَسَلَّم I started narrating Aḥādīš from him.) *(Ash-Shifā, vol. 2, pp. 41, 42)*

40. I will present my Salām in the blessed court of the Holy Prophet صَلَّى اللهُ تَعَالٰى عَلَيْهِ وَاٰلِهٖ وَسَلَّم with respect, honour and devotion in a soft voice with humility.

41. I will keep my voice rather low acting upon the Quranic commandment:

يٰۤاَيُّهَا الَّذِيْنَ اٰمَنُوْا لَا تَرْفَعُوْۤا اَصْوَاتَكُمْ فَوْقَ صَوْتِ النَّبِيِّ وَلَا تَجْهَرُوْا لَهٗ بِالْقَوْلِ كَجَهْرِ بَعْضِكُمْ لِبَعْضٍ اَنْ تَحْبَطَ اَعْمَالُكُمْ وَاَنْتُمْ لَا تَشْعُرُوْنَ ﴿۲﴾

O those who believe! Do not raise your voices over the voice of the one (the Holy Prophet) who reveals Ghayb, nor speak loudly in his presence the way you shout to one another, lest your deeds end in vain, whilst you are unaware.

[Kanz-ul-Īmān (Translation of Quran)] (Part 26, Sūraĥ Al-Ḥujurāt, verse 2)

42. I will beg for intercession by repeatedly uttering

اَسْئَلُكَ الشَّفَاعَةَ يَا رَسُوْلَ اللهِ

(Yā Rasūlallāĥ صَلَّى اللهُ تَعَالٰى عَلَيْهِ وَاٰلِهٖ وَسَلَّم! I beg you for intercession).

43. I will also present my Salām in the blessed courts of Sayyidunā Abū Bakr Ṣiddīq and Sayyidunā Fārūq A'ẓam رَضِىَ اللّٰهُ تَعَالٰى عَنْهُمَا.

44. Whilst present in the blessed courts, I will avoid looking here and there and peeping into the Golden Grilles.

45. I will present the Salām of the people who have requested me to do so in the court of the Prophet of Raḥmaĥ, the Intercessor of Ummaĥ صَلَّى اللهُ تَعَالٰى عَلَيْهِ وَاٰلِهٖ وَسَلَّم.

46. I will not turn my back on the Golden Grilles.

47. I will present Salām to those buried in Jannat-ul-Baqī'.

48. I will humbly visit the shrines of Sayyidunā Ḥamzah رَضِیَ اللّٰہُ تَعَالٰی عَنۡہُ and martyrs of the Uḥud battle. I will make Du'ā and Īṣāl-e-Šawāb, and will behold the mount Uḥud.

49. I will humbly attend the Qubā Masjid.

50. I will respect each and every thing of Madīnaĥ, even its doors and walls, fruits and leaves, flowers and thorns and stones and dust. (**Parable:** Sayyidunā Imām Mālik عَلَیْہِ رَحْمَۃُ اللّٰہِ الْخَالِق never defecated in Madīnaĥ زَادَھَا اللّٰہُ شَرَفًا وَّ تَعْظِیْمًا in respect of its soil. He would go out of Ḥaram for this. However, he was unable to go out of Ḥaram when severely ill.) *(Bistān-ul-Muḥaddiśīn, pp. 19)*

51. I will not find fault with anything of Madīna-tul-Munawwaraĥ زَادَھَا اللّٰہُ شَرَفًا وَّ تَعْظِیْمًا. (**Parable:** In Madīna-tul-Munawwaraĥ زَادَھَا اللّٰہُ شَرَفًا وَّ تَعْظِیْمًا, there was a person who would always weep and seek forgiveness. When asked about it, he replied, 'Once I said that the blessed curd of Madīna-tul-Munawwaraĥ زَادَھَا اللّٰہُ شَرَفًا وَّ تَعْظِیْمًا was sour and tasteless. As soon as I said this, I was deprived of my spiritual attachment and was rebuked in these words, 'O the one who has said that the curd of Madīnaĥ is sour and tasteless! See with the eyes of a devotee! Each and every thing of the street of the Beloved is nice and great.' *(Derived from Baĥār-e-Mašnawī, pp. 128)*

Parable: In the presence of Sayyidunā Imām Mālik عَلَیْہِ رَحْمَۃُ اللّٰہِ الْخَالِق, someone said that the soil of Madīnaĥ was bad. Listening to this, he gave the Fatwā that the impudent person be given 30 lashes and be imprisoned.) *(Ash-Shifā, vol. 2, pp. 57)*

52. In order to give gifts to my relatives and Islamic brothers, I will bring Zam Zam water, dates of Madīna-tul-Munawwaraĥ زَادَھَا اللّٰہُ شَرَفًا وَّ تَعْظِیْمًا and simple inexpensive rosaries.

(A'lā Ḥaḍrat رَحْمَةُ اللّٰهِ تَعَالٰی عَلَیْه was asked the following question: What should a rosary be made up of? Wood or stone etc? He رَحْمَةُ اللّٰهِ تَعَالٰی عَلَیْه replied, 'Whether a rosary is made up of wood or stone, it is permissible, but it should not be expensive as it is Makrūĥ. If it is made up of silver or gold, it is Ḥarām).

(Fatāwā Razawiyyaĥ, vol. 23, pp. 597)

53. I will recite Ṣalāt-'Alan-Nabī in abundance during my stay in Madīna-tul-Munawwaraĥ زَادَهَا اللّٰهُ شَرَفًا وَّ تَعْظِيْمًا.

54. During my stay in Madīna-tul-Munawwaraĥ زَادَهَا اللّٰهُ شَرَفًا وَّ تَعْظِيْمًا, whenever I pass by the Grand Green Dome, I will immediately turn towards it and will recite Ṣalāt-'Alan-Nabī whilst standing with my hands folded out of respect.

(**Parable:** In Madīna-tul-Munawwaraĥ زَادَهَا اللّٰهُ شَرَفًا وَّ تَعْظِيْمًا, a person came to Sayyidunā Abū Ḥāzim رَحْمَةُ اللّٰهِ تَعَالٰی عَلَیْه and told him that he saw the Holy Prophet صَلَّى اللّٰهُ تَعَالٰی عَلَيْهِ وَاٰلِهٖ وَسَلَّم in his dream. The Beloved and Blessed Prophet صَلَّى اللّٰهُ تَعَالٰی عَلَيْهِ وَاٰلِهٖ وَسَلَّم said, 'Tell it to Abū Ḥāzim! You pass by me even without stopping to say Salām to me.' Since then, whenever Sayyidunā Abū Ḥāzim رَحْمَةُ اللّٰهِ تَعَالٰی عَلَیْه passed by the blessed tomb, he would present Salām whilst standing with respect).

(Al-Manāmāt ma' Mawsū'aĥ Ibn Abid Dunyā, vol. 3, pp. 153, Ḥadīš 323)

55. If I am not blessed with burial in Jannat-ul-Baqī' and the heartrending moment of departure from Madīna-tul-Munawwaraĥ زَادَهَا اللّٰهُ شَرَفًا وَّ تَعْظِيْمًا approaches, I will make my farewell visit to the blessed court of the Holy Prophet صَلَّى اللّٰهُ تَعَالٰی عَلَيْهِ وَاٰلِهٖ وَسَلَّم and will plead tearfully for visits to Madīnaĥ again and again.

56. If possible, I will leave like a child who is being separated from his loving mother, crying and looking at the blessed court with wistful eyes.

اَلۡحَمۡدُ لِلّٰہِ رَبِّ الۡعٰلَمِیۡنَ وَ الصَّلٰوۃُ وَالسَّلَامُ عَلٰی سَیِّدِ الۡمُرۡسَلِیۡنَ

اَمَّا بَعۡدُ فَاَعُوۡذُ بِاللّٰہِ مِنَ الشَّیۡطٰنِ الرَّجِیۡمِ ؕ بِسۡمِ اللّٰہِ الرَّحۡمٰنِ الرَّحِیۡمِ ؕ

Congratulations for Your Intention of Visiting Madīna-tul-Munawwaraĥ!

The Noble Prophet صَلَّى اللهُ تَعَالٰى عَلَيْهِ وَاٰلِهٖ وَسَلَّم has said, 'It is Farḍ upon every Muslim to seek knowledge.' *(Ibn Mājaĥ, vol. 1, pp. 146, Ḥadīš 224)* In the exegesis of the foregoing Ḥadīš, it is stated that the one for whom Hajj has become Farḍ, it is also Farḍ for him to seek enough knowledge by which he can perform Hajj correctly. Usually people are more interested in learning Du'ās recited during Ṭawāf and Sa'ī, etc. No doubt, this is a good thing provided one can recite them correctly. However, if one doesn't recite these Du'ās, he will not be a sinner but if he does not acquire the knowledge of important rulings of Hajj, he will be a sinner.

Rafīq-ul-Ḥaramayn will help you refrain from a great deal of sins. In some Urdu books on Hajj distributed for free, extreme carelessness has been observed in Shar'ī rulings. This raises the concern that the Ḥujjāj receiving guidance from those books are prone to commit major mistakes.

اَلْحَمْدُ لِلّٰه عَزَّوَجَلَّ, *Rafīq-ul-Ḥaramayn* has been published for many years in millions. Extracted from authentic books like *Fatāwā Razawiyyaĥ* and *Bahār-e-Sharī'at*, most of the rulings contained in it are stated in an easily understandable way. Some amendments and additions have also been made. Dawat-e-Islami's Majlis 'Al-Madīna-tul-'Ilmiyyaĥ' has reviewed it and Dār-ul-Iftā Aĥl-e-Sunnat has scrutinized each and every ruling mentioned in it, providing useful guidance on its completion. اَلْحَمْدُ لِلّٰه عَزَّوَجَلَّ, *Rafīq-ul-Ḥaramayn* has been brought out with many good intentions. By Allah عَزَّوَجَلَّ! The publication of this book is only aimed at gaining the pleasure of Allah عَزَّوَجَلَّ by guiding the pilgrims to Madīnaĥ without any intent to obtain any worldly or monetary benefit. Although satan will be trying his utmost to make you feel lazy, do study this book in its entirety without losing courage.

Pay close attention to the rulings mentioned. If you don't understand them, ask the scholars of Aĥl-us-Sunnaĥ. اَلْحَمْدُلِلّٰه عَزَّوَجَلَّ! Many rulings are mentioned in *Rafīq-ul-Ḥaramayn* regarding Hajj and 'Umraĥ, including the Arabic Du'ās with their translations. If you take *Rafīq-ul-Ḥaramayn* with you during this blessed journey to Madīnaĥ, you will hardly need any other book of Hajj, اِنْ شَآءَالله عَزَّوَجَلَّ. However, if you want to learn even more rulings; study part 6 of *Baĥār-e-Sharī'at.*

Madanī request: If possible, buy 12 *Rafīq-ul-Ḥaramayn*, 12 pocket-sized booklets on any topic and 12 VCDs of Sunnaĥ-Inspiring speeches from Maktaba-tul-Madīnaĥ and distribute them among Muslims in Makkaĥ or Madīnaĥ with the intention of reaping reward. Before you return to your country, gift your own *Rafīq-ul-Ḥaramayn* to any Islamic brother of Ḥaramayn Ṭayyibayn with the intention of earning reward.

Please present my Salām in the courts of the Beloved Prophet صَلَّى اللّٰهُ تَعَالٰى عَلَيْهِ وَاٰلِهٖ وَسَلَّم, Shaykhayn Karīmayn رَضِىَ اللّٰهُ تَعَالٰى عَنْهُمَا, Sayyidunā Ḥamzaĥ رَضِىَ اللّٰهُ تَعَالٰى عَنْهُ, martyrs of Uḥud and those buried in Baqī' and Ma'lā. It is a Madanī request that you pray during the journey for the forgiveness of mine without accountability and that of the entire Muslim Ummaĥ. May Allah عَزَّوَجَلَّ make it easy for you to perform Hajj and visit Madīnaĥ, and accept your efforts in His blessed court!

اٰمِيْن بِجَاهِ النَّبِيِّ الْاَمِيْن صَلَّى اللّٰهُ تَعَالٰى عَلَيْهِ وَاٰلِهٖ وَسَلَّم

Muhammad Ilyas 'Attar Qadiri

اَلۡحَمۡدُ لِلّٰهِ رَبِّ الۡعٰلَمِيۡنَ وَ الصَّلٰوةُ وَالسَّلَامُ عَلٰى سَيِّدِ الۡمُرۡسَلِيۡنَ

اَمَّا بَعۡدُ فَاَعُوۡذُ بِاللّٰهِ مِنَ الشَّيۡطٰنِ الرَّجِيۡمِ ؕ بِسۡمِ اللّٰهِ الرَّحۡمٰنِ الرَّحِيۡمِ ؕ

Rafiq-ul-Haramayn

Travellers of Madīnaĥ and help from Mustafa ﷺ

A young man was seen reciting only Ṣalāt-'Alan-Nabī during Ṭawāf. Someone said to him, 'Do you not know the supplication of Ṭawāf or if there is any other reason? He replied, 'I can recite other supplications but there is a particular reason for reciting Ṣalāt-'Alan-Nabī only.' Explaining the matter in some detail, he said, 'My father and I left for Makka-tul-Mukarramaĥ to perform Hajj. During the journey, my father fell severely ill and passed away. After a while, the face of my father turned black and his belly swelled. I wept a lot and said, اِنَّا لِلّٰهِ وَ اِنَّآ اِلَيۡهِ رٰجِعُوۡنَ.

When the night fell, I slept. When I was asleep, I saw a dream in which I beheld a beautiful and fragrant personality dressed in white attire. Approaching my deceased father, he stroked his refulgent hand onto the face and belly of my father. In no time, the face of my deceased father became brighter and whiter than milk and his belly also normalized.

When he began to leave, I said, 'Your Eminence! For the sake of the One Who has sent you as a mercy for my father in this deserted place, let me know who you are.' He replied, 'Don't you recognize me? I am Allah's Prophet Muhammad (صَلَّى اللهُ تَعَالٰى عَلَيۡهِ وَاٰلِهٖ وَسَلَّم). Your father was a great sinner, but he would recite Ṣalāt upon me in abundance. When he got into this trouble, he pleaded to me. Therefore, I have come to help him. I help every such person who recites Ṣalāt abundantly upon me in the world.' *(Rauḍ-ur-Riyāḥīn, pp. 125)*

صَلُّوْا عَلَى الْحَبِيْب صَلَّى اللهُ تَعَالٰى عَلٰى مُحَمَّد

16 Useful Madanī pearls for Ḥujjāj

1. O beloved Ḥujjāj seeking the pleasure of Allah عَزَّوَجَلَّ and His Prophet صَلَّى اللهُ تَعَالٰى عَلَيْهِ وَاٰلِهٖ وَسَلَّم! Congratulations to you on pilgrimage of Hajj and Madīnaĥ. Ensure that your provisions for this journey are ready at least 3 to 4 days before departure. It is also beneficial to seek guidance from some experienced Ḥājī.

2. Ḥujjāj are not allowed by authorities to carry with them fruits, cooked food, sweet-meats etc.

3. Ḥujjāj have to walk to Masjid-ul-Ḥarām from their accommodation besides performing Ṭawāf and Sa'ī on foot. As a whole, they will have to walk almost 7 kilometres. In addition, they will also have to walk a lot in Minā, 'Arafāt and Muzdalifaĥ. Therefore, it is advisable for Ḥujjāj to make a habit of walking 45 minutes daily long before Hajj. Otherwise, they may get into trouble as a result of walking a lot during Hajj. (To walk 45 minutes a day is also very beneficial from medical point of view.)

4. Make a habit of eating less, and you will see its benefit for yourself. Stick to a strict diet particularly during the five days of Hajj so that you would not need to go to the toilet over and over again. There are long queues for the toilets in Minā, Muzdalifaĥ and 'Arafāt.

5. When performing Ṭawāf Islamic sisters should not wear bangles made of glass as these types of bangles may break during Ṭawāf and injure them and others.

6. Islamic sisters should not wear high-heeled slippers as this would cause difficulty in walking.

7. Commodes are installed in the bathrooms of Makkaĥ and Madīnaĥ. It is advisable to learn in your country how to use them; otherwise, it would be very difficult to keep your clothes clean.

8. Never carry with you anyone's packet unless you have opened and checked it, otherwise you may get into trouble at the airport if the packet contains anything illegal or impermissible.

9. Keep your necessary medicines along with prescription in your bag hung around your neck so that you would avoid difficulty in case of emergency.

10. Apply the Madanī guard to your tongue and eyes. If you have the habit of unnecessary talking, it will be extremely difficult to avoid backbiting, accusations and hurting others. Similarly, if you do not keep your eyes in control, it will be extremely difficult to refrain from unlawful gazing. Therefore, keep them lowered. As a good deed performed in Ḥaram is equivalent to a hundred thousand good deeds, a sin committed in Ḥaram is also equivalent to a hundred thousand sins. Ḥaram includes not only Masjid-ul-Ḥarām but also all limits of Ḥaram.

11. During Ṣalāĥ, some part of the Muḥrim's chest or abdomen is exposed. There is no harm in it because it is normal and acceptable in the state of Iḥrām. To be cautious about this matter is also very difficult.

12. To bring a shroud to one's country after it was soaked in Zam Zam water is better as the winds of Makkah̄ and Madīnah̄ will also kiss the shroud. When squeezing the shroud, ensure that not even a single drop of water goes into the drain. Squeeze the water onto some plant etc. (One can also sprinkle Zam Zam water over the shroud in his country.)

13. When performing Ṭawāf or Sa'ī, the pages of Hajj books are sometimes found lying on the ground. Pick them up, if possible. However, ensure that your back or chest should not face the Ka'bah̄ during the Ṭawāf. Do not pick up someone's money or wallet lying on the ground. (Some years ago, a Ḥājī from Pakistan found someone's money lying on the ground, so he picked it up to return it to its owner but the owner suspected him and handed him over to the police. Eventually, he was imprisoned for a long time.)

14. It is good to remain barefooted in Ḥijāz Muqaddas but wear slippers before entering toilets and when there is mud on the way. Do not enter any Masjid with dirty feet. Take special care before you enter both the sacred Masājid. Wear slippers if you cannot maintain cleanliness.

15. Avoid wearing used slippers when making Wuḍū at a washbasin because water is often spread over the floor near the washbasin. During Wuḍū, drops of water will fall on the floor causing the splashes of water to come onto your clothes etc. If the slippers are unclean, there is the risk of unclean splashes coming onto clothes. (Keep it in mind that slippers, water or anything else will be considered clean unless it is known for sure that they are unclean.)

16. Usually the flow of water is high in the toilets of Minā, so open the tap slowly to remain safe from the splashes of water.

List of items for pilgrims

1. Madanī Panj Sūraĥ
2. Shajaraĥ of your Murshid
3. Take with you and read the book entitled '*Rafīq-ul-Ḥaramayn*' and sixth volume of '*Baĥār-e-Sharī'at*'. Distribute twelve copies of *Rafīq-ul-Ḥaramayn* among Ḥujjāj and reap reward.
4. Pen and pad (5. Diary
6. Compass (buy it in Ḥijāz; it would help you locate the direction of Qiblaĥ in Minā, 'Arafāt etc.)
7. A small pouch to be hung around the neck for keeping books, traveller's cheques, passport, health certificate, ticket etc.
8. Iḥrām
9. Pocket belt made up of nylon or leather to be tied around Taĥband of Iḥrām.
10. 'Iṭr (perfume) (11. Prayer mat (12. Rosary
13. Clothes as per requirement (according to the weather conditions)
14. A shawl or blanket for covering the body
15. Pillow
16. 'Imāmaĥ (turban) with head-cloth and cap
17. Mat or cloth to be laid on the ground
18. It is Sunnaĥ to carry these things during a journey: mirror, oil, comb, Miswāk, kohl, sewing needle, thread and scissors.
19. Nail cutter
20. A marker pen for writing the name and address on luggage.
21. Towel (22. Kerchief

23. Two pairs of spectacles (if you use).

24. Soap (25. Tooth powder (26. Safety razor (27. Ewer

28. Glass (29. Plate (30. Cup (31. Dining mat

32. Water bottle that can be hung around the neck.

33. Spoon (34. Kitchen knife

35. Pills for headache, cold etc. Moreover, take the medicines you need.

36. Water sprayer to spray water over the face and the body when it is hot (as it is extremely hot in Minā and 'Arafāt).

37. Necessary cooking utensils

5 Madanī pearls for luggage

1. A strong hand bag for stuff that is used frequently.

2. A large bag for luggage (Write your name, address, contact number and other essential details with a tip marker and also mark it with a symbol such as "★". Tie a coloured piece of cloth or a lace in the metallic ring of the bag or at any other appropriate place in such a way that it is clearly visible.)

3. Lock the bag but keep its key in the pocket of Iḥrām's belt and also in the handbag. If the keys are lost, then the bags are usually opened with large scissors at Jeddah customs, which will put you to a lot of trouble.

4. Keep the tag of your name, address and contact number in the handbag as well.

5. It will be comfortable for you to use wheel-attached bags, اِنْ شَآءَاللّٰہ عَزَّوَجَلَّ.

Madanī pearls about health certificate

All Hajj pilgrims should ensure that all of their travelling documents as per legal requirements are prepared in advance, e.g. health certificate. This will be delivered to you after you get vaccinated against cholera, chickenpox etc. at the Ḥājī camp. If even a single of these documents is incomplete in any way, you may be prevented from boarding the aircraft or you may also face problem at Jeddah airport.

- To get vaccinated against diseases just a few days before departure is not very beneficial. It would be extremely effective to get vaccinated about fifteen days before leaving for the journey. Otherwise there will be a possibility of being affected by dangerous and even deadly disease during the blessed journey.

- It is better for you to get vaccinated against flu and hepatitis though it is not a legal requirement. Do not consider these precautionary treatments as a burden as these are for your own benefit.

- Most of travel agents or caravan organisations usually deliver you a health certificate without requiring you to undergo any medical treatment. It is dangerous for your health as well as a deceitful and Ḥarām act leading to Hell. The travel agent and the doctor who deliberately sign such a certificate and the Ḥājī (or Mu'tamir) who deliberately uses this certificate are all sinners and deserve torment of Hell. People who have committed such sins should repent sincerely.

When should pilgrims travelling by air put on Iḥrām?

It takes almost 4 hours to reach Jeddah from Karachi by air. Whilst airborne, it will be difficult to observe Mīqāt (no matter one travels from any country of the world). Hence make initial preparations at home before leaving. If it is not Makrūĥ time, offer the Nafl Ṣalāĥ of Iḥrām and put on Iḥrām as well at home. However, do not make the intention of Iḥrām at home as making intention causes certain restrictions to be imposed. The aircraft may get delayed owing to some reason.

Further, Muḥrim is not even allowed to wear garland around his neck because of the fragrance of flowers[1]. Hence it is convenient to reach the airport in Iḥrām or normal dressing. Bathrooms, Wuḍū facilities and prayer halls are available at the airport. You may also put on Iḥrām, offer Nafl Ṣalāĥ and make the intention of Iḥrām at the airport, but it will still be convenient to make the intention of Iḥrām and recite Labbayk after the aircraft has taken off. However, the knowledgeable ones who can observe the restrictions of Iḥrām will start getting the Šawāb of Iḥrām if they become Muḥrim as early as possible. (See the details of Mīqāt and intention on page 32 and 41 respectively.)

Fragrant tissue paper in an aircraft

Be aware! Crew of the aircraft often provides the passengers with the small packets of the perfumed tissue papers. The one in the state of Iḥrām must not open it. If much amount of fragrance has come into contact with the hand, *Dam*[2] (dʌm) will be Wājib. If they consider it less, Ṣadaqaĥ will be due. If the liquid of the fragrance has not come into contact, but rather it has only made the hand fragrant, there will be no expiation in this case.

---

[1] Precautions of using fragrance in the state of Iḥrām have been described in question/answer section of this book. Anyway, if someone has put on Iḥrām but has not yet made the intention, nor has he recited 'Labbayk' it is permissible for him to apply fragrance and put on garland.

[2] In this book, the word '*Dam*' has been used in the sense of an expiation with its pronunciation as 'dʌm.' It must not be pronounced as 'dæm.' Note that this word has been italicized in the whole book with its '*D*' capitalized. [Translator's Note]

Jeddah to Makkaĥ

On arriving at Jeddah airport, disembark from the plane with your hand-luggage reciting Labbayk (لَبَّيْكَ) with utmost devotion. Make your way towards the custom's counter. After collecting baggage and getting your passport and documents checked, proceed to the bus organized by your Mu'allim.

The formalities of clearing customs and arrival of the bus may take around 6 to 8 hours; therefore, show great patience in this situation. The distance between Makka-tul-Mukarramaĥ and Jeddah airport is covered in about one or one and half hours, but there may be some delay due to traffic jams and legal formalities. You may also have to wait for the bus. On every occasion, remain contented and have patience, and keep reciting Labbayk.

Stirred up with anger, if you quarrel with organizers and shout [at them], you will end up exploiting the situation instead of improving it. You may also fall into committing the sins of wasting the Šawāb of patience, hurting the Muslims, backbiting, accusing, bad suspicion, etc. As the bus is organized by your Mu'allim, get on it with your luggage while reciting Labbayk to lead towards Makkaĥ Mu'aẓẓamaĥ.

Iḥrām of those flying to Madīnaĥ

Those who directly reach Madīna-tul-Munawwaraĥ from their country are advised to cover this journey without Iḥrām. When they move towards Makkaĥ from Madīnaĥ, they should make the intention of Iḥrām from Madīnaĥ or at Żul-Ḥulayfaĥ (Abyār-e-'Alī).

Transport organized by Mu'allim

Whether you travel by air or by sea, all transportations from Jeddah to Makkaĥ, 'Arafāt, Minā, Madīnaĥ etc. and finally back to Jeddah from Makkaĥ are to be arranged by your Mu'allim, the cost of which has already been included in your fare. In addition, serving you with meal at the time of your first arrival at the Mu'allim's office in Makkaĥ and with lunch in 'Arafāt, is also the responsibility of the Mu'allim.

Twenty eight (28) Madanī pearls regarding travelling

1. When you are about to depart, seek forgiveness from your family members, friends and associates regarding the rights which you may have violated. It becomes incumbent upon the people from whom forgiveness is sought to forgive whole-heartedly.

   It is stated in a Ḥadīš that whomsoever is approached for forgiveness by an Islamic brother, it becomes Wājib for that person to forgive him, otherwise he will not be able to come to the pond of Kawšar. *(Fatāwā Razawiyyaĥ, vol. 10, pp. 627)*

2. If you possess belongings of others or owe debt to someone, return it. If you have unjustly seized someone's estate (i.e. property, possession, money etc.), return it or get it waived. If you cannot trace the owner, donate an equivalent amount in charity.

3. Fulfil the acts of worship which are still outstanding such as Ṣalāĥ, fasts of Ramadan, Zakāĥ etc. Repent of the sin of delaying them. The sole purpose of this journey must be to please Almighty Allah عَزَّوَجَلَّ and His Beloved Prophet صَلَّى اللّٰهُ تَعَالٰى عَلَيْهِ وَاٰلِهٖ وَسَلَّم. Refrain from ostentation and arrogance.

4. Islamic sister should not travel without husband or a trustworthy Maḥram (one with whom marriage is Ḥarām forever) otherwise, sin will be recorded for every step till her return. *(Baĥār-e-Sharī'at, vol. 1, pp. 1051)* (This ruling applies not only to Hajj-pilgrimage but also to every journey.)

5. Show the luggage to be loaded on the hired transport to the transporter in advance. Do not load extra luggage without his consent.

A parable

It is reported that once Sayyidunā 'Abdullāĥ Ibn Mubārak رحمۃ اللہ تعالی علیہ was about to go on a journey. A person gave him a letter to deliver to somebody. Sayyidunā 'Abdullāĥ Ibn Mubārak رحمۃ اللہ تعالی علیہ said, 'I have hired the camel, so I will have to seek permission from its owner as I have shown him my entire luggage and this letter is an extra thing.' *(Derived from: Iḥyā-ul-'Ulūm, vol. 1, pp. 353)*

6. It is stated in a Ḥadīš, 'Whenever three people depart for a journey, they should choose any one of them as Amīr.' *(Abū Dāwūd, vol. 3, pp. 51, Ḥadīš 2608)* This helps manage the affairs.
7. The Amīr should be a well-mannered, wise and religious person and a follower of Sunnaĥ.
8. The Amīr should serve his companions, striving for their comfort and convenience.
9. When leaving for the journey, leave as if one is going to depart from the world. Recite the following Du'ā whilst departing:

اَللّٰهُمَّ اِنَّا نَعُوْذُبِكَ مِنْ وَّعْثَآءِ السَّفَرِ وَكَاٰبَةِ الْمُنْقَلَبِ وَسُوْٓءِ

الْمَنْظَرِ فِى الْمَالِ وَالْاَهْلِ وَالْوَلَدِ ط

By virtue of this Du'ā, your wealth and family members will remain safe till return.

10. After putting on the travelling clothes, if it is not Makrūĥ time (for Ṣalāĥ), offer four Rak'āt Nafl Ṣalāĥ with Sūraĥ Al-Fātiḥaĥ and Sūraĥ Al-Ikhlāṣ in each Rak'at. This Ṣalāĥ will secure estate and family members till return.

11. Before leaving home, recite Āyat-ul-Kursī and five Sūraĥs from Sūraĥ Al-Kāfirūn to Sūraĥ An-Nās excluding Sūraĥ Laĥab with بِسْمِ اللّٰه before each Sūraĥ. Recite بِسْمِ اللّٰه once in the end as well. You will remain comfortable throughout the journey, اِنْ شَآءَاللّٰه عَزَّوَجَلَّ. Furthermore, if you also recite the following Du'ā, you will return safe and sound:

اِنَّ الَّذِیْ فَرَضَ عَلَیْکَ الْقُرْاٰنَ لَرَآدُّکَ اِلٰی مَعَادٍ ؕ

Undoubtedly, He who has made the Quran binding on you will bring you back where you desire to return.

[Kanz-ul-Īmān (Translation of Quran)] (Part 20, Sūraĥ Al-Qaṣaṣ, verse 85)

12. If it is not a Makrūĥ time, offer 2 Rak'āt Nafl Ṣalāĥ in the Masjid of your area.

Du'ā for the protection of aeroplane from falling and burning

13. After you have boarded the aeroplane, recite the following Du'ā of Beloved Mustafa صَلَّى اللّٰهُ تَعَالٰى عَلَيْهِ وَاٰلِهٖ وَسَلَّم with Ṣalāt-'Alan-Nabī once before and after it.

اَللّٰھُمَّ اِنِّیْۤ اَعُوْذُبِکَ مِنَ الْھَدْمِ وَاَعُوْذُبِکَ مِنَ التَّرَدِّیْ ؕ وَاَعُوْذُبِکَ مِنَ الْغَرَقِ وَالْحَرَقِ وَالْھَرَمِ وَ اَعُوْذُبِکَ اَنْ یَّتَخَبَّطَنِیَ الشَّیْطٰنُ عِنْدَ الْمَوْتِ ؕ وَاَعُوْذُبِکَ اَنْ اَمُوْتَ فِیْ سَبِیْلِکَ مُدْبِرًا وَ اَعُوْذُبِکَ اَنْ اَمُوْتَ لَدِیْغًا ؕ

Translation: *O Allah عَزَّوَجَلَّ! I seek Your refuge from the collapse of the building, and I seek Your refuge from falling from a higher place, and I seek Your refuge from drowning, burning and old age*[1]*. And I seek Your refuge from satanic whispering at the time of death, and I seek Your refuge from dying whilst showing my back to Your path, and I seek Your refuge from dying of the sting of a snake.*

Madanī pearl: The Arabic words for 'falling from a higher place' and 'burning' are تَرَدِّیْ and حَرَق respectively. The Beloved and Blessed Prophet صَلَّى اللهُ تَعَالٰى عَلَيْهِ وَاٰلِهٖ وَسَلَّم would make this Du'ā. In fact, this Du'ā is not specific to air travel. Since refuge is sought in this Du'ā from 'falling from a higher place' and 'burning', and air travel involves both of these risks, it is therefore hoped that the aeroplane will remain safe from any crash by the blessing of reciting this Du'ā.

14. While travelling by bus, train etc., recite the following invocations, the conveyance will remain safe from all sorts of accidents, اِنْ شَآءَاللّٰہ عَزَّوَجَلَّ.

- بِسْمِ اللهِ اَللهُ اَكْبَرُ Thrice
- اَلْحَمْدُ لِلّٰهِ Thrice
- سُبْحٰنَ اللهِ Thrice
- لَآ اِلٰهَ اِلَّا اللهُ Once

The following Quranic Du'ā once:

سُبْحٰنَ الَّذِیْ سَخَّرَ لَنَا هٰذَا وَ مَا

كُنَّا لَهٗ مُقْرِنِیْنَ ﴿۱۳﴾ وَ اِنَّاۤ اِلٰی رَبِّنَا لَمُنْقَلِبُوْنَ ﴿۱۴﴾

[1] The old age here implies the physical and mental condition in which a person loses his knowledge and is unable to perform deeds. *(Mirāt, vol. 4, pp. 3)*

Glory be to the One Who has given this conveyance in our control, and we did not have control over it. And no doubt we are to return to our Rab.

[Kanz-ul-Īmān (Translation of Quran)] (Part 25, Sūraĥ Zukhruf, verse 13-14)

15. After getting to the destination, perform two Rak'āt Nafl Ṣalāĥ provided the time is not Makrūĥ. To offer this Ṣalāĥ is a Sunnaĥ.

16. After reaching the destination, make the following Du'ā from time to time. You will remain safe from every harm, اِنْ شَآءَاللّٰه عَزَّوَجَلَّ.

اَعُوْذُ بِكَلِمَاتِ اللّٰهِ التَّآمَّاتِ مِنْ شَرِّ مَا خَلَقَ

I seek refuge from the harm of creatures by (virtue of) the complete and perfect words of Allah عَزَّوَجَلَّ.

17. Recite يَا صَمَدُ 134 times daily; you will be protected from thirst and hunger.

18. If there is a fear of an enemy, recite Sūraĥ Quraysh. You will remain safe from every calamity, اِنْ شَآءَاللّٰه عَزَّوَجَلَّ.

19. If there is a fear of an enemy, it is extremely useful to recite the following Du'ā:

اَللّٰهُمَّ اِنَّا نَجْعَلُكَ فِيْ نُحُوْرِهِمْ وَنَعُوْذُبِكَ مِنْ شُرُوْرِهِمْ

***Translation:** O Allah* عَزَّوَجَلَّ*, we keep You in front of their chests (to stop them from reaching us), and we seek Your refuge from their evils.*

20. If something is lost, recite the following:

يَا جَامِعَ النَّاسِ لِيَوْمٍ لَّا رَيْبَ فِيْهِ ؕ اِنَّ اللّٰهَ لَا يُخْلِفُ الْمِيْعَادَ ۞

اِجْمَعْ بَيْنِيْ وَبَيْنَ ضَآلَّتِيْ

***Translation:** O the One gathering people on the day about which there is no doubt! Indeed Allah (عَزَّوَجَلَّ) does not go against the promise. Make me find my lost thing.*

By the blessing of reciting it, the lost thing will turn up, اِنْ شَآءَاللّٰه عَزَّوَجَلَّ.

21. When moving to a higher place, say 'اَللّٰهُ اَكْبَرُ' and when moving from a higher to a lower place, say 'سُبْحٰنَ اللّٰهِ'.

22. Recite Āyat-ul-Kursī once at the time of sleeping, it provides refuge from satan and thief.

23. According to a Hadīš, if someone facing a difficulty needs help, he should call out the following words thrice:

***Translation:** O servants of Allah! Help me.* يَا عِبَادَ اللّٰهِ اَعِيْنُوْنِيْ

(Ḥiṣn-e-Ḥaṣīn, pp. 82)

24. Observe the foregoing manners and etiquettes during the return journey as well.

25. People should welcome the Ḥājī and request him for Du'ā before he reaches his home as the Du'ā made by a Ḥājī is accepted until he has reached his home.

26. On returning from the journey, offer two Rak'āt Nafl Ṣalāĥ before going home in the Masjid of your locality (provided the time is not Makrūĥ for Ṣalāĥ).

27. Likewise, offer two Rak'āt Nafl Ṣalāĥ after reaching home (provided the time is not Makrūĥ for Ṣalāĥ).

28. Then meet everyone warmly.

For detailed information, study from page 1051 to 1066 of the 6th part of *Baĥār-e-Sharī'at* (volume-1) and from page 726 to 731 of the referenced *Fatāwā Razawiyyaĥ* (volume-10).

6 Madanī pearls of offering Ṣalāĥ during journey

1. By Sharī'aĥ, the person who has been out of his staying place, i.e. his city or village with the intention of travelling up to the distance of three days is considered a traveller. The distance of three days during a journey-on-land refers to 57.5 miles (i.e. almost 92 kilometres). *(Fatawa Razawiyyaĥ – referenced, vol. 8, pp. 243, 270; Baĥār-e-Sharī'at, vol. 1, pp. 740, 741)*

2. On reaching the destination, if one intends to stay over there for 15 days or more, he will not be regarded a traveller by Sharī'aĥ. Instead, he will now be considered a Muqīm (resident). In this case, he will not offer Qaṣr Ṣalāĥ (shortened Ṣalāĥ where 4 Farḍ Rak'āt are reduced to 2). There is no reduction in the Farḍ Ṣalāĥ of Fajr and Maghrib. Likewise, Sunnaĥ and Witr Ṣalāĥ will also be offered as usual without any reduction.

3. A large number of Ḥujjāj reach Makka-tul-Mukarramaĥ in Shawwāl-ul-Mukarram and Żul-Qa'daĥ, whereas many days are still left in the commencement of Hajj. After some days they are shifted to Madīna-tul-Munawwaraĥ for almost nine days. In this case, they stay as travellers in Madīna-tul-Munawwaraĥ; in fact, they also stay as travellers in Makka-tul-Mukarramaĥ because they have to stay for less than 15 days. However, if anyone gets a chance to stay in Makkaĥ or Madīnaĥ for 15 days or more, his intention of stay is correct.

4. If someone makes the intention of stay but his condition indicates that he will not be staying in Makkaĥ nor in Madīnaĥ, then his intention is not correct. For example, he intends to perform Hajj and makes the intention of staying in Makkaĥ, whereas the month of Żul-Ḥijjaĥ has arrived then his intention is worthless. As he has intended to perform Hajj, he will not be staying for 15 days because he will be moving to Minā and 'Arafāt on 8 and 9 Żul-Ḥijjaĥ respectively. How is it possible for him to stay in Makkaĥ Mukarramaĥ (for 15 consecutive days)? If he makes the intention of stay after he has returned from Minā, it is correct because it is now possible for him to stay in Makkaĥ Mukarramaĥ for 15 days or more. If it is highly likely that he will move to Madīna-tul-Munawwaraĥ or to his own country, then he will be considered as a traveller.

5. By the time of the writing of this account, the distance between the end of the populated areas of Jeddah and the beginning of the populated areas of Makkaĥ is 53 kilometres by road and 47 kilometres by air. The distance between the end of the populated areas of Jeddah and the beginning of 'Arafāt is 78 kilometres by one route, 80 kilometres by two other routes and 67 kilometres by air. Therefore, whether residents of Jeddah go to Makkaĥ from Jeddah or they directly go to 'Arafāt, they are to offer complete Ṣalāĥ without Qaṣr.

6. You can offer the Ṣalāĥ of Farḍ, Witr, Sunnaĥs, Nawāfil, etc. while travelling by air. There is no need to repeat these Ṣalāĥs. Offer Farḍ, Witr, Sunnaĥ of Fajr while facing Qiblaĥ as usual. It is possible to offer the Ṣalāĥ while standing by washroom or kitchen or at the tail of the airplane. You can also offer the rest of Sunnaĥs and Nawāfil whilst sitting during travel. To face the Qiblaĥ in this situation is not a condition. [For more details, read '*Traveller's Ṣalāĥ*', a booklet included in '*Laws of Ṣalāĥ*'.]

3 Sayings of the Holy Prophet ﷺ

1. The Prophet of Raḥmah صَلَّى اللهُ تَعَالٰى عَلَيْهِ وَاٰلِهٖ وَسَلَّم has stated, 'The Ḥājī will intercede for his 400 family members and will be as free from sins as he was on the day he was born.'

   (Musnad-ul-Bazzār, vol. 8, pp. 169, Ḥadīš 3196)

2. The Holy Prophet صَلَّى اللهُ تَعَالٰى عَلَيْهِ وَاٰلِهٖ وَسَلَّم has stated, 'The Ḥājī is forgiven and the one for whom the Ḥājī asks forgiveness is also forgiven.' *(Majma'-uz-Zawāid, vol. 3, pp. 483, Ḥadīš 5287)*

3. The Beloved and Blessed Prophet صَلَّى اللهُ تَعَالٰى عَلَيْهِ وَاٰلِهٖ وَسَلَّم has stated, 'There will be no accountability for the one who departs for Hajj or 'Umraĥ and dies on the way. He will be ordered to enter Paradise.' *(Al-Mu'jam-ul-Awsaṭ, vol. 4, pp. 111, Ḥadīš 8835)*

70 Million virtues on every step

Giving encouragement to go on foot to perform Hajj-rites Sayyidī A'lā Ḥaḍrat Imām Aḥmad Razā Khān عَلَيْهِ رَحْمَةُ الرَّحْمٰن has stated in his book '*Anwar-ul-Bishāraĥ*', 'If possible one should go to Minā, 'Arafāt etc. from Makka-tul-Mukarramaĥ on foot as 70 million virtues will be written for his every step till his return to Makka-tul-Mukarramaĥ. This adds up to approximately seventy eight trillion and forty billion virtues. Without doubt, Allah عَزَّوَجَلَّ has showered innumerable blessings upon this Ummaĥ for the sake of His Beloved and Blessed Prophet صَلَّى اللهُ تَعَالٰى عَلَيْهِ وَاٰلِهٖ وَسَلَّم.'

Sag-e-Madīnaĥ (the author) states that Sayyidī Imām Aḥmad Razā Khān عَلَيْهِ رَحْمَةُ الرَّحْمٰن has made this estimation on the basis of the distance of the old longer route. Since tunnels have now been constructed in the mountains leading from Makka-tul-Mukarramaĥ to Minā, shortening the route and facilitating the travel for pedestrians, the number of virtues will also reduce accordingly. وَاللهُ وَرَسُوْلُهٗ اَعْلَم

The angels embrace those going for Hajj on foot

The Prophet of Raḥmaĥ, the Intercessor of Ummaĥ صَلَّى اللهُ تَعَالٰى عَلَيْهِ وَاٰلِهٖ وَسَلَّم has stated, 'When the Ḥujjāj come riding, the angels shake hands with them and those who come on foot, the angels embrace them. *(Itḥāf-us-Sādaĥ liz-Zubaydī, vol. 4, pp. 465)*

Commandment of Holy Quran during Hajj

Allah عَزَّوَجَلَّ has said in verse 197 of Sūraĥ Al-Baqaraĥ, part 2:

فَلَا رَفَثَ وَلَا فُسُوْقَ ۙ وَلَا جِدَالَ فِي الْحَجِّ ۭ

Then there should be no mention of copulation before women; nor any sin nor quarrelling with anyone till the time of Hajj.

[Kanz-ul-Īmān (Translation of Quran)] (Part 2, Sūraĥ Al-Baqaraĥ, verse 197)

Commenting on this sacred verse, 'Allāmaĥ Maulānā Muftī Muhammad Amjad 'Alī A'ẓamī عَلَيْهِ رَحْمَةُ اللهِ القَوِى has said: During the Hajj, such activities must be avoided! When you get angry or are prone to quarrel or even have the thought of committing any sin, just lower your head and recite the same verse with لَاحَوْل one or two times with full concentration; this condition will come to an end.

Sometimes, a quarrel breaks out between Ḥujjāj and at times even strange pedestrians are made to use foul language and quarrel with the Ḥājī unreasonably. This is a tough test for the Ḥājī. He should always be cautious and avoid quarrels so that the efforts he has made and the money he has spent on the journey would not go to waste just because of a few words. *(Bahār-e-Sharī'at, vol. 1, pp. 1061)*

صَلُّوْا عَلَى الْحَبِيْب صَلَّى اللهُ تَعَالٰى عَلٰى مُحَمَّد

Treasure of devotion is essential for Ḥājī

O fortunate Ḥujjāj! As the physical means are necessary for the Ḥājī, inner spiritual treasure is also a significant requirement for him. This treasure is that of true love and devotion which is attained from the true devotees of Rasūl.

Parable: Once a person entered the blessed court of Sayyidunā Ghauš-e-A'ẓam رَحْمَةُ اللّٰهِ تَعَالٰى عَلَيْه. Addressing the audience, Ghauš-e-A'ẓam رَحْمَةُ اللّٰهِ تَعَالٰى عَلَيْه declared, 'This person has just arrived here in a single step from Bayt-ul-Muqaddas (Jerusalem) in order to learn the manners of true devotion from me.' *(Akhbār-ul-Akhyār, pp. 4)*

May Allah عَزَّوَجَلَّ shower mercy on them and forgive us for their sake without accountability!

آمِيْن بِجَاهِ النَّبِيِّ الْاَمِيْن صَلَّى اللّٰهُ تَعَالٰى عَلَيْهِ وَاٰلِهٖ وَسَلَّم

Adopt affiliation with true devotee

سُبْحٰنَ اللّٰه عَزَّوَجَلَّ! Even a saint possessing saintly miracle (Karāmaĥ) needs to attend the court of a greater saint so as to attain the treasure of true devotion. How greatly we will be in the need of learning the manners of devotion! We should also have affiliation with some true devotee of the Holy Prophet to learn devotion from him and then depart for Madīnaĥ.

Beloved Ḥujjāj! Two parables of the true devotees of the Beloved and Blessed Prophet are being presented. Read them with a dejected heart shedding tears in the desire of being blessed with love and devotion of Allah عَزَّوَجَلَّ and Mustafa صَلَّى اللّٰهُ تَعَالٰى عَلَيْهِ وَاٰلِهٖ وَسَلَّم.

1. Mysterious Ḥājī

Sayyidunā Fuḍayl Bin 'Iyāḍ رَحْمَةُ اللّٰهِ تَعَالٰى عَلَيْه has narrated, 'People were busy making Du'ā in the plains of 'Arafāt when I spotted a young man standing with his head hung in shame. Approaching him, I said, 'O young man, you too make Du'ā.' He replied, 'I fear that I have lost the time granted to me, so how can I make Du'ā?' Then I said to him, 'Make Du'ā hoping to be blessed by Allah عَزَّوَجَلَّ for the sake of these people's supplications.'

Sayyidunā Fuḍayl Bin 'Iyāḍ رَحْمَةُ اللهِ تَعَالٰی عَلَيْه has stated, 'As the young man tried to raise his hands for Du'ā, he became overwhelmed, letting out a piercing cry. He then fell onto the ground and his soul left his body.' *(Kashf-ul-Maḥjūb, pp. 363)* May Allah عَزَّوَجَلَّ shower mercy on them and forgive us for their sake without accountability!

اٰمِیْن بِجَاہِ النَّبِیِّ الْاَمِیْن صَلَّی اللہُ تَعَالٰی عَلَیْہِ وَاٰلِہٖ وَسَلَّم

2. Ḥājī who slaughtered himself

Sayyidunā Żunnūn Miṣrī رَحْمَةُ اللهِ تَعَالٰی عَلَيْه has reported that once he saw a young man in Minā who was quietly sitting at a side while other people were busy performing their sacrifices (of animals). The young man cried out suddenly, 'O my Beloved Allah عَزَّوَجَلَّ! Your servants are busy offering their sacrifices. I wish to sacrifice myself in Your court. O my Creator! Accept my sacrifice.' Saying this, he ran his finger across his throat and fell down. Sayyidunā Żunnūn Miṣrī رَحْمَةُ اللهِ تَعَالٰی عَلَيْه stated, 'I hurriedly approached him and was astonished to see that he had passed away.' *(Kashf-ul-Maḥjūb, pp. 364)* May Allah عَزَّوَجَلَّ shower mercy on them and forgive us for their sake without accountability!

اٰمِیْن بِجَاہِ النَّبِیِّ الْاَمِیْن صَلَّی اللہُ تَعَالٰی عَلَیْہِ وَاٰلِہٖ وَسَلَّم

How is it to call oneself Ḥājī?

Respected Ḥujjāj! Did you notice! This is the Hajj of true devotees! May Allah عَزَّوَجَلَّ bless us with a deeply sincere heart by virtue of these two Ḥujjāj. Remember, sincerity is a prerequisite for the acceptance of any worship. Alas! As a result of drifting away from

Islamic teachings and righteous company, most of our worships are now ruined by ostentation. Unfortunately, these days, ostentation and showing-off seem to have become an integral part in most of our affairs including even Hajj, a great worship. For example, many people call themselves Ḥājī after having performed Hajj. Sometimes they add the title of Ḥājī before their name.

Perhaps you would be thinking as to what is wrong with this. Although there is no harm if other people call you Ḥājī without you desiring it but dear Ḥujjāj! Ponder calmly, if one calls himself Ḥājī, isn't he informing others of his worship unnecessarily! This can better be understood with the help of the following example.

An anecdote

A train was moving towards its destination. Two persons who were sitting close to each other started conversation. One of them asked the other, 'What's your name?' The other person replied, 'Ḥājī Shafiq.' The second person also asked, 'And what's your name please?' The first one replied, 'Namāzī Rafīq.'

Astonished, Ḥājī Sahib remarked, 'Namāzī Rafīq! It sounds very strange.' Rafīq Sahib asked, 'Would you please let me know as to how many times have you performed Hajj?' The Ḥājī Sahib replied, 'اَلْحَمْدُ لِلّٰه عَزَّوَجَلَّ I performed Hajj just last year.' Rafīq responded immediately, 'You have performed Hajj just once in your life and you are openly calling yourself a Ḥājī showing-off your Hajj whereas I have been offering Namāz (Ṣalāĥ) five times daily for many years, so what is strange if I call myself Namāzī Rafīq?'

How is it to display a 'Hajj congratulations board'?

You may have taken my point. Nowadays the trend of showing off has grown to extreme limits! On departure or arrival of the Ḥājī

Sahib, his home is adorned with lights along with a board 'Hajj congratulation' displayed at the front side of the home. Allah عَزَّوَجَلَّ forbid, at some places, even the photographs of the Ḥājī Sahib dressed in Iḥrām are taken. What is all this? Is it appropriate for an escaped slave to return to the blessed court of his Master صَلَّى اللهُ تَعَالٰى عَلَيْهِ وَاٰلِهٖ وَسَلَّم with such pomp and show? Definitely not, one should proceed for Hajj with tears in eyes and remorse in heart for all the sins committed.

Hajj-pilgrimage on foot

Presented here is a parable containing a lesson of humility for those displaying a board that reads 'Hajj Congratulations' at the front side of their homes without any good intention just for gaining the pleasure of their Nafs and showing off.

Sayyidunā Sufyān Šaurī عَلَيْهِ رَحْمَةُ اللّٰهِ الْقَوِی once departed from Basra for Hajj on foot. Someone asked him as to why he was not going by any transport. He رَحْمَةُ اللهِ تَعَالٰى عَلَيْه replied, 'Should the escaped slave be on a carriage whilst returning to the court of his Master for asking pardon?' I feel shy of entering this sacred land. ***(Tanbīh-ul-Mughtarrīn, pp. 267)***

May Allah عَزَّوَجَلَّ shower mercy on them and forgive us for their sake without accountability!

اٰمِيْن بِجَاهِ النَّبِيِّ الْاَمِيْن صَلَّى اللهُ تَعَالٰى عَلَيْهِ وَاٰلِهٖ وَسَلَّم

Even unable to perform Ṭawāf

Ḥujjat-ul-Islam Sayyidunā Imām Abū Ḥāmid Muhammad Bin Muhammad Bin Muhammad Ghazālī عَلَيْهِ رَحْمَةُ اللّٰهِ الْوَالِی has stated: A question was asked to a saint رَحْمَةُ اللهِ تَعَالٰى عَلَيْه, 'Have you ever entered the Holy Ka'baĥ?' He replied humbly, 'How can I be able to enter the Holy Ka'baĥ? I do not even consider myself able enough to perform the Ṭawāf of the Ka'baĥ because I know the [inappropriate] places where I used to go.' *(Iḥyā-ul-'Ulūm, vol. 1, pp. 345)*

May Allah عَزَّوَجَلَّ shower mercy on them and forgive us for their sake without accountability!

آمِيْن بِجَاهِ النَّبِيِّ الْاَمِيْن صَلَّى اللهُ تَعَالٰى عَلَيْهِ وَاٰلِهٖ وَسَلَّم

صَلُّوْا عَلَى الْحَبِيْب صَلَّى اللهُ تَعَالٰى عَلٰى مُحَمَّد

Attack of 'ostentation' and 'desire for respect' on Ḥājī

Dear Ḥujjāj and travellers of Madīnaĥ! There are probably greater risks of ostentation in Hajj compared to Ṣalāĥ and fast etc. Hajj is such a form of worship that is performed publicly, and anyway not everyone is blessed with it. Therefore, people meet the Ḥājī with humility, honour him, kiss his hand with respect, make him wear garlands around his neck and request him to make Du'ā for them.

On such occasions, the Ḥājī faces a tough test because humility and reverence on the part of people give such pleasure to the Ḥājī that he considers even the toughest act of worship as the easiest one; sometimes falling into the deep and deadly abyss of desire for respect and ostentation without noticing it at all. He desires that all people be informed about his Hajj so that they would come to meet and greet him, give him gifts, offer him garlands, request him to make Du'ā for them, implore him to convey their Salām to the Holy Prophet صَلَّى اللهُ تَعَالٰى عَلَيْهِ وَاٰلِهٖ وَسَلَّم in Madīnaĥ and come to the airport to see him off etc. Due to these desires and lack of religious knowledge, satan sometimes plays with such a Ḥājī as children play with a toy. Therefore, remaining alert to the attack of satan, create humility in your heart and avoid bragging. By Allah عَزَّوَجَلَّ! No one will be able to bear the torment of ostentation.

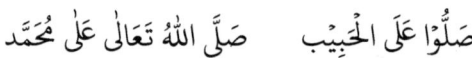

It is stated on page 79 of the 616-page book '*Naykī kī Da'wat*' (part 1) published by Maktaba-tul-Madīnaĥ, the publishing department of Dawat-e-Islami: The Beloved Prophet صَلَّى اللهُ تَعَالٰى عَلَيْهِ وَاٰلِهٖ وَسَلَّم has stated, 'Without doubt, there is a valley in Hell from which Hell seeks refuge four hundred times daily. Allah عَزَّوَجَلَّ has prepared this valley for those ostentatious people from the Ummaĥ of Muhammad who are the Ḥāfiẓ of Quran, give charity for [something or someone] other than Allah, perform the Hajj of the House of Allah عَزَّوَجَلَّ and travel in Divine path.' *(Al-Mu'jam-ul-Kabīr, vol. 12, pp. 136, Ḥadīš 12803)*

Two examples of ostentation of Ḥujjāj

Stated on page 76 of the 1st part of the book '*Naykī kī Da'wat*' are two examples of ostentation of Ḥujjāj:

1. To inform people about the number of performed Hajj and 'Umraĥ, the amount of daily recitation of the Quran, all the observed fasts in Rajab and Sha'bān and other Nafl fasts, Nafl Ṣalāĥ and Ṣalāt-'Alan-Nabī recited in abundance so that people would admire him and treat him with respect.

2. To perform Hajj or let others know that one has performed it so that people would call him as Ḥājī Sahib, come to meet him, implore him to make Du'ā for them, offer him garlands and give him gifts etc. (If one has no intention of being treated with respect and given gifts but rather he has good intentions such as expressing gratitude for a Divine bounty etc. there is no prohibition for him to let others know about his Hajj, to hold 'Maḥfil-e-Madīnaĥ' and to invite his relatives and friends etc. It is an act of reward of the Hereafter for him in this case.)

   (In order to get detailed information regarding ostentation, go through from page 63 to 106 of Maktaba-tul-Madīnaĥ's published book '*Naykī kī Da'wat*' part 1.)

55 Terms

Those intending to perform Hajj should first go through the following terms and names of sacred places keeping them in mind so that it may become easier for them to understand the rulings etc. described in the book.

1. Ashĥur-ul-Hajj [اَشْهُرُ الْحَجّ]

The holy months of Hajj which include Shawwāl, Żul-Qa'daĥ and the first ten days of Żul-Ḥijjaĥ.

2. Iḥrām [اِحْرام]

Iḥrām refers to the state in which even certain Ḥalāl things become Ḥarām for the one who recites Talbiyaĥ with the intention of performing Hajj or 'Umraĥ or both. Further, the unstitched shawls put on in the state of Iḥrām are also called Iḥrām metaphorically.

3. Talbiyaĥ [تَلْبِيَه]

The invocation repeatedly recited in the state of Iḥrām during Hajj and 'Umraĥ, i.e.

لَبَّيْكَ ط اَللّٰهُمَّ لَبَّيْكَ ط لَبَّيْكَ لَا شَرِيْكَ لَكَ لَبَّيْكَ ط

اِنَّ الْحَمْدَ وَالنِّعْمَةَ لَكَ وَالْمُلْكَ ط لَا شَرِيْكَ لَكَ ط

4. Iḍṭibā' [اِضْطِبَاع]

The act of wearing upper shawl of Iḥrām in such a way that it passes underneath the armpit of the right hand and remains on the left shoulder, keeping the right shoulder uncovered.

5. Raml [رَمْل]

Raml implies walking with small steps at a slightly increased pace whilst moving the shoulders and stiffening the chest.

6. Ṭawāf [circumambulation] (طَواف)

To circumambulate the Ka'baĥ 7 times is called Ṭawāf. One round is called a 'Shauṭ' while its plural is referred to as 'Ashwāṭ.'

7. Maṭāf [مَطاف]

The specific area where Ṭawāf is performed.

8. Ṭawāf-ul-Qudūm [طَوافُ الْقُدُوْم]

The very first Ṭawāf performed on arriving in Makka-tul-Mukarramaĥ is called 'Ṭawāf-ul-Qudūm' that is Sunnat-ul-Muakkadaĥ for those making the intention of Hajj Ifrād or Hajj Qirān.

9. Ṭawāf-uz-Ziyāraĥ [طَوافُ الزِّيَارَة]

It is also called Ṭawāf Ifāḍaĥ. It is an essential pillar of Hajj. It can be performed from the Ṣubḥ-e-Ṣādiq of 10th Żul-Ḥijjaĥ till the sunset on 12th Żul-Ḥijjaĥ. However, it is preferable to perform it on the 10th of Żul-Ḥijjaĥ.

10. Ṭawāf-ul-Wadā' [طَوافُ الْوَدَاع]

This is also called 'Ṭawāf-ur-Rukhṣat' and 'Ṭawāf-e-Ṣadr'. This Ṭawāf is performed after Hajj before departing from Makka-tul-Mukarramaĥ. It is Wājib for every Āfāqī Ḥājī (the definition of an Āfāqī Ḥājī is given ahead).

11. Ṭawāf-ul-'Umraĥ [طَوَافُ الْعُمْرَة]

This Ṭawāf is Farḍ for the person performing 'Umraĥ.

12. Istilām [اِسْتِلَام]

Istilām is the act of kissing Ḥajar-ul-Aswad or touching it with one's hand or with a stick and then kissing the hand/stick or pointing towards it with one's hands and then kissing the hands.

13. Sa'ī [سَعْی]

To walk between Ṣafā and Marwaĥ 7 times is called 'Sa'ī.' (One round implies going from Ṣafā to Marwaĥ; hence the 7th walk will end at Marwaĥ.)

14. Ramī [رَمْی]

To stone Jamarāt, i.e. satans

15. Ḥalq [حَلْق]

To shave one's head completely within Ḥaram in order to be out of the restrictions of Iḥrām.

16. Qaṣr [قَصْر]

To trim each hair of a quarter (¼) of the head equal to a finger digit in length. (A finger has three digits while the thumb has two.)

17. Masjid-ul-Ḥarām [اَلْمَسْجِدُ الْحَرَام]

The Masjid in which the Holy Ka'baĥ is situated.

18. Bāb-us-Salām [بَابُ السَّلَام]

A blessed door of Masjid-ul-Ḥarām situated towards the east. When making first visit to the Masjid, it is preferable to enter through this door. (But now it usually remains closed.)

19. Ka'baĥ [كَعْبَة]

It is also called 'بَيْتُ الله', i.e. the 'House of Allah عَزَّوَجَلَّ.' It is situated at the very centre of the earth. People throughout the world offer their Ṣalāĥ facing it. The Muslims make Ṭawāf (i.e. circumambulation) of it with great fervour.

Names of 4 corners of Ka'baĥ

20. Rukn Aswad [رُكْن اَسْوَد]

The south-east corner of the Ka'baĥ where Ḥajar-ul-Aswad is affixed.

21. Rukn 'Irāqī [رُكْن عِرَاقِی]

The north-east corner of the Ka'baĥ towards Iraq

22. Rukn Shāmī [رُكْن شَامِی]

The north-west corner of the Ka'baĥ towards Syria

23. Rukn Yamānī [رُكْن يَمَانِی]

The western corner of the Ka'baĥ towards Yemen

24. Bāb-ul-Ka'baĥ [بَابُ الْكَعْبَة]

The blessed door of the Ka'baĥ made of gold. It is elevated from the ground. It is located in eastern wall between Rukn Aswad and Rukn 'Irāqī.

25. Multazam [مُلْتَزَم]

The wall section between Rukn Aswad and the sacred door of the Ka'baĥ.

26. Mustajār [مُسْتَجَار]

The western wall section situated exactly behind Multazam, between Rukn Yamānī and Rukn Shāmī.

27. Mustajāb [مُسْتَجَاب]

The southern wall between Rukn Yamānī and Rukn Aswad. At this place 70,000 angels are present to say Āmīn for Du'ās. Sayyidī A'lā Ḥaḍrat رَحْمَةُ الله تَعَالٰى عَلَيْه has named it 'Mustajāb' (i.e. the place where one's Du'ās are accepted).

28. Ḥaṭīm [حَطِيْم]

The section inside the semi-circled small wall on the northern side of the Ka'baĥ. Ḥaṭīm is a part of the Ka'baĥ and entering it is just like entering the Ka'baĥ.

29. Mīzāb-ur-Raḥmaĥ [مِيْزَابُ الرَّحْمَة]

The drain pipe made of gold, affixed on the roof of the northern wall, between Rukn Shāmī and Rukn 'Irāqī. The rain water pours from it into Ḥaṭīm.

30. Maqām-u-Ibrāĥīm [مَقَامُ اِبْرَاهِيْم]

The heavenly stone situated under a small dome in front of the door of the Ka'baĥ. Sayyidunā Ibrāĥīm عَلٰى نَبِيِّنَا وَعَلَيْهِ الصَّلٰوةُ وَالسَّلَام stood onto this sacred stone to construct the Ka'baĥ. It is a living Prophetic miracle of Sayyidunā Ibrāĥīm عَلٰى نَبِيِّنَا وَعَلَيْهِ الصَّلٰوةُ وَالسَّلَام that his blessed footprints are still imprinted on it.

Hajar-ul-Aswad
Multazam
Hateem

Hajar-ul-Aswad
Multazam
Hateem

Bab-ul-Ka'bah

Bab-ul-Ka'bah

31. Zam Zam well [بِئْرُ زَم زَم]

This is the blessed well which sprang out when Sayyidunā Ismā'īl عَلٰی نَبِیِّنَا وَعَلَیْهِ الصَّلٰوۃُ وَالسَّلَام rubbed his delicate blessed feet on the ground in his infancy. *(Tafsīr Na'īmī, vol. 1, pp. 694)*

Looking at its water, drinking it and pouring it onto one's body are all acts of reward and it is a cure for diseases. This blessed well is situated in the south of Maqām-u-Ibrāĥīm. (Now no one can behold this well.)

32. Bāb-uṣ-Ṣafā [بَابُ الصَّفَا]

It is one of the southern doors of Masjid-ul-Ḥarām near which lies the mount Ṣafā.

33. Mount Ṣafā [کوہِ صَفَا]

It is situated on the southern side of the Ka'baĥ.

34. Mount Marwaĥ [کوہِ مَرْوَہ]

It is situated opposite the mount Ṣafā.

35. Mīlayn-e-Akhḍarayn [مِیْلَیْنِ اَخْضَرَیْن]

These are 2 green marks visible in the passage between Ṣafā and Marwaĥ. To make these marks prominent, green tube lights have been installed to the walls and the ceiling. During Sa'ī, males are to run between these two green marks.

36. Mas'ā [مَسْعٰی]

The passage between Mīlayn-e-Akhḍarayn is called Mas'ā. It is a Sunnaĥ for males to run along this passage during Sa'ī.

37. Mīqāt [مِيْقَات]

It refers to the place which cannot be passed by the Āfāqī, without Iḥrām, who is going to Makkaĥ, whether for trading or for any other purpose. Even the residents of Makkaĥ going out of Mīqāt (e.g. Madīnaĥ or Ṭāif) are not permitted to re-enter Makkaĥ without Iḥrām.

There are 5 Mīqāt

38. Żul-Ḥulayfaĥ [ذُوْالْحُلَيْفَه]

It is approximately 10 kilometres away from Madīnaĥ towards Makkaĥ. It is the Mīqāt for those coming from the direction of Madīnaĥ. Its present name is 'Abyār-e-'Alī.'

39. Żāt 'Irq [ذَات عِرْق]

It is the Mīqāt for those coming from the direction of Iraq.

40. Yalamlam [يَلَمْلَم]

It is the Mīqāt for those coming from the direction of Yemen. The Mīqāt for the Indo-Pak pilgrims is the area parallel to Yalamlam.

41. Juḥfaĥ [جُحْفَه]

It is the Mīqāt for those coming from the direction of Syria.

42. Qarn-ul-Manāzil [قَرْنُ الْمَنَازِل]

It is the Mīqāt for those coming from the direction of Najd (whose present name is Riyadh) which is near Ṭāif.

43. Ḥaram [حَرَم]

'Ḥaram' refers to the area around Makkaĥ whose limits have spread out up to several miles. This land is called Ḥaram because of its sacredness. Its limits are marked in all directions. It is Ḥarām (unlawful) for any person, whether Ḥājī or not, to hunt in its jungle and to cut its naturally growing trees and live grass. The people who dwell within the limits of Ḥaram are called Ḥaramī or Aĥl-e-Ḥaram.

44. Ḥil [حِلّ]

This is the area beyond the limits of Ḥaram but within the limits of Mīqāt. Certain acts which are Ḥarām within Ḥaram are Ḥalāl here. The people who live in this area are called Ḥillī.

45. Āfāqī [آفاقِی]

The person who lives outside the limits of Mīqāt is called an Āfāqī.

46. Tan'īm [تَنْعِيم]

It is the place outside Ḥaram where people whilst staying in Makkaĥ go in order to put on Iḥrām for 'Umraĥ. It lies at about 7 kilometres from Masjid-ul-Ḥarām towards Madīnaĥ. Masjid 'Āishaĥ has been built here. People refer to this place as 'small 'Umraĥ.'

47. Ji'irrānaĥ [جِعِرَّانَه]

It is situated about 26 kilometres from Makkaĥ on the way to Ṭāif. This is another place where people whilst staying in Makkaĥ go in order to put on Iḥrām for 'Umraĥ. People refer to this place as 'big 'Umraĥ'.

48. Minā [مِنٰی]

A valley 5 kilometres away from Masjid-ul-Ḥarām where the Ḥujjāj stay. Minā lies within Ḥaram.

49. Jamarāt [جَمَرَات]

The three places in Minā where stones are thrown (at satan). The first one is called Jamra-tul-Ukhrā or Jamra-tul-'Aqabaĥ, it is also called the big satan. The second one is called Jamra-tul-Wusṭā (the medium satan) and the third one is called Jamra-tul-Aūlā (the little satan).

50. 'Arafāt [عَرَفَات]

About 11 kilometres from Minā lies the plain of 'Arafāt where all Ḥujjāj gather on the 9th of Żul-Ḥijjaĥ. 'Arafāt is situated outside Ḥaram.

51. Jabal-ur-Raḥmaĥ [جَبَلُ الرَّحْمَة]

The sacred mountain in 'Arafāt near which Wuqūf (ritual stay) is preferable.

52. Muzdalifaĥ [مُزْدَلِفَه]

The plains about 5 kilometres away from Minā towards 'Arafāt. To spend night here on return from 'Arafāt is Sunnaĥ and to stay here for at least a moment between Ṣubḥ-e-Ṣādiq and sunrise is Wājib.

53. Muḥassir [مُحَسِّر]

Adjacent to Muzdalifaĥ is a plain called Muḥassir where Divine retribution was inflicted upon Aṣḥāb-ul-Fīl. One should cross it fast, seeking refuge from the Divine retribution.

54. Baṭn 'Uranaĥ [بَطْن عُرَنَه]

A jungle near 'Arafāt where Wuqūf for Hajj is invalid.

55. Mad'ā [مَدْعٰی]

An area in between Masjid-ul-Ḥarām and Jannat-ul-Ma'alā, the graveyard of Makka-tul-Mukarramaĥ, where it is Mustaḥab to make Du'ā.

❋❋❋

29 Places where one's Du'ā is accepted

Respected Ḥujjāj! Although the whole Ḥaram is full of blessings, I am going to quote some special places from the book '*Aḥsan-ul-Wi'ā li Ādāb-id–Du'ā*' where Du'ā is accepted so that you would make Du'ā there with more concentration and fervour. The places in Makka-tul-Mukarramaĥ where Du'ā is accepted include:

1. Maṭāf (2. Multazam (3. Mustajār
4. Inside the Holy Ka'baĥ
5. Below Mīzāb-ur-Raḥmaĥ
6. Ḥaṭīm (7. Ḥajar-ul-Aswad
8. Rukn Yamānī, especially when passing by it during Ṭawāf
9. Behind Maqām-u-Ibrāĥīm
10. Near Zam Zam well
11. Ṣafā (12. Marwaĥ
13. In between Ṣafā and Marwaĥ, especially between Mīlayn-e-Akhḍarayn.

14. 'Arafāt, especially the area where the Prophet of Raḥmaĥ, the Intercessor of Ummaĥ صَلَّى اللهُ تَعَالٰى عَلَيْهِ وَاٰلِهٖ وَسَلَّم stayed.

15. Muzdalifaĥ, especially Mash'ar-ul-Ḥarām

16. Minā

17. Near the three Jamarāt

18. Whenever one glances at the Holy Ka'baĥ.

The places in Madīna-tul-Munawwaraĥ where Du'ā is accepted include:

19. Masjid-un-Nabawī

20. The sacred Muwājaĥaĥ (near the Golden Grille). Imām Ibn-ul-Jazarī رَحْمَةُ اللهِ تَعَالٰى عَلَيْه has stated that if one's Du'ā is not accepted at this place, where else will it be accepted! *(Ḥiṣn Ḥaṣīn, pp. 31)*

21. Near the blessed Mimbar (pulpit)

22. Near the sacred pillars of Masjid-un-Nabawī

23. Masjid Qubā

24. In Masjid-ul-Fatḥ, especially on Wednesday between Ẓuĥr and 'Aṣr.

25. All those Masājid which have affiliation with the Blessed Prophet صَلَّى اللهُ تَعَالٰى عَلَيْهِ وَاٰلِهٖ وَسَلَّم (like Masjid Ghamāmaĥ, Masjid Qiblatayn etc.).

26. All those wells which have affiliation with the Beloved and Blessed Prophet صَلَّى اللهُ تَعَالٰى عَلَيْهِ وَاٰلِهٖ وَسَلَّم.

27. The mount Uḥud

28. Mashāĥid-e-Mubārakaĥ[1]

29. Shrines of Baqī' graveyard

According to historical narrations, about 10,000 Ṣaḥābaĥ (companions رَضِیَ اللّٰہُ تَعَالٰی عَنْھُم) are resting in Jannat-ul-Baqī'. Alas! In 1926, the tombs of this blessed graveyard were demolished and roads were made over the sites of the sacred graves. Therefore, Sag-e-Madīnaĥ hasn't dared to enter Jannat-ul-Baqī' to date lest he steps on some sacred grave unknowingly.

As per religious rulings, it is Ḥarām to place foot on a Muslim's grave or to sit on it. It is stated on page 34 of '*25 Tales of Graveyard*' [the 48-page publication of Maktaba-tul-Madīnaĥ, the publishing department of Dawat-e-Islami], 'It is Ḥarām to walk on the new path made (in the graveyard) by demolishing the graves.'

(Rad-dul-Muḥtār, vol. 1, pp. 612)

In fact, if there is even a doubt about a path being new, it is impermissible and a sin to walk on it. ***(Durr-e-Mukhtār, vol. 3, pp. 183)*** Therefore, devotees of Rasūl are requested to make Salām outside the graveyard. It is not necessary to make Salām at the main entrance of Baqī'. The proper manner is to stand at such a place where your back faces the Qiblaĥ. By doing this, you will be facing those buried in Baqī'.

صَلُّوْا عَلَى الْحَبِيْب صَلَّى اللّٰهُ تَعَالٰى عَلٰى مُحَمَّد

[1] Mashāĥid is the plural of Mashĥad which implies 'The place where one is present.' Here this refers to the places which the Holy Prophet صَلَّی اللّٰہُ تَعَالٰی عَلَیْہِ وَاٰلِہٖ وَسَلَّم visited. At such places Du'ās are accepted. There are countless places in Makkaĥ and Madīnaĥ which the Beloved Prophet صَلَّی اللّٰہُ تَعَالٰی عَلَیْہِ وَاٰلِہٖ وَسَلَّم visited, e.g. the sacred orchard of Sayyidunā Salmān Fārsī رَضِیَ اللّٰہُ تَعَالٰی عَنْہُ etc. [Sag-e-Madīnaĥ]

Types of Hajj

There are three types of Hajj:

1.) Qirān (2. Tamattu' (3. Ifrād

1. Qirān

It is the most preferred type of Hajj. The performer of this Hajj is called a Qārin. For this Hajj, the intention of both Hajj and 'Umraĥ is made together after Iḥrām has been put on. After performing 'Umraĥ, a Qārin cannot get Ḥalq or Qaṣr done; rather, he will remain in the state of Iḥrām as usual. On the 10th, 11th or 12th of Żul-Ḥijjaĥ, after having Ḥalq or Qaṣr done and offering sacrifice (Qurbānī), he will remove his Iḥrām.

2. Tamattu'

The performer of this type of Hajj is called a Mutamatte'. Those coming from outside Mīqāt in the months of Hajj can perform this Hajj. For example, the people from Indo-Pak usually perform Tamattu'. The convenience that lies in it is that a Mutamatte', after performing 'Umraĥ, can get Ḥalq or Qaṣr done and remove his Iḥrām. Then, on the 8th of Żul-Ḥijjaĥ or before it, Iḥrām of Hajj is put on.

3. Ifrād

The performer of this type of Hajj is called a Mufrid. This type of Hajj does not include 'Umraĥ. Only the Iḥrām for Hajj is put on. The residents of Makkaĥ and Ḥillī, i.e. those living between Ḥaram area and Mīqāt (e.g. the people of Jeddah) perform Hajj Ifrād. If they perform Hajj Qirān or Hajj Tamattu', *Dam* will become Wājib. However, Āfāqī can perform 'Ifrād'.

Method of putting on Iḥrām

There is the same manner of putting on Iḥrām for both Hajj and 'Umraĥ. However, there is a slight difference in intention and its wording. The details of intention have been described in the next pages. First note the method of putting on Iḥrām.

1. Trim nails
2. Remove armpits' hair and under navel hair including the hair of the rear private part.
3. Use Miswāk (4. Make Wuḍū (5. Perform Ghusl thoroughly
6. Apply perfume to the body and Iḥrām shawls, as it is a Sunnaĥ but don't use any perfume that stains clothing like dry ambergris (umber).
7. Removing sewn clothes Islamic brothers should put on a piece of new or washed shawl to cover the upper body and use a similar cloth as Taĥband[1]. (You will feel comfortable if the Taĥband is of cotton cloth and the upper shawl is of towelling. The Taĥband cloth should be thick so that the colour of skin is not exposed. Take a fairly big-sized upper shawl, you will find it comfortable.
8. Belt with pocket may also be worn to keep passport or money etc. Rexine belt often rips; therefore, a nylon or leather belt with a wallet having front zipper is very strong, reliable and durable.

Iḥrām of Islamic sisters

Islamic sisters are to wear their sewn clothes as usual. They may wear socks and gloves as well. They should keep their heads covered but should not wear such a veil that touches their face. However, they

[1] Taĥband must be thick enough to prevent the skin colour to be noticed and the other cloth could be of towelling.

may use a book or handheld fan in order to conceal their face from non-Maḥram men, when necessary. It is Ḥarām for women to hide the face in the state of Iḥrām with such a thing that is in contact with the face.

Nafl Ṣalāĥ of Iḥrām

If it is not a Makrūĥ time, offer two Rak'āt Nafl Ṣalāĥ with the intention of Iḥrām (men should also keep their heads covered whilst offering this Ṣalāĥ). It is better to recite Sūraĥ Al-Kāfirūn and Sūraĥ Al-Ikhlāṣ after Sūraĥ Al-Fātiḥaĥ in the first and the second Rak'at respectively.

***

Intention for 'Umraĥ

Now the Islamic brothers with their heads uncovered and the Islamic sisters with their heads covered should make the following intention whether they are performing normal 'Umraĥ of any day (other than the Hajj season) or 'Umraĥ for Hajj Tamattu'.

اَللّٰهُمَّ اِنِّیۡ اُرِیۡدُ الۡعُمۡرَةَ فَیَسِّرۡهَا لِیۡ وَتَقَبَّلۡهَا مِنِّیۡ وَاَعِنِّیۡ عَلَیۡهَا
وَبَارِكۡ لِیۡ فِیۡهَا ط نَوَیۡتُ الۡعُمۡرَةَ وَاَحۡرَمۡتُ بِهَا لِلّٰهِ تَعَالٰی ط

***Translation:** Yā Allah عَزَّوَجَلَّ, I make the intention of 'Umraĥ, make it easy for me and accept it from me. Help me in performing it and make it blessed for me. I have made intention for 'Umraĥ and put on its Iḥrām for the sake of Allah عَزَّوَجَلَّ.*

Intention for Hajj

After putting on the Iḥrām of Hajj, a Mufrid should make the following intention. Similarly, after putting on Iḥrām, a Mutamatte' should also make the following intention on 8th of Żul-Ḥijjaĥ or before it.

اَللّٰهُمَّ اِنِّیۡۤ اُرِيۡدُ الۡحَجَّ فَيَسِّرۡهُ لِیۡ وَتَقَبَّلۡهُ مِنِّیۡ وَاَعِنِّیۡ عَلَيۡهِ

وَبَارِكۡ لِیۡ فِيۡهِ ط نَوَيۡتُ الۡحَجَّ وَ اَحۡرَمۡتُ بِهٖ لِلّٰهِ تَعَالٰی ط

Translation: Yā Allah عَزَّوَجَلَّ! I make the intention of Hajj, make it easy for me and accept it from me. Help me in offering it and make it blessed for me. I have made the intention for Hajj and have put on its Iḥrām for the sake of Allah عَزَّوَجَلَّ.

Intention for Hajj Qirān

A Qārin should make intention for both Hajj and 'Umraĥ in the following words:

اَللّٰهُمَّ اِنِّیۡۤ اُرِيۡدُ الۡعُمۡرَةَ وَالۡحَجَّ فَيَسِّرۡهُمَا لِیۡ وَتَقَبَّلۡهُمَا مِنِّیۡ ط

نَوَيۡتُ الۡعُمۡرَةَ وَالۡحَجَّ وَاَحۡرَمۡتُ بِهِمَا مُخۡلِصًا لِّلّٰهِ تَعَالٰی ط

Translation: Yā Allah عَزَّوَجَلَّ! I make the intention of Hajj and 'Umraĥ, make both of them easy for me and accept them from me. I have made the intention of Hajj and 'Umraĥ and have put on the Iḥrām of both solely for the sake of Allah عَزَّوَجَلَّ.

Labbayk

After making the intention (whether it is the intention of 'Umraĥ, Hajj or that of Hajj Qirān), it is essential to utter Labbayk at least once; uttering it thrice is preferable. Labbayk is as follows:

لَبَّيْكَ ط اَللّٰهُمَّ لَبَّيْكَ ط لَبَّيْكَ لَا شَرِيْكَ لَكَ لَبَّيْكَ ط

اِنَّ الْحَمْدَ وَالنِّعْمَةَ لَكَ وَالْمُلْكَ ط لَا شَرِيْكَ لَكَ ط

I am in attendance. Yā Allah عَزَّوَجَلَّ I am in attendance. I am in attendance (and) You have no partners. I am in attendance. No doubt, all glorification and bounties are for You and also the sovereignty (is Yours), You have no partners.

O travellers of Madīnaĥ! You are now in the state of Iḥrām. Now Labbayk is the greatest invocation of yours. Recite it in abundance whilst sitting, standing and walking. Two blessed sayings of the Beloved Prophet صَلَّى اللّٰهُ تَعَالٰى عَلَيْهِ وَاٰلِهٖ وَسَلَّم are stated below for your inspiration:

1. When the reciter of Labbayk recites it, he is given a piece of good news. It was asked, 'Yā Rasūlallāĥ! Is he given the good news of being blessed with Paradise?' He صَلَّى اللّٰهُ تَعَالٰى عَلَيْهِ وَاٰلِهٖ وَسَلَّم replied, 'Yes.' *(Al-Mu'jam-ul-Awsaṭ, vol. 5, pp. 410, Ḥadīš 7779)*

2. 'When a Muslim recites Labbayk, each and every stone, tree and clod up to the edge of the earth towards his right and left, all recite Labbayk.' *(Tirmižī, vol. 2, pp. 226, Ḥadīš 829)*

Recite Labbayk considering its meaning

It is better to recite Labbayk with extreme humility of heart and full concentration of mind instead of reciting it inattentively looking here and there. When the person who has put on Iḥrām recites Labbayk, it is as if he humbly addresses Allah عَزَّوَجَلَّ and says: '*Labbayk*' that is, I am in attendance. If someone addresses his parents with the same words, he will certainly be attentive whilst saying them. This shows that the person imploring his Creator عَزَّوَجَلَّ by saying Labbayk should be greatly attentive. This is why Sayyidunā 'Allāmaĥ Mullā 'Alī Qārī عَلَيْهِ رَحْمَةُ اللّٰهِ الْبَارِى has stated, 'If a person recites the words of Labbayk aloud so that others would also be repeating each word loudly in the form of a group, this is not Mustaḥab. Everyone should recite it individually.' *(Al-Maslak-ul-Mutaqassiṭ lil-Qārī, pp. 103)*

One Sunnaĥ after reciting Labbayk

It is a Sunnaĥ to make Du'ā after reciting Talbiyaĥ (i.e. Labbayk). It is stated in a blessed Ḥadīš that our Beloved Rasūl صَلَّى اللهُ تَعَالٰى عَلَيْهِ وَاٰلِهٖ وَسَلَّم would make Du'ā to Allah عَزَّوَجَلَّ, after reciting Labbayk, for the attainment of Allah's pleasure, bounties and Paradise and for protection from Hell. *(Musnad Imām Shāfi'ī, pp. 123)* Without doubt, Allah عَزَّوَجَلَّ is pleased with the Beloved Prophet صَلَّى اللهُ تَعَالٰى عَلَيْهِ وَاٰلِهٖ وَسَلَّم. Doubtlessly, the Most Blessed Prophet صَلَّى اللهُ تَعَالٰى عَلَيْهِ وَاٰلِهٖ وَسَلَّم is not only predestined to enter Paradise but he صَلَّى اللهُ تَعَالٰى عَلَيْهِ وَاٰلِهٖ وَسَلَّم is also the Master of Paradise by the grace of Allah عَزَّوَجَلَّ. In fact, besides many other acts of wisdom, these Du'ās are aimed at teaching us so that we will also make Du'ā with the intention of acting upon a Sunnaĥ.

9 Madanī pearls of Labbayk

1. Recite Labbayk in abundance whilst sitting, standing and walking both with and without Wuḍū.
2. Recite it while going upstairs or downstairs, when your caravan meets the other one, at dawn, dusk and at night and after Ṣalāĥ of five times.
3. Whenever you recite Labbayk, recite it at least thrice.
4. As soon as a Mu'tamir as well as a Mutamatte' perform first Istilām of Ḥajar-ul-Aswad for commencing Ṭawāf of 'Umraĥ, they should stop reciting Labbayk.

5. Mufrid and Qārin should stay in Makkaĥ and keep reciting Labbayk. Their recitation of Labbayk will end on 10th of Żul-Ḥijjaĥ when they throw the first stone at Jamra-tul-'Aqabaĥ (big satan).

6. Islamic brothers should recite Labbayk loudly but it should not be so loud as to cause difficulty to themselves or others.

7. Islamic sisters should recite Labbayk in low voice. Both Islamic brothers and sisters should note down the following ruling. Besides Hajj, whenever you recite anything, it is essential to recite it loud enough for you to hear but not so loud as to disturb others.

8. Intention is a condition for Iḥrām. If Labbayk is uttered without intention, Iḥrām will not be valid. Similarly, a mere intention is not sufficient unless Labbayk or its alternative is recited. *('Ālamgīrī, vol. 1, pp. 222)*

9. For Iḥrām, it is essential to recite Labbayk at least once. If, in lieu of Labbayk, someone uttered سُبْحٰنَ اللّٰهِ, اَلْحَمْدُ لِلّٰهِ, لَآ اِلٰهَ اِلَّا اللّٰهُ or some other invocation regarding glorification of Allah عَزَّوَجَلَّ, making intention of Iḥrām, his Iḥrām will be valid but it is Sunnaĥ to recite Labbayk. *(ibid)*

Important ruling regarding intention

Remember! The intention of heart (willingness in heart) is, in fact, a valid intention. Whether one makes intention for Ṣalāĥ, fast, Iḥrām or for any other deed, if the intention is not present in his heart, mere verbal utterance of the words of the intention is not sufficient, and such an intention is not valid.

Also keep in mind that uttering the words of intention in Arabic is not necessary; one can also utter it in his mother tongue. Similarly, uttering the words of intention in any language is not necessary either; just the presence of intention in heart is sufficient. However, uttering it verbally is better and uttering it in Arabic is even more preferable as Arabic is the elegant language of the Noble Prophet صَلَّى اللّٰهُ تَعَالٰى عَلَيْهِ وَاٰلِهٖ وَسَلَّم. Whenever one makes intention in Arabic, it is necessary that he understands its meaning.

Meaning of Iḥrām

The literal meaning of Iḥrām is to declare a thing Ḥarām because even some Ḥalāl (lawful) acts become Ḥarām (unlawful) for the person who is in the state of Iḥrām. The Islamic brother who is in the state of Iḥrām is called Muḥrim, whereas the Islamic sister is called Muḥrimaĥ.

Ḥarām acts in Iḥrām

The following acts are Ḥarām in the state of Iḥrām.

1. For men to wear sewn clothes
2. To wear a cap or to tie a turban or handkerchief on the head
3. For men to place a bundle of clothes onto the head (Islamic sisters should keep their heads covered with shawls; they are not prohibited to place bundle of clothes onto the head).
4. For men to wear gloves (no prohibition for women)
5. For men to wear such socks or shoes that hide the instep (i.e. the raised middle part of the foot)
6. To apply perfume to the body, clothes or hair
7. To eat pure aroma e.g. cardamom, clove, cinnamon, saffron etc. or keep them into clothes. However, if these items are cooked with other food, there is no harm in eating them even if they are giving fragrance.

8. To have intercourse, to kiss, to touch or to hug the wife or to see her vagina provided that the last four things other than intercourse are done with lust.
9. Every indecent act and all types of sins were already Ḥarām and have been more severely Ḥarām in the state of Iḥrām.
10. Worldly conflicts and quarrels
11. Hunting in the forest or even assisting in hunting in any way. Eating, buying and selling meat, egg etc. of the hunted animal is also Ḥarām.
12. Trimming one's nails or getting the nails trimmed by somebody else or trimming the nails of someone else
13. Cutting the hair of the head or beard, removing armpits hair or hair under navel; removing even a single hair from any part of the body from head to foot.
14. Dyeing (hair) with henna (Meĥndī)
15. To apply olive or sesame oil to hair or the body even if the oil has no fragrance
16. Shaving someone's head whether he is in Iḥrām or not. (However, if the time of getting out of the restrictions of Iḥrām has arrived, one can shave one's own head as well as that of anyone else.)
17. Killing or throwing away a louse or signalling someone to kill it. Washing clothes or placing them in sunlight with the intention of killing the louse. Applying anti-lice medicine etc. to hair. In other words, causing the louse to be killed in any way. (All of these acts are Ḥarām in the state of Iḥrām.)

(Baĥār-e-Sharī'at, vol. 1, pp. 1078-1079)

Makrūĥ acts in Iḥrām

1. To remove dirt from the body
2. To wash hair or body with soap etc.

3. To comb hair
4. To scratch (the body) in such a manner that hair may fall out or louse may fall from the head
5. To place a shirt or a coat etc. on the shoulders like wearing it
6. To smell a perfume deliberately
7. To smell fragrant fruits or leaves like lemon, orange, mint etc. (There is no harm in eating such things)
8. To sit in a perfume shop with the intention of smelling fragrance.
9. To touch the emanating fragrance by the hand such that it does not come into contact with the hand; otherwise it would be Ḥarām.
10. To eat or drink such a thing in which uncooked fragrance has been added. However, if the fragrance has neutralized, there is no harm in eating/drinking it.
11. To get underneath the cover of the Holy Ka'baĥ such that it touches the head or the face
12. To cover the nose or any part of the face by a piece of cloth
13. To wear such unsewn cloth which is darned or patched
14. To lie on the stomach[1] with face on the pillow
15. It is Makrūĥ to tie a Ta'wiż even if wrapped in unsewn cloth. However, if a Ta'wiż wrapped in unsewn cloth is worn around the neck instead of being tied on the arm etc. there is no harm in it.
16. To wrap a bandage around the head or the face

[1] To sleep whilst lying on the stomach is forbidden at all times as it is a posture of the hell-dwellers as mentioned in a Ḥadīš.

17. To wrap a bandage around any part of the body without a valid reason.

18. To wear make-up (cosmetics).

19. To tie knots at the ends of a shawl having worn it around shoulders with the head uncovered. To cover the head with it is Ḥarām.

20. To tie a knot at both the ends of Taĥband (i.e. sarong).

21. It is permissible to tie a pocket-belt with the intention of keeping money etc. into it. However, it is Makrūĥ to wear such a belt or string with the intention of tightening the Taĥband. *(Baĥār-e-Sharī'at, vol. 1, pp. 1079-1080)*

Permissible acts in Iḥrām

1. Using Miswāk
2. Wearing a ring[1]

---

[1] Once a companion wearing a brass-ring came in the court of the Beloved and Blessed Rasūl صَلَّى اللهُ تَعَالٰى عَلَيْهِ وَاٰلِهٖ وَسَلَّم. He صَلَّى اللهُ تَعَالٰى عَلَيْهِ وَاٰلِهٖ وَسَلَّم said, 'Why is the smell of idol coming from you!' Hearing this, the companion removed that brass-ring and threw it away. He then came again with an iron ring in his finger. Seeing this, the Noble Prophet صَلَّى اللهُ تَعَالٰى عَلَيْهِ وَاٰلِهٖ وَسَلَّم said, 'Why are you wearing ornaments of the hell-dwellers!' The companion threw that iron-ring away either and asked, 'Yā Rasūlallāĥ صَلَّى اللهُ تَعَالٰى عَلَيْهِ وَاٰلِهٖ وَسَلَّم, what sort of ring should I get made?' The Holy Prophet صَلَّى اللهُ تَعَالٰى عَلَيْهِ وَاٰلِهٖ وَسَلَّم replied, 'Have a silver-ring made and do not let it weigh up to one Mišqāl (16 grams).' *(Abū Dāwūd, vol. 4, pp. 122, Ḥadīš 4223)* In other words, its weight must be less than 4.5 Māshaĥ.

Islamic brothers are allowed to wear only one silver-ring which weighs less than 4.5 Māshaĥ (4 grams and 374 milligrams). There must be only one gem in the ring; they shouldn't wear the ring without a gem either; there is no limit for the weight of the gem. A stoneless ring of silver or any other metal (even if it was made in Madīna-tul-Munawwaraĥ) cannot be worn. Similarly, a ring made of any other metal (e.g. gold, copper, brass, steel etc.) except that of silver with weight limitation described above cannot also be worn. For men to wear a chain made of gold, silver or any metal around the neck is a sin. Islamic sisters may wear rings and chains made of gold and silver. There is no limitation of weight or gem for them.

3. To apply unfragrant kohl into eyes. However, it is Makrūĥ Tanzīĥī for the Muḥrim to use kohl unnecessarily. (If the Muḥrim applied fragrant kohl into the eyes once or twice, he would have to give a Ṣadaqaĥ. If he applied it three times or more, he would have to give a *Dam*.)
4. To bathe without removing dirt from the body.
5. Washing clothes (but it is Ḥarām to do so with the intention of killing lice).
6. Scratching at the body or the head such that hair does not fall out.
7. To use an umbrella or to sit under shade.
8. To insert the ends of shawl into Taĥband.
9. To extract a molar.
10. To detach a broken nail.
11. To rupture a pimple.
12. To remove hair from the eye.
13. To perform circumcision.
14. To have cupping (provided no hair is removed).
15. To kill pest and harmful and evil creatures such as kite, crow, rat, lizard, chameleon, snake, scorpion, bug, mosquito, flea, fly etc. To kill them in Ḥaram is also allowed.
16. To wrap a bandage around any part of the body except for the head and the face. [Although a Muḥrim can wrap a bandage around the head or the face if inevitable but he will have to pay expiation for it].
17. To place a pillow under one's head or cheek.

18. To cover ears with a cloth.
19. To place one's own hand or someone else's hand onto the nose or the head. (Cloth or handkerchief cannot be placed.)
20. To cover the hair of the beard below the chin with a cloth.
21. For a Muḥrim to place a platter or a sack of cereals on the head is permissible but it is Ḥarām for him to place a bundle of clothes onto his head. However, a Muḥrimaĥ is allowed to place both the things onto her head.
22. To eat the food in which clove, cinnamon, cardamom etc. have been cooked; it does not matter even if fragrance is still emanating from it. Similarly, it is permissible to eat the food or drink the beverage in which uncooked fragrance has been added and the fragrance does not emanate from it.
23. To apply ghee or fat or bitter oil or the oil of almond or coconut or squash or lettuce to the body or hair provided it has no fragrance.
24. It is permissible to wear such shoes that do not hide the instep (i.e. the raised middle part of the foot). [Hence the Muḥrim is advised to wear flip-flops, i.e. an open sandal with a thong between the big and the second toe.]
25. To wear a Ta'wīż around the neck, wrapped in an unsewn piece of cloth.
26. To slaughter a domesticated animal such as camel, goat, hen, cow etc. To cook its meat and to eat it. To break its eggs, to fry and to eat them. *(Bahār-e-Sharī'at, vol. 1, pp. 1081-1082)*

Difference in Iḥrām of man and woman

The abovementioned rulings of Iḥrām apply equally to men and women both. However, there are some other permissible acts for women. These days, sewn scarves are sold in markets in the name of Iḥrām. Due to lack of knowledge, Islamic sisters consider those scarves to be a part of their Iḥrām, which is wrong. They should wear sewn clothes as usual. However, if they wear such scarves without deeming them necessary by Sharī'aĥ, there is no harm in it.

1. To conceal the head. It is Farḍ (for a woman) to conceal the head during Ṣalāĥ as well as in the presence of non-Maḥram males (including her maternal and paternal cousins, the husband of the sister of the mother, the husband of the sister of the father, the husband of the sister and especially the younger and elder brother of her own husband). It is Ḥarām for a woman to appear before non-Maḥram males whilst her head is not concealed or whilst wearing such a thin shawl that the blackness of her hair is visible. For a woman to come before non-Maḥram males with her head uncovered is Ḥarām and it is more strictly Ḥarām in the state of Iḥrām.
2. Since Muḥrimaĥ is allowed to conceal her head, she may also carry bundle of clothes onto her head.
3. To tie a sewn Ta'wīż on the arm or the neck.
4. To get underneath the cover of the Holy Ka'baĥ such that it remains on her head without coming into contact with her face as it is Ḥarām even for a woman to cover her face with a piece of cloth. (These days, people apply a lot of fragrance to the cover of the Holy Ka'baĥ, therefore, women should also be careful in the state of Iḥrām.)
5. To wear gloves, socks and sewn clothes.
6. Since it is Ḥarām for the Muḥrimaĥ to cover her face in the state of Iḥrām, she should keep some cardboard or handheld fan near her face (without it touching the face) for veiling from non-Maḥram males. *(Bahār-e-Sharī'at, vol. 1, pp. 1083)*

7. Islamic sisters can wear such caps that have veils attached to the brims, making sure that the veil does not touch the face. However, there is the risk of the veil coming into contact with the face when heavy wind is blowing. Moreover, there is also the chance that they might wipe sweat from the face with the same veil. Therefore, they must take great care.

9 Useful cautions in Iḥrām

1. When buying Iḥrām, unfold and check it whether it fits you. If you bought the Iḥrām without checking, and it turned out to be unfit at the time of your departure, you might face a troublesome ordeal.

2. Practise how to put on Iḥrām at home before your departure.

3. The upper shawl should be of towelling, whereas the Taĥband should be of thick cotton cloth. The Ḥājī would find it comfortable during Ṣalāĥ, reducing the chance of the shawl flying in Minā etc. when the wind is blowing.

4. Practise walking at home after you have put on Iḥrām and belt etc. One who has put on Iḥrām for the first time might face difficulty because the Iḥrām may be fastened very tightly or may get unfastened.

5. The cotton shawl of Iḥrām should be thick and of good quality. Thin cloth might stick to the body because of sweat, making the colour of thighs etc. visible. Some types of cloth are so thin that the colour of thighs etc. is visible even when the body is not sweating. It is stated on page 194 of the 496 pages-containing book '*Laws of Ṣalāĥ*' published by Maktaba-tul-Madīnaĥ, the publishing department of Dawat-e-Islami: 'If someone wears such thin clothing that exposes such a part of the body which is

Farḍ to be concealed in Ṣalāĥ, or that exposes the colour of skin (of that part), the Ṣalāĥ will not be valid. *(Fatāwā 'Ālamgīrī, vol. 1, pp. 58)* Nowadays, the trend of wearing thin clothing is growing. Wearing such thin clothes that expose any part of thigh or Satr is Ḥarām even when not offering Ṣalāĥ. *(Baĥār-e-Sharī'at, vol. 1, pp. 480)*

6. It is a Sunnaĥ to apply fragrance to Iḥrām before you have made the intention. Do apply fragrance to Iḥrām but do not put the bottle of fragrance into the pocket of the belt you are wearing, because fragrance may come into contact with your hand if you put the hand into the pocket after you have made the intention. If so much amount of fragrance has come into contact with the hand that others consider it to be 'more' *Dam* will be Wājib. If they consider it less, Ṣadaqaĥ will be due. If the liquid of the fragrance has not come into contact, but rather it has only caused the hand to have fragrance, there will be no expiation in this case. If you want to put the bottle of fragrance into your bag etc. wrap it in some polythene bag and then put it at such a place where it will not come into contact with your hand etc.

7. If the upper shawl has slipped down from shoulders and the Muḥrim is going to draw it up, he should take care that it neither touches his own head or face nor that of any other Muḥrim. I[1] have personally seen that the upper shawls of some Muḥrim when being drawn up in the crowd had caught on the bald heads of other Muḥrims.

8. Most of the Muḥrims tie Taĥband (i.e. sarong) of Iḥrām from beneath their navel. Sometimes the upper shawl falls from their shoulders due to carelessness, exposing some part of the body beneath the navel. Such Muḥrims do not usually care about it

---

[1] The author, Amīr-e-Aĥl-e-Sunnat دَامَتْ بَرَكَاتُهُمُ الْعَالِيَه

at all. Similarly sometimes thighs etc. become exposed to others when some Muḥrims walk or sit carelessly[1]. Remember this important ruling that the body of man from below the navel up to and including the knees is his 'Satr' (i.e. the body-parts which must be kept concealed), and exposing even a small portion of it to others, without Shar'ī exemption, is Ḥarām.

These rulings regarding veiling of man's 'Satr' are not confined to Iḥrām. Even when not in Iḥrām, it is Ḥarām to expose one's Satr to others or to look at the Satr of others.

9. Some Muḥrims tie Taĥband of Iḥrām from beneath their navel, carelessly exposing some portion of their under navel belly before others.

   It is stated in *Baĥār-e-Sharī'at*: If one fourth (1/4) portion of the area from under the navel till the root of the member[2] in roundness remains uncovered, Ṣalāĥ will not be valid. Some people are so careless in this matter that their knees and thighs are uncovered before others. This is Ḥarām (even when not in the state of Iḥrām or not offering Ṣalāĥ). If someone is habitual of doing this, he is a transgressor (Fāsiq).

   (Baĥār-e-Sharī'at, vol. 1, pp. 481)

An important caution

If the acts impermissible in the state of Iḥrām occur due to some compulsion or by mistake, though there will be no sin, the penalty imposed by Sharī'aĥ in this regard must be paid even if these acts take place unwillingly, forgetfully, during sleep or under coercion.

(ibid, pp. 1083)

صَلُّوْا عَلَى الْحَبِيْب   صَلَّى اللّٰهُ تَعَالٰى عَلٰى مُحَمَّد

[1] See the method of observing veil within veil in the glossary given at the end of the book.

[2] 'Member' is a polite word for a penis.

Explanation of Ḥaram

People generally assume that only Masjid-ul-Ḥarām is Ḥaram. No doubt Masjid-ul-Ḥarām is also within Ḥaram but Ḥaram has spread out[1] up to several miles around Makka-tul-Mukarramaĥ with its limits fixed in all directions.

For example, there lies a police check point on the road about 23 kilometres away from Makka-tul-Mukarramaĥ towards Jeddah. On this road, there is a sign board that read: 'لِلْمُسْلِمِيْنَ فَقَط' (i.e. *only for Muslims*). Ahead of it is Bīr-e-Shamīs[2], i.e. Ḥudaybiyaĥ wherefrom the limit of Ḥaram starts in this direction. According to the latest measurement made by a historian, the perimeter of Ḥaram is 127 kilometres, whereas its total area is 550 square kilometres. *(Tārīkh Makka-tul-Mukarramaĥ, pp. 15)* (The administration often makes new roads and routes by building tunnels, cutting mountains and deforestation, causing the area of the sacred territory to be increased or decreased. Therefore, the correct limits of Ḥaram are the very same as stated in blessed Aḥādīš.)

Ṫĥandī ṫĥandī ĥawā Ḥaram kī ĥay
Bārish Allah kay karam kī ĥay

Gentle breeze is blowing in Ḥaram
Rain of mercy is showering in Ḥaram

(Wasāil-e-Bakhshish, pp. 124)

Entering Makkaĥ

Anyway, enter the limits of Ḥaram with your head bowed and eyes lowered with humility and shame for the sins committed. Recite

[1] Obviously, the population of Makka-tul-Mukarramaĥ is increasing constantly, extending it beyond the limits of Ḥaram in some directions. For example, Tan'im is outside the limits of Ḥaram but probably within the municipality of Makka-tul-Mukarramaĥ. وَاللهُ وَرَسُوْلُهٗ اَعْلَم

[2] Name of a well

Ṣalāt-'Alan-Nabī and Labbayk and do Żikr in abundance. As soon as you have the sight of the sacred city of Makka-tul-Mukarramaĥ of Rab-bul-'Ālamīn, recite the following Du'ā:

اَللّٰهُمَّ اجْعَلْ لِّیْ قَرَارًا وَّارْزُقْنِیْ فِیْهَا رِزْقًا حَلَالًا

***Translation:** Yā Allah عَزَّوَجَلَّ! Bestow upon me peace and Ḥalāl sustenance in it.*

After reaching Makka-tul-Mukarramaĥ, make arrangements for accommodation and keep luggage etc. at a safe place. Then, come to Bāb-us-Salām reciting Labbayk. Kiss the holy door and enter Masjid-ul-Ḥarām placing your right foot first and reciting the Du'ā of entering the Masjid that is as follows:

بِسْمِ اللّٰهِ وَالسَّلَامُ عَلٰی

رَسُوْلِ اللّٰهِ ط اَللّٰهُمَّ افْتَحْ لِیْٓ اَبْوَابَ رَحْمَتِكَ ط

***Translation:** Allah عَزَّوَجَلَّ in Whose name I begin and salutations on the Rasūl of Allah, Yā Allah عَزَّوَجَلَّ, open the portals of Your mercy for me.*

Make intention of I'tikāf

Whenever you enter any Masjid and make the intention of I'tikāf, you will be granted reward. Therefore, make this intention in Masjid-ul-Ḥarām as well. One good deed here is equivalent to a hundred thousand deeds performed elsewhere. Hence one will get the reward of a hundred thousand I'tikāf. You will get the reward for as long as you stay in the Masjid. In addition, acts of eating, drinking Zam Zam water and sleeping will also become permissible; otherwise these acts are impermissible in the Masjid according to Sharī'aĥ.

نَوَيْتُ سُنَّتَ الْاِعْتِكَافِ ط

***Translation:* I make the intention of Sunnaĥ of I'tikāf.**

First glance at Holy Ka'baĥ

As soon as you have the first glance of the Holy Ka'baĥ, recite the following thrice:

لَآ اِلٰهَ اِلَّا اللّٰهُ وَاللّٰهُ اَكْبَرُ ط

Then, recite Ṣalāt-'Alan-Nabī and make Du'ā as the Du'ā made on having the first glance of the Holy Ka'baĥ is definitely accepted. You may also make this Du'ā: 'Yā Allah عَزَّوَجَلَّ, whenever I make any permissible Du'ā that is beneficial to me, accept it.' 'Allāmaĥ Shāmī قُدِّسَ سِرُّهُ السَّامِی has quoted Islamic jurists to have stated: When having the first glance of the Ka'baĥ, one should make Du'ā to be blessed with entry into Paradise without accountability, and should recite Ṣalāt-'Alan-Nabī. *(Rad-dul-Muḥtār, vol. 3, pp. 575)*

Most virtuous supplication

O devotees of Rasūl seeking the pleasure of Allah عَزَّوَجَلَّ and the Holy Prophet صَلَّى اللهُ تَعَالٰى عَلَيْهِ وَاٰلِهٖ وَسَلَّم! Instead of reciting different specific Du'ās, it is the most virtuous to recite Ṣalāt-'Alan-Nabī on every occasion e.g. during Ṭawāf, Sa'ī etc. اِنْ شَآءَاللّٰه عَزَّوَجَلَّ All of your problems will be resolved by virtue of Ṣalāt and Salām. You should do what is better than all Du'ās for you, as promised by the Prophet of Raḥmaĥ, the Intercessor of Ummaĥ صَلَّى اللهُ تَعَالٰى عَلَيْهِ وَاٰلِهٖ وَسَلَّم. Instead of making Du'ā for yourself, send Ṣalāt upon him on all occasions. The Beloved and

Blessed Prophet صَلَّى اللّٰهُ تَعَالٰى عَلَيْهِ وَاٰلِهٖ وَسَلَّم has stated, 'If you do so, Allah عَزَّوَجَلَّ will resolve all your problems and forgive all your sins.' *(Tirmiżī, vol. 4, pp. 207, Ḥadīš 2465; Fatāwā Razawiyyaĥ referenced, vol. 10, pp. 740)*

Halting for supplication during Ṭawāf is forbidden

Respected Ḥujjāj! If possible, recite only Ṣalāt and Salām as it is the most virtuous invocation in addition to being easier to be recited. However, Du'ās have also been presented for those who are keen to recite them. But remember that whether you recite Ṣalāt and Salām or Du'ās, recite them in a low voice. Some Ṭawāf-performing people recite Du'ās aloud like shouting. You should avoid it. Furthermore, recite it whilst walking. Do not halt during Ṭawāf for reciting anything.

METHOD OF 'UMRAH

Method of Ṭawāf

Before commencing Ṭawāf, men should do Iḍṭibā', i.e. put on shawl by bringing its one end from under the armpit of the right hand and placing its both ends over the left shoulder such that the right shoulder remains uncovered. You are now wholeheartedly ready for Ṭawāf of the Holy Ka'baĥ. Now in the state of Iḍṭibā', stand up facing the Holy Ka'baĥ such that the whole 'Ḥajar-ul-Aswad' is towards your right side. Now make intention for Ṭawāf in the following words without raising the hands:

اَللّٰهُمَّ اِنِّيْٓ اُرِيْدُ طَوَافَ

بَيْتِكَ الْحَرَامِ فَيَسِّرْهُ لِيْ وَتَقَبَّلْهُ مِنِّيْ ط

Translation: *Yā Allah عَزَّوَجَلَّ! I make intention for Ṭawāf of Your sacred House. Make it easier for me and accept it from me.*

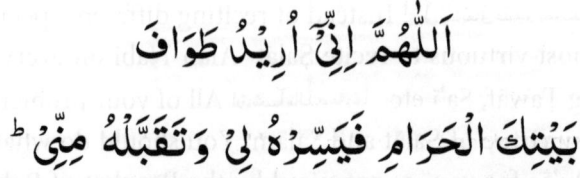

After making the intention, whilst facing the Holy Ka'baĥ, move a little towards your right so that Ḥajar-ul-Aswad is right in front of you. (This would happen after a slight movement of yours. Now Ḥajar-ul-Aswad is exactly in front of you and its recognition is that the green tube light fixed opposite Ḥajar-ul-Aswad will be right behind your back.)

(Please note that the intention made in Arabic for any act like Ṣalāĥ, fasting, I'tikāf, Ṭawāf etc. will be valid only when one understands its meaning. Intention may also be made in one's native language. In all cases, presence of intention in heart is a pre-condition. Even if one does not make a verbal intention, the intention of heart is sufficient. However making a verbal intention, in addition, is better).

سُبْحٰنَ اللّٰہ عَزَّوَجَلَّ! This is that lucky heavenly stone which has certainly been kissed by our Beloved Rasūl صَلَّى اللهُ تَعَالٰى عَلَيْهِ وَاٰلِهٖ وَسَلَّم. Now raise both hands such that both palms (of hands) face the direction of Ḥajar-ul-Aswad and recite the following:

بِسْمِ اللهِ وَالْحَمْدُ لِلّٰهِ وَاللهُ

اَكْبَرُ وَالصَّلٰوةُ وَالسَّلَامُ عَلٰى رَسُوْلِ اللهِ ط

***Translation:** Allah عَزَّوَجَلَّ in Whose name I begin and all glorifications are for Allah عَزَّوَجَلَّ and Allah عَزَّوَجَلَّ is the greatest and Ṣalāt & Salām be on the Rasūl of Allah صَلَّى اللهُ تَعَالٰى عَلَيْهِ وَاٰلِهٖ وَسَلَّم.*

Now, if possible, place both palms on Ḥajar-ul-Aswad and kiss it in between your palms without producing any sound. Do this thrice.

!سُبۡحٰنَ اللّٰہ عَزَّوَجَلَّ Be delighted with the thought that your lips have kissed that sacred stone which has certainly been touched by the blessed lips of our Beloved Rasūl صَلَّی اللہ تَعَالٰی عَلَیۡہِ وَاٰلِہٖ وَسَلَّم. Get ecstatic and overjoyed! Also shed tears.

Sayyidunā 'Abdullāĥ Ibn 'Umar رَضِیَ اللّٰہُ تَعَالٰی عَنۡھُمَا has narrated, 'Keeping his sacred lips on Ḥajar-ul-Aswad our Beloved and Blessed Prophet صَلَّی اللہ تَعَالٰی عَلَیۡہِ وَاٰلِہٖ وَسَلَّم kept on weeping. He صَلَّی اللہ تَعَالٰی عَلَیۡہِ وَاٰلِہٖ وَسَلَّم then turned and noticed that Sayyidunā 'Umar رَضِیَ اللہ تَعَالٰی عَنۡہُ was also weeping. Our Holy Prophet صَلَّی اللہ تَعَالٰی عَلَیۡہِ وَاٰلِہٖ وَسَلَّم said, 'Certainly, it is an occasion of weeping and shedding tears.' *(Ibn Mājaĥ, vol. 3, pp. 434, Ḥadīš 2945)*

Take care that you do not push anybody as this is not a place to display your strength but it is an occasion to express humility and humbleness. If it is difficult for you to kiss Ḥajar-ul-Aswad due to the crowd, then neither cause discomfort to others nor get stuck in the crowd. Instead, kiss your hand or a stick having touched it to Ḥajar-ul-Aswad. If it is not possible either, kiss your hand having pointed your palms towards Ḥajar-ul-Aswad. Even this is a great privilege to have glance at the spot which has been kissed by the Beloved and Blessed Prophet صَلَّی اللہ تَعَالٰی عَلَیۡہِ وَاٰلِہٖ وَسَلَّم.

To kiss Ḥajar-ul-Aswad or to kiss your hand or a stick having touched it to Ḥajar-ul-Aswad or to kiss your hand having pointed your palms towards Ḥajar-ul-Aswad is called Istilām.

The Beloved Prophet صَلَّی اللہ تَعَالٰی عَلَیۡہِ وَاٰلِہٖ وَسَلَّم has stated, 'On the Day of Judgement, this stone will be raised with eyes whereby it will see, and with the tongue whereby it will speak, and will give evidence for the one who kissed it with the truth.' *(Tirmiżī, vol. 2, pp. 286, Ḥadīš 963)*

اَللّٰهُمَّ اِيۡمَانًا بِكَ وَاتِّبَاعًا

لِّسُنَّةِ نَبِيِّكَ مُحَمَّدٍ صَلَّى اللّٰهُ تَعَالٰى عَلَيۡهِ وَسَلَّمْ ط

Translation: *O Almighty* عَزَّوَجَلَّ*! I have put belief in You and I am going to perform Ṭawāf following the Sunnaĥ of Your Prophet* صَلَّى اللهُ تَعَالٰى عَلَيۡهِ وَاٰلِهٖ وَسَلَّم*.*

Now whilst facing the Holy Ka'baĥ, move a little towards your right so that Ḥajar-ul-Aswad is not in front of your face (and this would happen after a slight movement of yours towards right). Then immediately turn rightward such that the Holy Ka'baĥ is on your left side. Now walk with care so that no one is bumped by you.

Men should perform Raml during the first three rounds i.e. walk briskly with small steps whilst moving the shoulders like strong and brave people. Some people perform it by jumping and running, this is not a Sunnaĥ. Raml may be discontinued on crowded spots or when it is painful for you or for others but do not halt for Raml; continue with Ṭawāf. As soon as you get a chance to do Raml, resume it.

It is preferable to remain closer to the Holy Ka'baĥ during Ṭawāf but not to such an extent that your cloth or body touches the wall of the Holy Ka'baĥ. If Raml cannot be performed in case of remaining closer to the Holy Ka'baĥ due to crowd, remaining farther is better. For Islamic sisters to remain away from the Holy Ka'baĥ is better. During first round, recite the following Du'ā after reciting Ṣalāt-'Alan-Nabī.

***

Supplication of first round

سُبۡحٰنَ اللّٰهِ وَالۡحَمۡدُ لِلّٰهِ وَلَآ اِلٰهَ اِلَّا اللّٰهُ وَاللّٰهُ اَكۡبَرُؕ وَلَا حَوۡلَ وَلَا قُوَّةَ اِلَّا بِاللّٰهِ الۡعَلِیِّ الۡعَظِیۡمِؕ وَالصَّلٰوةُ وَالسَّلَامُ عَلٰی رَسُوۡلِ اللّٰهِ صَلَّی اللّٰهُ تَعَالٰی عَلَیۡهِ وَاٰلِهٖ وَسَلَّمَؕ اَللّٰهُمَّ اِیۡمَانًا بِكَ وَتَصۡدِیۡقًا بِكِتَابِكَ وَوَفَآءً بِعَهۡدِكَ وَاتِّبَاعًا لِّسُنَّةِ نَبِیِّكَ وَحَبِیۡبِكَ مُحَمَّدٍ صَلَّی اللّٰهُ تَعَالٰی عَلَیۡهِ وَاٰلِهٖ وَسَلَّمؕ اَللّٰهُمَّ اِنِّیۡۤ اَسۡئَلُكَ الۡعَفۡوَ وَالۡعَافِیَةَ وَالۡمُعَافَاةَ الدَّآئِمَةَ فِی الدِّیۡنِ وَالدُّنۡیَا وَالۡاٰخِرَةِ وَالۡفَوۡزَ بِالۡجَنَّةِ وَالنَّجَاةَ مِنَ النَّارِؕ

Translation: *Allah عَزَّوَجَلَّ is pure (from all shortcomings). All glorifications are for Allah عَزَّوَجَلَّ and no one is worthy of worship except Allah عَزَّوَجَلَّ. And Allah عَزَّوَجَلَّ is the greatest. And the power (to refrain from sins) and the strength (to incline towards worship) is (bestowed) by Allah عَزَّوَجَلَّ Who is dignified and glorified. May blessings and salutations of Allah عَزَّوَجَلَّ be upon Rasūl of Allah صَلَّى اللهُ تَعَالٰى عَلَيْهِ وَاٰلِهٖ وَسَلَّم. Yā Allah عَزَّوَجَلَّ! I believe in You and testify Your commandments and affirm the oath made with You following the Sunnaĥ of Your Beloved Prophet Muhammad صَلَّى اللهُ تَعَالٰى عَلَيْهِ وَاٰلِهٖ وَسَلَّم (I have started Ṭawāf). Yā Allah عَزَّوَجَلَّ! I beg forgiveness from You (for my sins) and safety (from every affliction) and everlasting security (from every trouble)* *in our religion and in the world and in the Hereafter, and the gaining of Paradise and deliverance from the fire of Hell.* (Recite Ṣalāt-'Alan-Nabī)

Complete this Du'ā before reaching Rukn Yamānī. Now touch Rukn Yamānī (for acquiring blessings) with both hands or with right hand provided that there is no risk of trouble for you and for others due to crowd. Do not touch with left hand only. If you get a chance, kiss Rukn Yamānī. If one does not get the chance to kiss or touch, then kiss the hands having signalled to it. (As people apply a lot of fragrance to Rukn Yamānī these days, those in the state of Iḥrām should take care before they touch or kiss Rukn Yamānī.)

Now after completing the Ṭawāf of three corners of the Holy Ka'bah, you are approaching the fourth sacred corner Rukn Aswad. The wall between Rukn Yamānī and Rukn Aswad is called Mustajāb. Here 70,000 angels are deputed to say Āmīn for Du'ā. Ask whatever you desire in your mother tongue, for yourself as well as for all Muslims, or recite Ṣalāt-'Alan-Nabī once on behalf of the entire Ummah including me, a sinful devotee of Madīnah. Recite this Quranic Du'ā as well:

رَبَّنَآ اٰتِنَا فِی الدُّنْیَا حَسَنَةً

وَّفِی الْاٰخِرَةِ حَسَنَةً وَّقِنَا عَذَابَ النَّارِ ۝

Our Rab! Grant us good in this world and good in the Hereafter and save us from the torment of hell-fire.

[Kanz-ul-Īmān (Translation of Quran)]

Now you have reached Ḥajar-ul-Aswad, completing the first round. Here people are seen waving their hands from far away, imitating each other as they pass. Doing so is not a Sunnah. As described earlier, turn towards Ḥajar-ul-Aswad facing the Qiblah. There is no need of making intention as it has already been made. To start the second round raise both hands up to ears and recite this Du'ā:

بِسْمِ اللّٰهِ وَالْحَمْدُ لِلّٰهِ وَاللّٰهُ

اَكْبَرُ وَالصَّلٰوةُ وَالسَّلَامُ عَلٰى رَسُوْلِ اللّٰهِ ط

Perform Istilām i.e. if there is an opportunity, kiss Ḥajar-ul-Aswad, otherwise kiss the hands having signalled to it with them. Now keeping face towards the Holy Ka'baĥ, move a little towards your right. As soon as Ḥajar-ul-Aswad is not in front of you, start Ṭawāf such that the Holy Ka'baĥ is on your left side. Reciting Ṣalāt-'Alan-Nabī, recite Du'ā of second round.

Supplication of second round

اَللّٰهُمَّ اِنَّ هٰذَا الْبَيْتَ بَيْتُكَ وَالْحَرَمَ حَرَمُكَ وَالْاَمْنَ اَمْنُكَ

وَالْعَبْدَ عَبْدُكَ وَاَنَا عَبْدُكَ وَابْنُ عَبْدِكَ وَهٰذَا مَقَامُ الْعَآئِذِبِكَ

مِنَ النَّارِ ط فَحَرِّمْ لُحُوْمَنَا وَبَشَرَتَنَا عَلَى النَّارِ ط اَللّٰهُمَّ حَبِّبْ

اِلَيْنَا الْاِيْمَانَ وَزَيِّنْهُ فِيْ قُلُوْبِنَا وَكَرِّهْ اِلَيْنَا الْكُفْرَ وَالْفُسُوْقَ

وَالْعِصْيَانَ وَاجْعَلْنَا مِنَ الرَّاشِدِيْنَ ط اَللّٰهُمَّ قِنِيْ عَذَابَكَ

يَوْمَ تَبْعَثُ عِبَادَكَ ط اَللّٰهُمَّ ارْزُقْنِيَ الْجَنَّةَ بِغَيْرِ حِسَابٍ ط

***Translation:** Yā Allah عَزَّوَجَلَّ! No doubt, this House is Your House, this Ḥaram is Your Ḥaram, the peace and security (here) has been bestowed by You. And every servant is Your servant and I am also Your servant and I am a son of Your servant. This is the place to beg protection against the fire of Hell from You. So make our flesh and skin Ḥarām for the fire of Hell. Yā Allah عَزَّوَجَلَّ! Bless us with utmost devotion for (Islamic) faith and inculcate fondness for it in our hearts. And make infidelity, sin and transgression a displeasing thing for us and include us among those who are on the True Path. Yā Allah عَزَّوَجَلَّ! Save me from torment on the day when You will resurrect Your servants and Yā Allah عَزَّوَجَلَّ! Bestow upon me Paradise without accountability.* (Recite Ṣalāt-'Alan-Nabī)

***

Finish this supplication before reaching Rukn Yamānī. If you get a chance, kiss it. Otherwise just touch it (i.e. Rukn Yamānī), and move towards Ḥajar-ul-Aswad reciting Ṣalāt-'Alan-Nabī as well as this Qurānic Du'ā:

رَبَّنَآ اٰتِنَا فِی الدُّنْیَا حَسَنَةً

وَّفِی الْاٰخِرَةِ حَسَنَةً وَّقِنَا عَذَابَ النَّارِ ۝

Our Rab! Grant us good in this world and good in the Hereafter and save us from the torment of hell-fire.

[Kanz-ul-Īmān (Translation of Quran)]

Look! You have again approached Ḥajar-ul-Aswad. Now your second round has also completed. Then, like before, recite the following Du'ā raising both hands up to ears:

بِسۡمِ اللّٰہِ وَالۡحَمۡدُ لِلّٰہِ وَاللّٰہُ
اَکۡبَرُ وَالصَّلٰوۃُ وَالسَّلَامُ عَلٰی رَسُوۡلِ اللّٰہِ ط

Then perform Istilām of Ḥajar-ul-Aswad and complete the third round like previous ones. Reciting Ṣalāt-'Alan-Nabī recite the following Du'ā:

***

Supplication of third round

اَللّٰھُمَّ اِنِّیۡۤ اَعُوۡذُبِكَ مِنَ الشَّكِّ وَالشِّرۡكِ وَالنِّفَاقِ
وَالشِّقَاقِ وَسُوۡٓءِ الۡاَخۡلَاقِ وَسُوۡٓءِ الۡمَنۡظَرِ وَالۡمُنۡقَلَبِ فِی
الۡمَالِ وَالۡاَھۡلِ وَالۡوَلَدِ ط اَللّٰھُمَّ اِنِّیۡۤ اَسۡئَلُكَ رِضَاكَ وَالۡجَنَّۃَ
وَاَعُوۡذُبِكَ مِنۡ سَخَطِكَ وَالنَّارِ ط اَللّٰھُمَّ اِنِّیۡۤ اَعُوۡذُبِكَ مِنۡ
فِتۡنَۃِ الۡقَبۡرِ وَاَعُوۡذُبِكَ مِنۡ فِتۡنَۃِ الۡمَحۡیَا وَالۡمَمَاتِ ط

***Translation:** Yā Allah عَزَّوَجَلَّ! I seek Your refuge from doubting (in Your commandments) and from polytheism (in Your Being or in Your Attributes), and from discord and hypocrisy, from bad manners, and from bad condition and from doom of wealth and family. Yā Allah عَزَّوَجَلَّ! I beg for Your pleasure and Paradise, and I seek Your refuge from Your wrath* *and from Hell. Yā Allah عَزَّوَجَلَّ! I seek Your refuge from the calamity of the grave and seek Your refuge from every affliction of life and death.* (Recite Ṣalāt-'Alan-Nabī)

***

Finish this Du'ā before reaching Rukn Yamānī. If possible, kiss it. Otherwise only touch it (Rukn Yamānī) and move towards Ḥajar-ul-Aswad reciting Ṣalāt-'Alan-Nabī and this Qurānic Du'ā:

رَبَّنَآ اٰتِنَا فِي الدُّنْيَا حَسَنَةً

وَّفِي الْاٰخِرَةِ حَسَنَةً وَّقِنَا عَذَابَ النَّارِ ۝

Our Rab! Grant us good in this world and good in the Hereafter and save us from the torment of hell-fire.

[Kanz-ul-Īmān (Translation of Quran)]

Look! You have again reached Ḥajar-ul-Aswad. Now your third round has completed. Then, like before, recite the following Du'ā raising both hands up to ears:

بِسْمِ اللّٰهِ وَالْحَمْدُ لِلّٰهِ وَاللّٰهُ

اَكْبَرُ وَالصَّلٰوةُ وَالسَّلَامُ عَلٰى رَسُوْلِ اللّٰهِ ط

Then perform Istilām of Ḥajar-ul-Aswad and start the fourth round like previous ones. You do not need to perform Raml any longer as Raml is to be performed in the first three rounds only. Now you have to complete remaining rounds by walking at medium pace. Reciting Ṣalāt-'Alan-Nabī, recite the following Du'ā of the fourth round:

Supplication of fourth round

اَللّٰهُمَّ اجْعَلْهُ حَجًّا مَّبْرُوْرًا وَّ سَعْيًا مَّشْكُوْرًا وَّ ذَنْبًا

مَّغْفُوْرًا وَّعَمَلًا صَالِحًا مَّقْبُوْلًا وَّتِجَارَةً لَّنْ تَبُوْرَ ط

يَا عَالِمَ مَا فِى الصُّدُوْرِ اَخْرِجْنِىْ يَآ اَللّٰهُ مِنَ الظُّلُمَاتِ اِلَى

النُّوْرِ ط اَللّٰهُمَّ اِنِّىْٓ اَسْئَلُكَ مُوْجِبَاتِ رَحْمَتِكَ وَعَزَآئِمَ

مَغْفِرَتِكَ وَالسَّلَامَةَ مِنْ كُلِّ اِثْمٍ وَّالْغَنِيْمَةَ مِنْ كُلِّ

بِرٍّ وَّالْفَوْزَ بِالْجَنَّةِ وَالنَّجَاةَ مِنَ النَّارِ ط اَللّٰهُمَّ قَنِّعْنِىْ

بِمَا رَزَقْتَنِىْ وَبَارِكْ لِىْ فِيْهِ وَاخْلُفْ عَلٰى كُلِّ غَآئِبَةٍ

لِّىْ بِخَيْرٍ ط

Translation: *Yā Allah* عَزَّوَجَلَّ*! Make this (Hajj of mine) an accepted one, a successful effort and a basis for the forgiveness of my sins and an accepted pious deed and a trading with no loss. O the Knower of the affairs of hearts! Bring me out from darkness (of sins) towards the refulgence (of pious deeds). Yā Allah* عَزَّوَجَلَّ*! I ask You (the means of) that which makes Your mercy indispensable for me and the means of that which guarantees my forgiveness from You. I ask You to grant me protection from every sin and ability to adopt every good deed and to avail Paradise and to get* *freedom from Hell. Yā Allah* عَزَّوَجَلَّ*! Whatever sustenance You have bestowed upon me, make me content with it, increase virtue in the bounties which You have provided to me and, by Your grace, provide me with good substitute for every loss.* (Recite Ṣalāt-'Alan-Nabī)

***

As usual, complete the foregoing Du'ā before reaching Rukn Yamānī. Then reciting Ṣalāt-'Alan-Nabī, recite the following Du'ā:

رَبَّنَآ اٰتِنَا فِى الدُّنْيَا حَسَنَةً

وَّفِى الْاٰخِرَةِ حَسَنَةً وَّقِنَا عَذَابَ النَّارِ ۝

Our Rab! Grant us good in this world and good in the Hereafter and save us from the torment of hell-fire.

[Kanz-ul-Īmān (Translation of Quran)]

You have reached Ḥajar-ul-Aswad once again. Then, like before, recite the following supplication raising both hands up to ears:

بِسْمِ اللّٰهِ وَالْحَمْدُ لِلّٰهِ وَاللّٰهُ

اَكْبَرُ وَالصَّلٰوةُ وَالسَّلَامُ عَلٰى رَسُوْلِ اللّٰهِ ط

Then perform the Istilām of Ḥajar-ul-Aswad and begin the fifth round of Ṭawāf. Reciting Ṣalāt-'Alan-Nabī, recite the Du'ā for the fifth round of Ṭawāf which is as follows:

Supplication of fifth round

اَللّٰهُمَّ اَظِلَّنِیْ تَحْتَ ظِلِّ عَرْشِكَ یَوْمَ لَا ظِلَّ اِلَّا ظِلُّ عَرْشِكَ

وَلَا بَاقِیَ اِلَّا وَجْهُكَ وَاسْقِنِیْ مِنْ حَوْضِ نَبِیِّكَ سَیِّدِنَا

مُحَمَّدٍ صَلَّى اللّٰهُ تَعَالٰی عَلَیْهِ وَاٰلِهٖ وَسَلَّمَ شَرْبَةً هَنِیْٓـئَةً

مَّرِیْٓـئَةً لَّا نَظْمَأُ بَعْدَهَا اَبَدًا ط اَللّٰهُمَّ اِنِّیْٓ اَسْـَٔلُكَ مِنْ خَیْرِ

مَا سَـَٔلَكَ مِنْهُ نَبِیُّكَ سَیِّدُنَا مُحَمَّدٌ صَلَّى اللّٰهُ تَعَالٰی عَلَیْهِ

وَاٰلِهٖ وَسَلَّمَ وَاَعُوْذُبِكَ مِنْ شَرِّمَا اسْتَعَاذَكَ مِنْهُ نَبِیُّكَ

سَیِّدُنَا مُحَمَّدٌ صَلَّى اللّٰهُ تَعَالٰی عَلَیْهِ وَاٰلِهٖ وَسَلَّمَ ط اَللّٰهُمَّ

اِنِّیْٓ اَسْـَٔلُكَ الْجَنَّةَ وَ نَعِیْمَهَا وَمَا یُقَرِّبُنِیْٓ اِلَیْهَا مِنْ قَوْلٍ

اَوْ فِعْلٍ اَوْ عَمَلٍ ط وَاَعُوْذُبِكَ مِنَ النَّارِ وَمَا یُقَرِّبُنِیْٓ اِلَیْهَا

مِنْ قَوْلٍ اَوْ فِعْلٍ اَوْ عَمَلٍ ط

Translation: *Yā Allah* عَزَّوَجَلَّ*! Bless me with the shade of Your 'Arsh on the day there will be no shade except the shade of Your 'Arsh and nothing would survive except You. Let me drink such a pleasant and tasty sip from Your Prophet's pond (Kawšar) that I would never feel thirst thereafter.*

Yā Allah عَزَّوَجَلَّ*! I ask You for the goodness of those things which Your Prophet had asked from You, I ask You protection from the evil of the things which Your Prophet Muhammad* صَلَّى اللهُ تَعَالٰى عَلَيْهِ وَاٰلِهٖ وَسَلَّم *had sought protection from. Yā Allah* عَزَّوَجَلَّ*! I ask for Paradise and its bounties, and (the strength to adopt) all those statements, acts and deeds which would bring me closer to Paradise. I ask You protection from Hell and (the strength to refrain from) all those statements, acts and deeds which may bring me closer to Hell.* (Recite Ṣalāt-'Alan-Nabī)

❊❊❊

As usual, complete the foregoing Du'ā before reaching Rukn Yamānī. Then reciting Ṣalāt-'Alan-Nabī, recite the following Du'ā:

رَبَّنَآ اٰتِنَا فِی الدُّنْيَا حَسَنَةً

وَّفِی الْاٰخِرَةِ حَسَنَةً وَّقِنَا عَذَابَ النَّارِ ۝

Our Rab! Grant us good in this world and good in the Hereafter and save us from the torment of hell-fire.

[Kanz-ul-Īmān (Translation of Quran)]

Then recite the following facing Ḥajar-ul-Aswad with both hands raised up to ears:

بِسْمِ اللهِ وَالْحَمْدُ لِلّٰهِ وَاللهُ

اَكْبَرُ وَالصَّلٰوةُ وَالسَّلَامُ عَلٰى رَسُوْلِ اللهِ ط

Thereafter, perform the Istilām of Ḥajar-ul-Aswad and begin the sixth round whose Du'ā is as follows:

Supplication of sixth round

اَللّٰھُمَّ اِنَّ لَكَ عَلَیَّ حُقُوْقًا كَثِیْرَۃً فِیْمَا بَیْنِیْ وَ بَیْنَكَ وَحُقُوْقًا

كَثِیْرَۃً فِیْمَا بَیْنِیْ وَ بَیْنَ خَلْقِكَ اَللّٰھُمَّ مَا كَانَ لَكَ مِنْھَا

فَاغْفِرْہُ لِیْ وَمَا كَانَ لِخَلْقِكَ فَتَحَمَّلْہُ عَنِّیْ وَ اَغْنِنِیْ بِحَلَالِكَ

عَنْ حَرَامِكَ وَ بِطَاعَتِكَ عَنْ مَّعْصِیَتِكَ وَ بِفَضْلِكَ عَمَّنْ سِوَاكَ

یَا وَاسِعَ الْمَغْفِرَۃِ ؕ اَللّٰھُمَّ اِنَّ بَیْتَكَ عَظِیْمٌ وَّ وَجْھَكَ كَرِیْمٌ

وَّاَنْتَ یَآ اَللّٰہُ حَلِیْمٌ كَرِیْمٌ عَظِیْمٌ تُحِبُّ الْعَفْوَ فَاعْفُ عَنِّیْ ؕ

Translation: *Yā Allah عَزَّوَجَلَّ! There are many obligations (upon me) in the affairs between You and me, and there are many obligations (upon me) in the affairs between Your creation and me. Yā Allah عَزَّوَجَلَّ! Forgive me (for my sluggishness) in the fulfilment of those which are between You and me and kindly take on responsibility to get me forgiven for those which are between Your creation and me. Yā Allah عَزَّوَجَلَّ! Bless me with Ḥalāl sustenance saving me from Ḥarām, with obedience saving me from disobedience and with Your grace making me independent of everyone else. O the One Who is the Greatest Forgiver. Yā Allah عَزَّوَجَلَّ! Without doubt, Your House is indeed gracious and You are indeed glorious and Yā Allah عَزَّوَجَلَّ, You are gracious, grand, mighty and the One Who likes forgiveness, so forgive my mistakes.* (Recite Ṣalāt-'Alan-Nabī)

As usual, complete this before arriving at Rukn Yamānī. Then, reciting Ṣalāt-'Alan-Nabī, recite the following Du'ā:

رَبَّنَآ اٰتِنَا فِى الدُّنْيَا حَسَنَةً

وَّ فِى الْاٰخِرَةِ حَسَنَةً وَّ قِنَا عَذَابَ النَّارِ ۝

Our Rab! Grant us good in this world and good in the Hereafter and save us from the torment of hell-fire.

[Kanz-ul-Īmān (Translation of Quran)]

Then recite the following facing Ḥajar-ul-Aswad with both hands raised up to ears:

بِسْمِ اللّٰهِ وَالْحَمْدُ لِلّٰهِ وَاللّٰهُ

اَكْبَرُ وَالصَّلٰوةُ وَالسَّلَامُ عَلٰى رَسُوْلِ اللّٰهِ ط

Thereafter, perform Istilām of Ḥajar-ul-Aswad and begin the seventh round whose Du'ā is as follows:

Supplication of seventh round

اَللّٰهُمَّ اِنِّىْٓ اَسْئَلُكَ اِيْمَانًا كَامِلًا وَّيَقِيْنًا صَادِقًا وَّرِزْقًا

وَّاسِعًا وَّقَلْبًا خَاشِعًا وَّلِسَانًا ذَاكِرًا وَّرِزْقًا حَلَالًا طَيِّبًا وَّتَوْبَةً

نَّصُوْحًا وَّتَوْبَةً قَبْلَ الْمَوْتِ وَرَاحَةً عِنْدَ الْمَوْتِ وَمَغْفِرَةً

وَّرَحْمَةً بَعْدَ الْمَوْتِ وَالْعَفْوَ عِنْدَ الْحِسَابِ وَالْفَوْزَ بِالْجَنَّةِ

وَالنَّجَاةَ مِنَ النَّارِ بِرَحْمَتِكَ يَا عَزِيْزُ يَا غَفَّارُ ط رَبِّ زِدْنِىْ

عِلْمًا وَّاَلْحِقْنِىْ بِالصّٰلِحِيْنَ ط

Translation: *Yā Allah* عَزَّوَجَلَّ*! I implore You to bless me with perfect faith and undoubted belief and plentiful sustenance and a humble heart and a tongue glorifying You, Ḥalāl and pure sustenance, true repentance by heart, forgiveness before death, and tranquillity at the time of death, forgiveness and mercy after death, forgiveness at the time of accountability, entry in Paradise and security from the fire of Hell (all this I beg You) by virtue of Your grace. O the most respected One and the most forgiving. O my Creator, increase my knowledge and include me among (Your) pious servants.* (Recite Ṣalāt-'Alan-Nabī)

As usual, complete the foregoing Du'ā before reaching Rukn Yamānī. Then reciting Ṣalāt-'Alan-Nabī, recite the following Du'ā:

رَبَّنَآ اٰتِنَا فِی الدُّنْیَا حَسَنَةً

وَّفِی الْاٰخِرَةِ حَسَنَةً وَّقِنَا عَذَابَ النَّارِ ۝

Our Rab! Grant us good in this world and good in the Hereafter and save us from the torment of hell-fire.

[Kanz-ul-Īmān (Translation of Quran)]

Now on reaching Ḥajar-ul-Aswad, your all seven rounds of Ṭawāf have completed. Now, pick up both hands to your ears and recite the following for the eighth time:

بِسْمِ اللّٰهِ وَالْحَمْدُ لِلّٰهِ وَاللّٰهُ

اَكْبَرُ وَالصَّلٰوةُ وَالسَّلَامُ عَلٰى رَسُوْلِ اللّٰهِ ط

Remember that a Ṭawāf consists of seven rounds and eight Istilāms.

Maqām-u-Ibrāĥīm

Now cover your right shoulder with the upper shawl of Iḥrām. Come at Maqām-u-Ibrāĥīm, and recite the following Quranic verse:

وَاتَّخِذُوْا مِنْ مَّقَامِ اِبْرٰهٖمَ مُصَلًّى ؕ

And make the standing place of Ibrāĥīm a spot for (offering) Ṣalāĥ.

[Kanz-ul-Īmān (Translation of Quran)]

Ṣalāĥ for Ṭawāf

Offer two Rak'āt Ṣalāĥ of Ṭawāf near Maqām-u-Ibrāĥīm, if space is available near it, otherwise offer it anywhere in Masjid-ul-Ḥarām provided the time is not Makrūĥ for Ṣalāĥ. Recite Sūraĥ Al-Kāfirūn and Sūraĥ Al-Ikhlāṣ after Sūraĥ Al-Fātiḥaĥ in the first and the second Rak'at respectively. This Ṣalāĥ is Wājib and it is a Sunnaĥ to offer it right after the completion of Ṭawāf. Most people keep their shoulder uncovered even during Ṣalāĥ; it is Makrūĥ to do so.

The act of Iḍṭibā' (i.e. keeping the right shoulder uncovered) is done during all the seven rounds of only such Ṭawāf which is followed by Sa'ī. If the time is Makrūĥ, offer this Ṣalāĥ later. Keep in mind that it is essential to offer this Ṣalāĥ.

Make Du'ā at Maqām-u-Ibrāĥīm after having offered two Rak'āt Ṣalāĥ. It is stated in a Ḥadīš that Allah عَزَّوَجَلَّ has said: Whoever makes this Du'ā, I will forgive his wrongdoing, remove his grief, bring him out of deprivation, grant him blessings in his trade more than any other trader, and the world will helplessly and miserably approach him even if he does not desire it. *(Ibn 'Asākir, vol. 7, pp. 431)*

The Du'ā is as follows:

Supplication of Maqām-u-Ibrāĥīm

اَللّٰهُمَّ اِنَّكَ تَعۡلَمُ سِرِّیۡ وَ عَلَانِیَتِیۡ فَاقۡبَلۡ مَعۡذِرَتِیۡ وَ تَعۡلَمُ
حَاجَتِیۡ فَاَعۡطِنِیۡ سُؤۡلِیۡ وَ تَعۡلَمُ مَا فِیۡ نَفۡسِیۡ فَاغۡفِرۡ لِیۡ ذُنُوۡبِیۡ ط
اَللّٰهُمَّ اِنِّیۡۤ اَسۡئَلُكَ اِیۡمَانًا یُّبَاشِرُ قَلۡبِیۡ وَ یَقِیۡنًا صَادِقًا حَتّٰۤی
اَعۡلَمَ اَنَّهٗ لَا یُصِیۡبُنِیۡۤ اِلَّا مَا كَتَبۡتَ لِیۡ وَ رِضًا بِمَا قَسَمۡتَ لِیۡ
یَاۤ اَرۡحَمَ الرّٰحِمِیۡنَ ط

Translation: *O Allah عَزَّوَجَلَّ! You are aware of all my concealed and open deeds; hence accept my apology. And You are aware of my needs, bestow upon me what I seek. And You are aware of my inner being; hence forgive my sins. O Allah عَزَّوَجَلَّ! I ask You for such a faith which overwhelms my heart and a true belief that I will be facing only what has been predestined for me, and contentment with what is in my fate from You, O the most merciful of all!*

4 Madanī pearls about offering Ṣalāĥ at Maqām-u-Ibrāĥīm

1. The Beloved and Blessed Prophet صَلَّى اللّٰهُ تَعَالٰى عَلَيْهِ وَاٰلِهٖ وَسَلَّم has stated, 'One who offers two Rak'āt Ṣalāĥ behind Maqām-u-Ibrāĥīm, his future and past sins will be forgiven, and he will be resurrected on the Day of Judgement with the ones granted peace.' *(Ash-Shifā, Al-Juz-uš-Šānī, pp. 93)*

2. Most people try to offer Ṣalāĥ behind Maqām-u-Ibrāĥīm at any cost even in a huge crowd, whereas some people stand round in a circle holding each others' hands so that their female

companions could offer Ṣalāĥ inside the circle near Maqām-u-Ibrāĥīm, blocking the way for others. Such people should avoid it in crowd. Instead, they should offer Ṣalāĥ some distance away from Maqām-u-Ibrāĥīm so that the Ṭawāf-performing people would not be inconvenienced and they would not also be pushed and shoved.

3. After Maqām-u-Ibrāĥīm, the most preferable place to offer this Ṣalāĥ is the inside of the Holy Ka'baĥ. Then in Ḥaṭīm under Mīzāb-ur-Raḥmaĥ, then any place throughout Ḥaṭīm, then any place near the Holy Ka'baĥ, then any place in Masjid-ul-Ḥarām and then any place throughout the Ḥaram of Makkaĥ.

(Lubāb-ul-Manāsik, pp. 156)

4. It is a Sunnaĥ to offer this Ṣalāĥ right after the Ṭawāf provided that the time is not Makrūĥ. There should be no delay. If a person who has not offered this Ṣalāĥ after the Ṭawāf, offers it any time in his life, this will be considered offered, and not Qaḍā. However, he has missed a Sunnaĥ, which is a wrongdoing. *(Al-Maslak-ul-Mutaqassiṭ, pp. 155)*

Now come at Multazam

After completing Ṣalāĥ and Du'ā, it is Mustaḥab to come at Multazam. Embrace Multazam! The section between Ḥajar-ul-Aswad and the sacred door of the Holy Ka'baĥ is called Multazam. The blessed door is not included in Multazam. Embrace Multazam with your chest, belly, right cheek and left cheek. Raise both hands above the head and spread them on Multazam or spread right hand towards the blessed door and the left towards Ḥajar-ul-Aswad. Let tears flow and make Du'ā sobbing with extreme humbleness and humility for yourself and the entire Ummaĥ in your native language. This is the place where Du'ā is accepted. One of the Du'ās made here is as follows:

يَا وَاجِدُ يَا مَاجِدُ لَا تُزِلْ عَنِّیْ نِعْمَةً اَنْعَمْتَهَا عَلَيَّ ط

O Omnipotent! O the most Honoured! Do not deprive me of the favour You have granted to me.

It is stated in a Ḥadīš: When I like, I see Jibrāīl (عَلَيْهِ السَّلَام) make this Du'ā whilst embracing Multazam. *(Bahār-e-Sharī'at, vol. 1, pp. 1104)* To recite Ṣalāt-'Alan-Nabī once before making this Du'ā is better.

Du'ā to be made at Multazam

اَللّٰهُمَّ يَا رَبَّ الْبَيْتِ الْعَتِيْقِ اَعْتِقْ رِقَابَنَا وَرِقَابَ اٰبَآئِنَا وَاُمَّهَاتِنَا وَاِخْوَانِنَا وَاَوْلَادِنَا مِنَ النَّارِ يَا ذَا الْجُوْدِ وَالْكَرَمِ وَالْفَضْلِ وَالْمَنِّ وَالْعَطَآءِ وَالْاِحْسَانِ ط اَللّٰهُمَّ اَحْسِنْ عَاقِبَتَنَا فِی الْاُمُوْرِ كُلِّهَا وَاَجِرْنَا مِنْ خِزْیِ الدُّنْيَا وَعَذَابِ الْاٰخِرَةِ ط اَللّٰهُمَّ اِنِّیْ عَبْدُكَ وَابْنُ عَبْدِكَ وَاقِفٌ تَحْتَ بَابِكَ مُلْتَزِمٌ بِاَعْتَابِكَ مُتَذَلِّلٌ بَيْنَ يَدَيْكَ اَرْجُوْ رَحْمَتَكَ وَاَخْشٰى عَذَابَكَ مِنَ النَّارِ يَا قَدِيْمَ الْاِحْسَانِ ط اَللّٰهُمَّ اِنِّیْ اَسْئَلُكَ اَنْ تَرْفَعَ ذِكْرِیْ وَتَضَعَ وِزْرِیْ وَتُصْلِحَ اَمْرِیْ وَتُطَهِّرَ قَلْبِیْ وَتُنَوِّرَ لِیْ فِیْ قَبْرِیْ وَتَغْفِرَ لِیْ ذَنْبِیْ وَاَسْئَلُكَ الدَّرَجَاتِ الْعُلٰى مِنَ الْجَنَّةِ ط اٰمِيْن بِجَاهِ النَّبِیِّ الْاَمِيْن صَلَّى اللّٰهُ عَلَيْهِ وَسَلَّم

Translation: *O Allah عَزَّوَجَلَّ! O Creator of this ancient House! Free our necks and those of our ancestors, our mothers (and sisters), our brothers and children from the fire of Hell! O the forgiver, the most merciful, the most beneficent, the most kind, the bestower and the most generous. O Allah عَزَّوَجَلَّ, bless us with good end in all our affairs and save us from remorse in this world and torment in the Hereafter. O Allah عَزَّوَجَلَّ! I am Your servant and the son of Your servant. I am standing beneath Your sacred door. I have clung to its doorstep and I am expressing my humbleness before You and I am begging for Your mercy and I fear the torment of Hell, O Ever-Kind (be kind with me at this moment). I implore You to raise my name and lighten the burden of my sins and reform my affairs, cleanse my inner self, illuminate my grave, and forgive my sins and I am begging You for high status in Paradise. Āmīn*

An important ruling

After performing the Ṭawāf which is followed by Sa'ī, offer Ṣalāĥ of Ṭawāf before coming to Multazam. In case of performing the Ṭawāf which is not followed by Sa'ī, e.g. a Nafl Ṭawāf or Ṭawāf-uz-Ziyārāĥ (provided Sa'ī of Hajj has already been performed), one should approach and embrace Multazam prior to offering the Ṣalāĥ of Ṭawāf at Maqām-u-Ibrāĥīm. *(Al-Maslak-ul-Mutaqassiṭ, pp. 138)*

Come at Zam Zam well

A large number of coolers containing Zam Zam water are placed in Masjid-ul-Ḥarām at different points. Come to any water-cooler and drink Zam Zam water in three breaths until your stomach is full, whilst standing and facing the Qiblaĥ. (Remember that it is necessary to make the intention of I'tikāf before you drink Zam Zam water in any Masjid.)

The Beloved and Blessed Prophet صَلَّى اللهُ تَعَالٰى عَلَيْهِ وَاٰلِهٖ وَسَلَّم has stated, 'The difference between us and the hypocrites is that they do not drink

Zam Zam to their full stomach.' *(Ibn Mājaĥ, vol. 3, pp. 489, Ḥadīš 3061)* Recite بِسْمِ اللّٰه every time you drink Zam Zam water and say اَلْحَمْدُ لِلّٰه عَزَّوَجَلَّ afterwards. Look at the Holy Ka'baĥ every time you drink it. Sprinkle the remaining water over the body or moisten the face and the head, etc. Take care that no drop of water falls over the ground. When drinking Zam Zam water, make Du'ā as it will be accepted. Here are two sayings of the Holy Prophet صَلَّى اللهُ تَعَالٰى عَلَيْهِ وَاٰلِهٖ وَسَلَّم:

1. 'This (Zam Zam water) is blessed and it is a meal for the hungry and a cure for the patient.' *(Abū Dāwūd Ṭayālsī, pp. 61, Ḥadīš 457)*

2. 'The purpose for which Zam Zam is drunk will be fulfilled.' *(Ibn Mājaĥ, vol. 3, pp. 490, Ḥadīš 3062)*

Recite this Du'ā after drinking Zam Zam water

اَللّٰهُمَّ اِنِّيْٓ اَسْئَلُكَ عِلْمًا نَّافِعًا وَّرِزْقًا وَّاسِعًا وَّشِفَآءً مِّنْ كُلِّ دَآءٍ ط

***Translation:** O Allah عَزَّوَجَلَّ! I ask You for useful knowledge, increased sustenance and cure for all diseases.*

How to make Du'ā whilst drinking Zam Zam water

The exegetist of *Ṣaḥīḥ Muslim* Sayyidunā Imām Nawavī Shāfi'ī عَلَيْهِ رَحْمَةُ اللهِ الْقَوِى has stated, 'If a person desires forgiveness or a cure for some disease etc. by drinking Zam Zam water, it is Mustaḥab for him to stand facing the Qiblaĥ and recite بِسْمِ اللهِ الرَّحْمٰنِ الرَّحِيْم and then say: O Allah (عَزَّوَجَلَّ)! I have heard a Ḥadīš of Your Prophet صَلَّى اللهُ تَعَالٰى عَلَيْهِ وَاٰلِهٖ وَسَلَّم who has said, 'The purpose for which Zam Zam is drunk will be fulfilled.' *(Musnad Imām Aḥmad, vol. 5, pp. 136, Ḥadīš 1855)* O Allah (عَزَّوَجَلَّ)! I am going to drink it so that You would forgive me or O Allah (عَزَّوَجَلَّ)! I am going to drink it to be cured of my disease. O Allah (عَزَّوَجَلَّ)! You grant me the cure. Many other Du'ās may be made in the same way. *(Al-Īḍāḥ fī Manāsik Al-Hajj lin-Nawavī, pp. 401)*

Do not drink very cold water

Avoid drinking very cold water lest it causes hindrance to the acts of worship. Crushing the desire of Nafs, drink water from such cooler that has been labelled زَمْ زَمْ غَيْرُ مُبَرَّد (i.e. *Zam Zam water that is not cold*).

Eyesight improves

To see Zam Zam water improves the eyesight and removes the sins. To sprinkle three handfuls of it onto the head protects against disgrace. *(Al-Baḥr-ul-'Amīq fil-Manāsik, vol. 5, pp. 2569-2573)*

Tū ĥar sāl Hajj per bulā Yā Ilāĥī
Waĥān Āb-e-Zam Zam pilā Yā Ilāĥī

May I perform Hajj every year, O Almighty!
And drink Zam Zam water there, O Almighty!

Sa'ī of Ṣafā and Marwaĥ*

Prepare for Sa'ī between Ṣafā and Marwaĥ now. However, if you are tired or occupied, you may take some rest before performing Sa'ī. Do not perform Iḍṭibā' in Sa'ī. Now, perform Istilām of Ḥajar-ul-Aswad for Sa'ī as usual by raising both hands up to ears and then recite the following Du'ā:

بِسْمِ اللهِ وَالْحَمْدُ لِلّٰهِ وَاللهُ
اَكْبَرُ وَالصَّلٰوةُ وَالسَّلَامُ عَلٰى رَسُوْلِ اللهِ ط

* Perform Sa'ī at the basement.

If it is not possible to perform Istilām, then face Ḥajar-ul-Aswad and recite اَللّٰهُ اَكْبَرُ وَلَآ اِلٰهَ اِلَّا اللّٰهُ وَالْحَمْدُ لِلّٰهِ with Ṣalāt-'Alan-Nabī and come at Bāb-uṣ-Ṣafā immediately. The mount Ṣafā is outside Masjid-ul-Ḥarām. Since it is a Sunnaĥ to step out left foot first whilst exiting a Masjid, do the same here while exiting Masjid-ul-Ḥarām and recite the following Du'ā with Ṣalāt-'Alan-Nabī once before it:

اَللّٰهُمَّ اِنِّيْٓ اَسْئَلُكَ مِنْ فَضْلِكَ وَ رَحْمَتِكَ

***Translation:** O Allah عَزَّوَجَلَّ! I beg You for Your mercy and grace.*

While reciting Ṣalāt-'Alan-Nabī, now go uphill at Ṣafā such that you may see the Holy Ka'baĥ from there. This can be achieved walking uphill just slightly. Therefore, avoid climbing the mount too high like the masses. You should then recite the following Du'ā:

اَبْدَءُ بِمَا بَدَأَ اللّٰهُ تَعَالٰى بِهٖ ﴿اِنَّ الصَّفَا وَالْمَرْوَةَ مِنْ شَعَآئِرِ اللّٰهِ ۚ فَمَنْ حَجَّ الْبَيْتَ اَوِ اعْتَمَرَ فَلَا جُنَاحَ عَلَيْهِ اَنْ يَّطَّوَّفَ بِهِمَا ؕ وَمَنْ تَطَوَّعَ خَيْرًا ۙ فَاِنَّ اللّٰهَ شَاكِرٌ عَلِيْمٌ ۝﴾

***Translation:** I begin with that which Allah عَزَّوَجَلَّ has begun with (this Holy Statement of His): Without doubt, Ṣafā and Marwaĥ are from amongst the signs of Allah عَزَّوَجَلَّ, whosoever performs Hajj or 'Umraĥ of this house, there is no sin on him for taking rounds of these two. And whoever performs a good deed at his own will, undoubtedly Allah عَزَّوَجَلَّ is the most rewarding and all knowing.*

Wrong way

Out of ignorance, many people are seen waving their palms towards the Ka'baĥ. Likewise, some signal with their hands and some raise hands up to their ears three times and then drop them, all these are incorrect manners. What you should do is to raise your hands up to your shoulders as in Du'ā, whilst facing the Ka'baĥ. Make Du'ā for as long as it takes to recite 25 verses of Sūraĥ Al-Baqaraĥ.

Make Du'ā humbly whilst pleading and sobbing as this is a place where Du'ā is accepted. Pray for the betterment of yourself and all other Muslims including Muslim jinns. It will be a great favour if you make Du'ā of forgiveness for me, a sinner (Sag-e-Madīnaĥ). Reciting Ṣalāt-'Alan-Nabī make the following Du'ā.[1]

Du'ā of mount Ṣafā

اَللّٰهُ اَكْبَرُ ط اَللّٰهُ اَكْبَرُ ط لَآ اِلٰهَ اِلَّا اللّٰهُ وَاللّٰهُ
اَكْبَرُ ط اَللّٰهُ اَكْبَرُ ط وَلِلّٰهِ الْحَمْدُ ط اَلْحَمْدُ لِلّٰهِ عَلٰى مَا هَدٰنَا
اَلْحَمْدُ لِلّٰهِ عَلٰى مَآ اَوْلَانَا اَلْحَمْدُ لِلّٰهِ عَلٰى مَآ اَلْهَمَنَا ط اَلْحَمْدُ لِلّٰهِ
الَّذِیْ هَدٰنَا لِهٰذَا وَمَا كُنَّا لِنَهْتَدِیَ لَوْلَآ اَنْ هَدٰنَا اللّٰهُ ط
لَآ اِلٰهَ اِلَّا اللّٰهُ وَحْدَهٗ لَا شَرِیْكَ لَهٗ ط لَهُ الْمُلْكُ وَلَهُ الْحَمْدُ

[1] As intention is not a condition for the Ramī of Jamarāt and Wuqūf in 'Arafāt etc. it is not a condition for Sa'ī as well. If the Sa'ī is performed even without an intention, it will still be valid. However, it is Mustaḥab to make intention. If there is no intention, no reward will be granted. [Sag-e-Madīnaĥ]

يُحْيِيْ وَ يُمِيْتُ وَهُوَ حَيٌّ لَّا يَمُوْتُ بِيَدِهِ الْخَيْرُ وَ هُوَ عَلٰى كُلِّ شَيْءٍ

قَدِيْرٌ ط لَآ اِلٰهَ اِلَّا اللّٰهُ وَحْدَهٗ صَدَقَ وَعْدَهٗ وَنَصَرَ عَبْدَهٗ وَاَعَزَّ

جُنْدَهٗ وَهَزَمَ الْاَحْزَابَ وَحْدَهٗ ط لَآ اِلٰهَ اِلَّا اللّٰهُ وَلَا نَعْبُدُ اِلَّا اِيَّاهُ

مُخْلِصِيْنَ لَهُ الدِّيْنَ وَلَوْ كَرِهَ الْكَافِرُوْنَ ط ۞ فَسُبْحٰنَ اللّٰهِ حِيْنَ

تُمْسُوْنَ وَحِيْنَ تُصْبِحُوْنَ ﴿۱۷﴾ وَ لَهُ الْحَمْدُ فِي السَّمٰوٰتِ وَالْاَرْضِ

وَعَشِيًّا وَّحِيْنَ تُظْهِرُوْنَ ﴿۱۸﴾ يُخْرِجُ الْحَيَّ مِنَ الْمَيِّتِ وَيُخْرِجُ الْمَيِّتَ

مِنَ الْحَيِّ وَ يُحْيِ الْاَرْضَ بَعْدَ مَوْتِهَا ط وَ كَذٰلِكَ تُخْرَجُوْنَ ﴿۱۹﴾ ع ۞

اَللّٰهُمَّ كَمَا هَدَيْتَنِيْ لِلْاِسْلَامِ اَسْأَلُكَ اَنْ لَّا تَنْزِعَهٗ مِنِّيْ حَتّٰى

تَوَفَّانِيْ وَ اَنَا مُسْلِمٌ ط سُبْحٰنَ اللّٰهِ وَالْحَمْدُ لِلّٰهِ وَلَآ اِلٰهَ اِلَّا اللّٰهُ

وَاللّٰهُ اَكْبَرُ وَ لَاحَوْلَ وَ لَا قُوَّةَ اِلَّا بِاللّٰهِ الْعَلِيِّ الْعَظِيْمِ ط اَللّٰهُمَّ

اَحْيِنِيْ عَلٰى سُنَّةِ نَبِيِّكَ مُحَمَّدٍ صَلَّى اللّٰهُ تَعَالٰى عَلَيْهِ وَاٰلِهٖ وَسَلَّمَ

وَتَوَفَّنِيْ عَلٰى مِلَّتِهٖ وَاَعِذْنِيْ مِنْ مُّضِلَّاتِ الْفِتَنِ ط اَللّٰهُمَّ اجْعَلْنَا

مِمَّنْ يُّحِبُّكَ وَ يُحِبُّ رَسُوْلَكَ وَ اَنْبِيَآئَكَ وَ مَلٰئِكَتَكَ وَ عِبَادَكَ

الصّٰلِحِيْنَ ط اَللّٰهُمَّ يَسِّرْ لِيَ الْيُسْرٰى وَ جَنِّبْنِيَ الْعُسْرٰى اَللّٰهُمَّ
اَحْيِنِيْ عَلٰى سُنَّةِ رَسُوْلِكَ مُحَمَّدٍ صَلَّى اللّٰهُ تَعَالٰى عَلَيْهِ وَاٰلِهٖ وَسَلَّمَ
وَتَوَفَّنِيْ مُسْلِمًا وَّ اَلْحِقْنِيْ بِالصّٰلِحِيْنَ وَاجْعَلْنِيْ مِنْ وَّ رَثَةِ جَنَّةِ
النَّعِيْمِ وَاغْفِرْلِيْ خَطِيْٓـئَتِيْ يَوْمَ الدِّيْنَ ط اَللّٰهُمَّ اِنَّا نَسْئَلُكَ
اِيْمَانًا كَامِلًا وَّ قَلْبًا خَاشِعًا وَّ نَسْئَلُكَ عِلْمًا نَّافِعًا وَّ يَقِيْنًا
صَادِقًا وَّ دِيْنًا قَيِّمًا وَّ نَسْئَلُكَ الْعَفْوَ وَالْعَافِيَةَ مِنْ كُلِّ بَلِيَّةٍ
وَّنَسْئَلُكَ تَمَامَ الْعَافِيَةِ وَنَسْئَلُكَ دَوَامَ الْعَافِيَةِ وَنَسْئَلُكَ
الشُّكْرَ عَلَى الْعَافِيَةِ وَ نَسْئَلُكَ الْغِنٰى عَنِ النَّاسِ ط اَللّٰهُمَّ صَلِّ
وَسَلِّمْ وَ بَارِكْ عَلٰى سَيِّدِنَا مُحَمَّدٍ وَّ عَلٰى اٰلِهٖ وَ صَحْبِهٖ عَدَدَ
خَلْقِكَ وَرِضَا نَفْسِكَ وَ زِنَةَ عَرْشِكَ وَ مِدَادَ كَلِمَاتِكَ كُلَّمَا ذَكَرَكَ
الذَّاكِرُوْنَ وَغَفَلَ عَنْ ذِكْرِكَ الْغَافِلُوْنَ ط اٰمِيْن بِجَاهِ النَّبِيِّ
الْاَمِيْن صَلَّى اللّٰهُ عَلَيْهِ وَسَلَّم

Translation: *Allah* عَزَّوَجَلَّ *is the Greatest, Allah* عَزَّوَجَلَّ *is the Greatest, Allah* عَزَّوَجَلَّ *is the Greatest. No one is worthy to be worshipped except Allah* عَزَّوَجَلَّ*. And Allah* عَزَّوَجَلَّ *is the Greatest, Allah* عَزَّوَجَلَّ *is the Greatest.*

Glorification is for Allah عَزَّوَجَلَّ. Glorification is for Allah عَزَّوَجَلَّ as He has guided us. Glorification is for Allah عَزَّوَجَلَّ as He has granted us. Glorification is for Allah عَزَّوَجَلَّ as He has revealed to us [through Ilĥām]. Glorification is for Allah عَزَّوَجَلَّ Who has guided it to us and if He عَزَّوَجَلَّ had not guided us, we would not have got it (by our own). No one is worthy to be worshipped except Allah عَزَّوَجَلَّ Who is alone; no one is His partner. For Him is sovereignty and for Him is glorification. Only He عَزَّوَجَلَّ gives life and gives death. He عَزَّوَجَلَّ is alive such that He عَزَّوَجَلَّ cannot die. Goodness and virtues are under His authority. He عَزَّوَجَلَّ is Omnipotent. No one is worthy to be worshipped except Allah عَزَّوَجَلَّ Who is One and fulfilled His promise and helped His servant and made his forces dominant and He عَزَّوَجَلَّ defeated alone all the battalions of unbelievers. No one is worthy to be worshipped except Allah عَزَّوَجَلَّ. We purely worship Him only making the religion pure for Him even though the unbelievers get annoyed. [Therefore, glorify Allah عَزَّوَجَلَّ when you enter the evening and when you enter the morning. And His is praise in the heavens and in the earth, and at little before the setting of sun and when you enter the noon. He brings forth the living from the dead and brings forth the dead from the living, and gives life to the earth after its death. And in like manner you shall be brought forth.] O Allah عَزَّوَجَلَّ! You have guided me to walk into the path of Islam. I beg You not to disassociate me from this wealth. Let me die in Islam. Allah عَزَّوَجَلَّ is Pure (from all shortcomings). All glorifications are for Allah عَزَّوَجَلَّ and no one is worthy of worship except Allah عَزَّوَجَلَّ. And Allah عَزَّوَجَلَّ is the Greatest. And the power (to refrain from sins) and the strength (to incline towards worship) is (bestowed) by Allah عَزَّوَجَلَّ Who is Dignified and Glorified. O Allah عَزَّوَجَلَّ! Make me one who acts upon the Sunnaĥ of Your Beloved Prophet صَلَّى اللهُ تَعَالٰى عَلَيْهِ وَاٰلِهٖ وَسَلَّم, let me die in his religion, and save me from evils of heresy. O Allah عَزَّوَجَلَّ! Include me amongst those people who love You and love Your beloved Prophets, distinguished angels, and righteous people. O Allah عَزَّوَجَلَّ! Bestow easiness upon me and save me from severity. O Allah عَزَّوَجَلَّ! Make me one who acts upon the Sunnaĥ of Your Blessed Prophet صَلَّى اللهُ تَعَالٰى عَلَيْهِ وَاٰلِهٖ وَسَلَّم *and let me die a Muslim. And include me amongst the virtuous people. And make me the one who is worthy of Jannat-un-Na'īm. And excuse me for my mistakes on the Last Day. O Allah* عَزَّوَجَلَّ*! We beg You so we are blessed with a complete faith; we beg You so we are blessed with a pure heart; and we beg You so we are blessed with useful knowledge, absolute belief and straight path (Dīn). And we beg You so You save us from every affliction. And we beg You so You provide us with perfect safety, everlasting security, and gratitude for safety. And we beg You so You save us from relying upon human beings. Yā Allah* عَزَّوَجَلَّ*! [We beg You so You] send Ṣalāt, Salām, and blessing upon our Master* صَلَّى اللهُ تَعَالٰى عَلَيْهِ وَاٰلِهٖ وَسَلَّم*, his descendants and his companions equivalent to Your (living and non-living) creation, Your pleasure, and the weight of Your 'Arsh. [Send Ṣalāt, Salām, and blessing upon them] in a number equivalent to Your words until the people carry out Your Żikr and until the negligent people remain negligent in carrying out Your Żikr.*

Completing the Du'ā, lower your hands and make the intention of Sa'ī in your heart after having recited Ṣalāt-'Alan-Nabī. However, it is better to make verbal intention, provided you understand its meaning. Make the following intention:

Intention of Sa'ī

اَللّٰهُمَّ اِنِّیۡ اُرِیۡدُ السَّعۡیَ بَیۡنَ الصَّفَا وَ الۡمَرۡوَۃِ سَبۡعَۃَ اَشۡوَاطٍ

لِّوَجۡهِكَ الۡكَرِیۡمِ فَیَسِّرۡهُ لِیۡ وَ تَقَبَّلۡهُ مِنِّیۡ ط

Translation: *O Allah* عَزَّوَجَلَّ*! I intend to perform the seven rounds of Sa'ī between Ṣafā and Marwaĥ for Your pleasure. Make it easy for me and accept it from me.*

Du'ā when descending from Ṣafā/Marwaĥ

اَللّٰهُمَّ اسْتَعْمِلْنِیْ بِسُنَّةِ نَبِیِّكَ صَلَّى اللّٰهُ تَعَالٰی عَلَیْهِ وَاٰلِهٖ وَسَلَّمَ وَتَوَفَّنِیْ عَلٰی مِلَّتِهٖ وَاَعِذْنِیْ مِنْ مُّضِلَّاتِ الْفِتَنِ بِرَحْمَتِكَ یَآ اَرْحَمَ الرّٰحِمِیْنَ ط

***Translation:** O Allah عَزَّوَجَلَّ! Make me one who acts upon the Sunnaĥ of Your Beloved Prophet صَلَّى اللّٰهُ تَعَالٰی عَلَیْهِ وَاٰلِهٖ وَسَلَّم, let me die in his religion, and save me from evils of heresy by virtue of Your mercy, O the most merciful!*

Whilst busy with Żikr and Ṣalāt-'Alan-Nabī, walk from Ṣafā towards Marwaĥ at a medium pace. (Nowadays this passage has marble flooring and air coolers. There was a time when Sayyidatunā Ĥājiraĥ رَضِیَ اللّٰهُ تَعَالٰی عَنْهَا had performed Sa'ī. Just for a moment think of that heart-breaking situation when this area was barren with no sign of water and vegetation. Sayyidunā Ismā'īl عَلٰی نَبِیِّنَا وَعَلَیْهِ الصَّلٰوةُ وَالسَّلَام was an infant crying desperately out of extreme thirst and Sayyidatunā Ĥājiraĥ رَضِیَ اللّٰهُ تَعَالٰی عَنْهَا was restlessly searching for water in the scorching heat of this rocky land).

On reaching the first green mark, Islamic brothers should begin to run (but in a dignified way, not uncontrollably) and those on wheel-chairs should step up their speed. If there is a crowd, wait for a moment when there is hope of the crowd being decreased. Whilst running, take care that neither you nor any body else gets hurt as running here is a Sunnaĥ but causing pain to a Muslim is Ḥarām. Islamic sisters should not run. Now, Islamic brothers whilst running and Islamic sisters whilst walking should recite the following Du'ā.

Du'ā to be recited between green marks

رَبِّ اغْفِرْ وَارْحَمْ وَتَجَاوَزْ عَمَّا تَعْلَمُ اِنَّكَ تَعْلَمُ مَا لَا نَعْلَمُ ط
اِنَّكَ اَنْتَ الْاَعَزُّ الْاَكْرَمُ وَاهْدِنِيْ لِلَّتِيْ هِيَ اَقْوَمُ ط اَللّٰهُمَّ
اجْعَلْهُ حَجًّا مَّبْرُوْرًا وَّسَعْيًا مَّشْكُوْرًا وَّذَنْبًا مَّغْفُوْرًا ط

Translation: *O my Rab عَزَّوَجَلَّ, forgive me and have mercy on me. Forgive my wrongdoings that are known to You. Without doubt, You are fully aware but we are not. Without doubt, You are Great and Glorified. Keep me on the straight path. O Allah عَزَّوَجَلَّ! Accept my Hajj, make my Sa'ī, Mashkūr (i.e. liked) and forgive my sins.*

When you arrive at the next green mark, slow down and proceed towards Marwaĥ at a medium pace. Look! You are now at the blessed mount of Marwaĥ. Most people try to go as high as possible but you should not do so. You should go uphill a little only. Even by reaching as far as the check-marble floor starts, you are considered to have climbed Marwaĥ.

Although, nowadays, the Ka'baĥ is not visible from here due to various constructions, you should still face towards the direction of the Ka'baĥ and make Du'ā for the same amount of time as was spent on Ṣafā (in Du'ā). There is no need to make the intention again, as it has already been made. Now you have completed one round.

Now proceed towards Ṣafā reciting Du'ā. Perform the same act between the two green lights (Mīlayn-e-Akhḍarayn) as you did during the first round, i.e. Islamic brothers should run while Islamic sisters should just walk in this passage whilst reciting Du'ā. On reaching

Ṣafā, two rounds would be completed. Continue until all seven rounds are completed. The seventh round will finish at Marwaĥ. Your Sa'ī has now completed.

A precaution to be taken during Sa'ī

At times people are offering Ṣalāĥ at Mas'ā [the place where Sa'ī is performed]. For a Ṭawāf-performing person to pass across the front of a Ṣalāĥ-offering person is permissible but for a Sa'ī-performing person it is impermissible to do so. Therefore, if you come across such a situation during Sa'ī, wait until the Ṣalāĥ-offering person has finished his Ṣalāĥ. However, you can pass across the front of the Ṣalāĥ-offering person using an already passing person as Sutraĥ[1].

Ṣalāĥ of Sa'ī is Mustaḥab

If it is not a Makrūĥ time for Ṣalāĥ, perform two Rak'āt Ṣalāĥ in Masjid-ul-Ḥarām, as it is Mustaḥab. It is reported that the Holy Prophet صَلَّى اللّٰهُ تَعَالٰى عَلَيْهِ وَاٰلِهٖ وَسَلَّم offered two Rak'āt Ṣalāĥ having performed Sa'ī at the border of Maṭāf in the direction of Ḥajar-ul-Aswad.

(Musnad Imām Aḥmad, vol. 10, pp. 354, Ḥadīš 27313; Rad-dul-Muḥtār, vol. 3, pp. 589)

This act of performing Ṭawāf and Sa'ī is called 'Umraĥ. So 'Umraĥ has been completed for the Qārin and the Mutamatte'.

Ṭawāf-ul-Qudūm

For a Mufrid, this Ṭawāf is, in fact, Ṭawāf-ul-Qudūm i.e. a ritual for attendance in the court of Allah عَزَّوَجَلَّ. A Qārin should perform one more Ṭawāf and Sa'ī with the intention of Ṭawāf-ul-Qudūm which is a Sunnat-ul-Muakkadaĥ for both a Qārin and a Mufrid. Although missing it is a bad act, no *Dam* etc. will be Wājib.

(Bahār-e-Sharī'at, vol. 1, pp. 1111)

---

[1] **Sutraĥ:** A barrier placed in front of the Ṣalāĥ-offering person so that others may pass across the front of him without committing the sin.

Ḥalq or Taqṣīr

Men should now either do Ḥalq, i.e. get their entire head shaved or Taqṣīr, i.e. get their hair trimmed. It is preferable for them to get Ḥalq done. The Noble Prophet صَلَّى اللّٰهُ تَعَالٰى عَلَيْهِ وَاٰلِهٖ وَسَلَّم got Ḥalq done during Ḥijja-tul-Wadā' and made the Du'ā of mercy three times for those getting the head shaved and one time for those getting the hair trimmed. *(Bukhārī, vol. 1, pp. 574, Ḥadīš 1728)*

Definition of Taqṣīr

Taqṣīr implies cutting the hair of a quarter of the head equal to a finger digit[1] in length. As a caution, cut a bit more than this length to ensure that the shorter hair present in the centre of the head also gets cut equal to a finger digit in length. Some people just cut a few strands of hair with a pair of scissors, which is absolutely wrong for the Ḥanafīs, and the restrictions of Iḥrām will not be terminated either in this case.

Taqṣīr for Islamic sisters

It is Ḥarām for Islamic sisters to shave their entire head. They should perform Taqṣīr only. An easy way of it is to cut hair from the end of the plait of hair a little more than the length of a finger digit. It is important that at least the hair of one quarter of the head must be cut.

Advice for those performing Ṭawāf-ul-Qudūm

It is not necessary to perform Iḍṭibā', Raml and Sa'ī for Ṭawāf-ul-Qudūm. However, if these acts are not performed in Ṭawāf-ul-Qudūm, they must be performed with Ṭawāf-uz-Ziyāraĥ. Since it may be difficult to perform these acts in Ṭawāf-uz-Ziyāraĥ due to massive crowd or tiredness, my suggestion is that these acts be

[1] Each finger has 3 digits and the thumb has 2.

performed in Ṭawāf-ul-Qudūm so that one would no longer need to perform them in Ṭawāf-uz-Ziyāraĥ.

Advice for Mutamatte'

The Mufrid and the Qārin have completed the Raml and Sa'ī of Hajj through Ṭawāf-ul-Qudūm but a Mutamatte' cannot do so as Ṭawāf-ul-Qudūm is not a Sunnaĥ for him. The Ṭawāf and Sa'ī which the Mutamatte' performed were in connection with 'Umraĥ and not the Hajj. Hence if a Mutamatte' also wants to fulfill these acts in advance, he can do so. After putting on Iḥrām for Hajj, he should perform a Nafl Ṭawāf with Raml and Sa'ī. Now, there would be no need for him to perform these acts during Ṭawāf-uz-Ziyāraĥ. *(Baĥār-e-Sharī'at, vol. 1, pp. 1112)*

Normally, there is a huge crowd on the 6th, 7th and 8th of Żul-Ḥijjaĥ. Therefore, one should not perform a Nafl Ṭawāf for the Raml and Sa'ī of Hajj during these days. One can perform them with Ṭawāf-uz-Ziyāraĥ because it is likely that there will be relatively a small crowd and he will not need to put on Ihram as well. However, there is a big crowd on the 10th of Żul-Ḥijjaĥ but it thins out on the 11th and 12th of Żul-Ḥijjaĥ.

Advice for all Ḥujjāj

Now all the Ḥujjāj whether they are Mufrid, Mutamatte' or Qārin will be spending the pleasant moments of their lives in Makka-tul-Mukarramaĥ eagerly waiting for 8th Żul-Ḥijjaĥ to leave for Minā.

Dear devotees of Prophet! This is the sacred city where the Beloved and Blessed Prophet صَلَّى اللّٰهُ تَعَالٰى عَلَيْهِ وَاٰلِهٖ وَسَلَّم has spent nearly 53 years of his blessed life. It is the city which brings back the memories of our Noble Prophet صَلَّى اللّٰهُ تَعَالٰى عَلَيْهِ وَاٰلِهٖ وَسَلَّم. Therefore, show utmost respect and reverence here. Beware! Refrain from even the intention of sin as one sin is also equivalent to a hundred thousand sins here and one good deed is equivalent to a hundred thousand deeds.

Swearing, backbiting, tale-telling, lying, unlawful gazing, having ill opinion etc. are always Ḥarām, but committing any of these sins and every other sin here is equivalent to committing one hundred thousand sins. Moreover, do not be like those unwise people who shave off their beards whilst doing Ḥalq, مَعَاذَاللهعَزَّوَجَلَّ.

Remember that shaving off beard or trimming it less than a fist-length are both Ḥarām acts leading towards Hell and doing so here is equivalent to committing one hundred thousand Ḥarām acts.

O devotees of Rasūl! Now the sacred breeze of Makkaĥ and Madīnaĥ is kissing your face, therefore, let the blessed beard grow and repent of the sin of shaving or shortening it less than a fist-length so far. Adorn your face with this holy Sunnaĥ of the Beloved and Blessed Rasūl صَلَّى اللهُ تَعَالٰى عَلَيْهِ وَاٰلِهٖ وَسَلَّم forever.

Sarkār kā 'āshiq bĥī kyā ḋārĥī munḋātā ĥay?
Kyūn 'ishq kā cheĥray say iẓĥār nahīn ĥotā

Can a Prophet devotee shave his beard
Why does his face not express his devotional love?

(Wasāil-e-Bakhshish, pp. 234)

صَلُّوْا عَلَى الْحَبِيْب صَلَّى اللهُ تَعَالٰى عَلٰى مُحَمَّد

What to do during stay in Makkaĥ*?

1. Perform as many Nafl Ṭawāf as possible as this is more preferable for you than even Nafl Ṣalāĥ. Remember! After performing a Nafl Ṭawāf, one should first embrace Multazam before offering 2 Rak'āt Ṣalāĥ at Maqām-u-Ibrāĥīm.

* Details regarding the visits of holy places are given ahead.

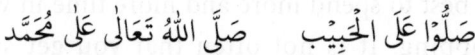

2. Perform Ṭawāfs on behalf of the Holy Prophet صَلَّى اللهُ تَعَالٰى عَلَيْهِ وَاٰلِهٖ وَسَلَّم, Sayyidunā Ghauš-e-A'ẓam رَحْمَةُ اللهِ تَعَالٰى عَلَيْه, your parents, spiritual guide (Shaykh/Murshid) etc.

3. Keep as many Nafl fasts as possible, reaping the reward of a hundred thousand Nafl fasts for each. Take care that whenever you break the fast (i.e. do Ifṭār) within Masjid-ul-Ḥarām or whenever you drink Zam Zam water or eat date etc. there, do not forget to make the intention of I'tikāf first.

4. Whenever you glance at the Holy Ka'baĥ, recite لَآ اِلٰهَ اِلَّا اللهُ وَاللهُ اَكْبَرُ thrice, Ṣalāt-'Alan-Nabī once and make Du'ā afterwards, Du'ā will be accepted, اِنْ شَآءَاللّٰه عَزَّوَجَلَّ.

5. Those who have intended to perform Hajj on foot should go to Minā, Muzdalifaĥ, and 'Arafāt two to four days earlier and mark their camps. Further, they should take the route that can easily lead them to their camps; otherwise they may have a tough time in the crowd. (It is better for Islamic sisters to travel by bus. For them to go on foot may pose the risk of them being lost or mingled with Islamic brothers. Furthermore, it is extremely difficult to look after Islamic sisters in the crowd of millions at the time of entering Muzdalifaĥ.)

6. Try your best to spend more and more time in worship rather than shopping. It is not often that you get such a golden opportunity.

Very important caution

It is often observed that some people keep their shoes/slippers outside the sacred gates of Masjid-ul-Ḥarām and Masjid-un-Nabawī and, on their return from the Masjid; they wear any pair of shoes they like.

The person using such slippers/shoes without Shar'ī exemption will be sinner for as many times as he wears them. For example, if he wears them 100 times without Shar'ī exemption, he will become sinner 100 times for wearing them even if he has taken just one pair of shoes. The rulings for such shoes are like those of Luqṭaĥ (i.e. lost belongings of someone else). If the owner cannot be traced, whoever finds this Luqṭaĥ can use it only when he is Faqīr. Otherwise, he has to donate it to some Faqīr.

Ruling on taking others shoes unlawfully

Whoever has committed such a mistake anywhere in the world is a sinner. It is Farḍ for the one who has made personal use of Luqṭaĥ (i.e. lost belongings of someone else) to repent of it and return slippers, shoes and all such things to their owners. If the owners have passed away, he must give these things to the heirs of the owners. If it is not possible either, he must give the things to some Miskīn. If he has lost the things, he must pay their price to the Miskīn or some Masjid or Madrasaĥ, provided it is impossible to pay the price to the owners or to their heirs. (For detailed rulings on Luqṭaĥ, study from page 471 to 484 of *Baĥār-e-Sharī'at*, volume 2.)

Advice for Islamic sisters

Islamic sisters should offer Ṣalāĥ where they are staying. For them to come to Masjidayn Karīmayn to offer Ṣalāĥ is a mistaken idea. The objective is to earn reward, and our Beloved and Blessed Prophet صَلَّى اللهُ تَعَالٰى عَلَيْهِ وَاٰلِهٖ وَسَلَّم has stated, 'There is more reward for woman in offering Ṣalāĥ at her home rather than offering it in my Masjid (i.e. Masjid-un-Nabawī).' *(Baĥār-e-Sharī'at, vol. 1, pp. 1112; Musnad Imām Aḥmad Bin Ḥanbal, vol. 10, pp. 310, Ḥadīš 27158)*

Seven Ḥarām acts during Ṭawāf

The following acts are Ḥarām in Ṭawāf, even if it is a Nafl one:

1. To perform Ṭawāf without Wuḍū
2. To make Ṭawāf on some carriage or on someone's back or in someone's lap without a valid excuse
3. To crawl or drag oneself whilst sitting during Ṭawāf without a valid excuse
4. To make Ṭawāf in the opposite direction keeping the Ka'baĥ at right side
5. To pass from inside the Ḥaṭīm during Ṭawāf
6. To perform less than seven rounds
7. Unveiling of a quarter of that part of the body which is included in 'Satr.' For example, unveiling of a quarter of thigh is Ḥarām. Likewise, unveiling of a quarter of the ear or the wrist of a free woman is Ḥarām. *(Bahār-e-Sharī'at, vol. 1, pp. 1112)*

   Islamic sisters pay very little attention to this. During Ṭawāf, especially when doing Istilām of Ḥajar-ul-Aswad, a quarter of the wrists of several Islamic sisters is unveiled, even sometimes complete wrist is unveiled, which is Ḥarām and a sin. Unveiling the hair of head, the ear or the wrist to a non-Maḥram male is Ḥarām and a sin even when not performing Ṭawāf. (In order to learn detailed rulings about Islamic veiling, study the 397-page book '*Parday kay bāray mayn Suwāl Jawāb*' published by Maktaba-tul-Madīnaĥ, the publishing department of Dawat-e-Islami.)

Eleven Makrūĥ acts during Ṭawāf

1. Useless talking
2. To make Du'ā, do Żikr, recite Quran, Na'at, Munājāt etc. aloud

3. To recite couplets other than the ones containing Ḥamd, Ṣalāt and Manqabat
4. To perform Ṭawāf in impure clothes. (As a caution, don't carry used shoes/slippers with you during Ṭawāf).
5. Not to do Raml whenever required or
6. not to do Iḍṭibā' whenever required or
7. not to kiss Ḥajar-ul-Aswad whenever required.
8. To perform Ṭawāf with longer intervals in between the rounds of Ṭawāf. However, there is no harm if one needs to go to the toilet or to make Wuḍū. He may leave. He should resume Ṭawāf from where he had left; there is no need to restart from the beginning.
9. To start the next Ṭawāf without offering the two Rak'āt Ṣalāĥ of the previous one. However, if the time is Makrūĥ for Ṣalāĥ, there is no harm in doing so. For example, several Ṭawāfs may be performed without offering Ṣalāĥ of Ṭawāf from Ṣubḥ-e-Ṣādiq till 20 minutes after the appearance of the edge of the sun at sunrise or after offering Ṣalāt-ul-'Aṣr till sunset. However, after the elapsing of Makrūĥ timing, two Rak'āt Ṣalāĥ will have to be offered for each Ṭawāf.
10. To eat anything during Ṭawāf
11. To perform Ṭawāf in the intense need of passing urine or breaking wind etc. *(Bahār-e-Sharī'at, vol. 1, pp. 1113; Al-Maslak-ul-Mutaqassiṭ lil-Qārī, pp. 165)*

Seven permissible acts during Sa'ī and Ṭawāf

1. To make Salām
2. To reply to Salām

3. To talk when necessary
4. To drink water (eating is also allowed during Sa'ī)
5. To recite verses of Ḥamd, Na'at or Manqabat in low voice
6. To pass across the front of someone offering Ṣalāĥ, as Ṭawāf is also like Ṣalāĥ. However, such passing is impermissible during Sa'ī.
7. To ask or answer an Islamic ruling

(ibid, vol. 1, pp. 1114; Al-Maslak-ul-Mutaqassiṭ, pp. 162)

Ten Makrūĥ acts in Sa'ī

1. Performing Sa'ī with longer intervals in between its rounds without any need. However, one may leave to relieve oneself or to make Wuḍū if it is broken, although Wuḍū is not a requisite for Sa'ī, it is Mustaḥab.
2. Buying
3. Selling
4. Useless talking
5. Looking here and there uselessly is Makrūĥ in Sa'ī and more Makrūĥ in Ṭawāf.
6. Not to climb Ṣafā or
7. Marwaĥ (climb a little, not up to the top)
8. For males not to run between the green marks without a valid reason
9. Delaying Sa'ī too much after Ṭawāf
10. Unveiling of Satr-e-'Awrat

(Baĥār-e-Sharī'at, vol. 1, pp. 1115)

Four miscellaneous rulings regarding Sa'ī

1. Performing Sa'ī by walking on foot is Wājib provided there is no valid exemption. (If someone performs it by sliding whilst sitting or riding without a valid exemption, *Dam* will be Wājib). *(Lubāb-ul-Manāsik, pp. 178)*

2. Purity is not a conditional requirement for Sa'ī. A woman suffering from menses or post-natal bleeding may also perform Sa'ī. *('Ālamgīrī, vol. 1, pp. 227)*

3. It is Mustaḥab to perform Sa'ī in the state of Wuḍū with purity of body and clothes. *(Bahā̂r-e-Sharī'at, vol. 1, pp. 1110)*

4. Whilst starting Sa'ī, first recite Du'ā of Ṣafā and then make the intention for Sa'ī. There are several rituals performed before Sa'ī such as Istilām of Ḥajar-ul-Aswad, climbing Ṣafā and making Du'ā, etc. It is better to make a separate intention before performing each of them. However, if the intention of performing the pre-Sa'ī rituals for earning reward is present in the heart, this is also sufficient.

Important advice for Islamic sisters

Islamic sisters should keep themselves apart from males. Most of the unwise women intrude into the males' crowd in order to touch Ḥajar-ul-Aswad and Rukn Yamānī or to become closer to the Holy Ka'baĥ. How shameful it is! It is advisable for Islamic sisters to perform Ṭawāf at 10 noon as the crowd is small at that time.

Rain and Mīzāb-ur-Raḥmaĥ

A huge crowd gathers at Ḥātim when it rains. Ḥujjāj rush devotedly to obtain the holy water falling from Mīzāb-ur-Raḥmaĥ. This poses the risk of Ḥujjāj being injured or even crushed to death in an effort to obtain the holy water. On such occasions, it is necessary for Islamic sisters to stay away.

Put on the Iḥrām of Hajj

If you have not yet put on the Iḥrām of Hajj, you can do on the 8th of Żul-Ḥijjaĥ. But it will be better to put on it on the 7th of Żul-Ḥijjaĥ because the Mu'allim starts sending Ḥujjāj to Minā after the Ṣalāt-ul-'Ishā of 7th Żul-Ḥijjaĥ. Offer two Rak'āt Nafl in Masjid-ul-Ḥarām at the time that is not Makrūĥ and make intention of Hajj in these words keeping the meaning in mind.

اَللّٰھُمَّ اِنِّیۡۤ اُرِیۡدُ الۡحَجَّ فَیَسِّرۡہُ لِیۡ وَ تَقَبَّلۡہُ مِنِّیۡ وَاَعِنِّیۡ عَلَیۡہِ

وَبَارِكۡ لِیۡ فِیۡہِ ؕ نَوَیۡتُ الۡحَجَّ وَاَحۡرَمۡتُ بِہٖ لِلّٰہِ تَعَالٰی ؕ

Translation: *Yā Allah عَزَّوَجَلَّ, I make the intention of Hajj, make it easy for me and accept it from me. Help me in offering it and make it blessed for me. I have made intention for Hajj and put on Iḥrām of it for the sake of Allah عَزَّوَجَلَّ.*

After making the intention, loudly recite Labbayk thrice but Islamic sisters should recite it in low voice. Now the restrictions of Iḥrām have become effective once again.

A Madanī advice

Now it would be convenient for you to perform a Nafl Ṭawāf along with Idṭibā', Raml and Sa'ī of Hajj. In this way, you will not be required to perform Raml and Sa'ī in Ṭawāf-uz-Ziyāraĥ. But keep it in mind that there is a large crowd on 7th and 8th Żul-Ḥijjaĥ. Similarly, there is a large crowd on 10th Żul-Ḥijjaĥ and it is not easy to perform Ṭawāf-uz-Ziyāraĥ. However, the crowd thins out on 11th and 12th of Żul-Ḥijjaĥ and one can perform Ṭawāf-uz-Ziyāraĥ without much difficulty. It also becomes easy to perform Sa'ī.

Leaving for Minā

It is the 8th night of Żul-Ḥijjaĥ. After Ṣalāt-ul-'Ishā, excitement has filled the air. Everybody is eager to move for Minā. Take the necessary items, e.g. rosary, prayer-mat, compass, some utensils, water bottle that can be hung around the neck, necessary medicines and address of the Mu'allim. The address of the Mu'allim should always be with you as it will prove to be beneficial in case of getting lost or, Allah عَزَّوَجَلَّ forbid, passing out or meeting an accident. If women are accompanying you, they should have a green or any dark colour piece of cloth sewn at the back of their veil so that they can be identified in the crowd. Make them walk ahead of you, especially in the crowd. If you are ahead of them and they are left far behind, they can get lost.

Don't forget to take money for meeting the expenses of Qurbānī, meal etc. Don't carry the cooker as it is prohibited. If possible, make the journey to Minā, 'Arafāt and Muzdalifaĥ on foot as 70 million good deeds will be written for every step until your return to Makka-tul-Mukarramaĥ. وَاللّٰهُ ذُوالْفَضْلِ الْعَظِيْم

Recite Talbiyaĥ and Ṣalāt-'Alan-Nabī and do Żikr abundantly all the way. As soon as Minā appears, recite Ṣalāt-'Alan-Nabī and the following Du'ā:

اَللّٰهُمَّ هٰذِهٖ مِنٰى فَامْنُنْ عَلَيَّ بِمَا مَنَنْتَ بِهٖ عَلٰى اَوْلِيَآئِكَ

***Translation:** O Allah عَزَّوَجَلَّ! This is Minā. Bless me with the boon that you bestowed upon Your Awliyā (beloveds).*

Look! You have now entered the glorious valley of Minā. How captivating is the scene here! Tents are everywhere in the plains and on the plateaus. Stay in the tent provided by your Mu'allim. You will be offering five Ṣalāĥ (from Ṣalāt-uẓ-Ẓuĥr of 8th Żul-Ḥijjaĥ to Ṣalāt-ul-Fajr of 9th Żul-Ḥijjaĥ) in Minā as the Beloved and Blessed Prophet صَلَّى اللّٰهُ تَعَالٰى عَلَيْهِ وَاٰلِهٖ وَسَلَّم did the same.

❋❋❋

Quarrels over staying place in Minā first day

The ritual stay in Minā today is a great worship. Millions of people have gathered for this worship, which is why satan is furious and is infuriating people on trivial matters. Some Ḥujjāj are quarrelling and shouting in order to find a place in the camps. You should be alert to the attack of satan. If a Ḥājī has unfairly occupied your space, you should politely draw his attention towards his mistake and request him to vacate your space. If he does not listen to you and you do not have any other place, contact the deputy of Mu'allim instead of quarrelling. Your problem will be solved, اِنْ شَآءَاللّٰه عَزَّوَجَلَّ.

Anyhow you should have a heart of gold and behave with the guests of Allah Almighty in a polite and forgiving manner. This is a very important day. Some people may be wasting their time in chat but you should remain busy in worship. If possible, call them to righteousness for it is also a great worship. The approaching tonight is the night of 'Arafaĥ. If possible, spend this night in worship; there are many other nights to sleep and rest. It is not often that you get such an opportunity.

Du'ā of night of 'Arafaĥ

The Beloved and Blessed Prophet صَلَّى اللهُ تَعَالٰى عَلَيْهِ وَاٰلِهٖ وَسَلَّم has stated: The person reciting the following Du'ā one thousand times at the night of 'Arafaĥ will be granted whatever he asks Allah عَزَّوَجَلَّ for, provided he does not ask for sin or cutting ties.

سُبْحٰنَ الَّذِیْ فِی السَّمَآءِ عَرْشُهٗ ط سُبْحٰنَ الَّذِیْ فِی الْاَرْضِ مَوْطِئُهٗ ط سُبْحٰنَ الَّذِیْ فِی الْبَحْرِ سَبِیْلُهٗ ط سُبْحٰنَ الَّذِیْ فِی النَّارِ سُلْطَانُهٗ ط سُبْحٰنَ الَّذِیْ فِی الْجَنَّةِ رَحْمَتُهٗ ط سُبْحٰنَ الَّذِیْ فِی الْقَبْرِ قَضَائُهٗ ط سُبْحٰنَ الَّذِیْ فِی الْهَوَآءِ رُوْحُهٗ ط سُبْحٰنَ الَّذِیْ رَفَعَ السَّمَآءَ ط سُبْحٰنَ الَّذِیْ وَضَعَ الْاَرْضَ ط سُبْحٰنَ الَّذِیْ لَا مَلْجَاَ وَلَا مَنْجٰی مِنْهُ اِلَّا اِلَیْهِ ط

Translation: *Pure is He عَزَّوَجَلَّ Whose 'Arsh is in the Heavens, Pure is He عَزَّوَجَلَّ Whose sovereignty is in the earth, Pure is He عَزَّوَجَلَّ Whose path is in the oceans, Pure is He عَزَّوَجَلَّ Whose sultanate is in Hell, Pure is He عَزَّوَجَلَّ Whose mercy is in Paradise, Pure is He عَزَّوَجَلَّ Whose commandment is in the grave, Pure is He عَزَّوَجَلَّ under Whose authority are the souls present in the air, Pure is He عَزَّوَجَلَّ Who has elevated the skies and Pure is He عَزَّوَجَلَّ Who has lowered the earth, Pure is He عَزَّوَجَلَّ from Whose torment there is no refuge and salvation except towards Him.*

Spending night of 9th Żul-Ḥijjaĥ in Minā is Sunnat-ul-Muakkadaĥ

The buses of Mu'allim leave for 'Arafāt at night and thousands of Ḥujjāj miss the Sunnat-ul-Muakkadaĥ of spending the night of 9th Żul-Ḥijjaĥ in Minā.

It is stated in *Baĥār-e-Sharī'at*: If someone spends night in Minā but goes to 'Arafāt before Ṣubḥ-e-Ṣādiq or before Ṣalāt-ul-Fajr or before sunrise, he has done wrong. *(Baĥār-e-Sharī'at, vol. 1, pp. 1120)* Due to lack of knowledge many Ḥujjāj offer Ṣalāt-ul-Fajr before Ṣubḥ-e-Ṣādiq. Instead of leaving in a hurry, Ḥujjāj should talk to the Mu'allim and spend the night in Minā. Buses will also be available after the sunrise.

Leaving for 'Arafāt

Today is the 9th of Żul-Ḥijjaĥ. After offering Ṣalāt-ul-Fajr in its Mustaḥab time, remain busy reciting Talbiyaĥ, doing Żikr and making Du'ā until the sun rises and shines on the mount Šabīr which is situated opposite Masjid Khayf. Now proceed towards 'Arafāt with a trembling heart whilst doing Żikr and reciting Talbiyaĥ and Ṣalāt-'Alan-Nabī abundantly.

Try to cleanse your heart from the thoughts of others. Today is the day when the Hajj of some Ḥujjāj will be accepted and some will be forgiven for their sake. Deprived is the person who is deprived today. If you have satanic whispering do not fight them because it is also a success of satan that he has engaged you in any other task. Thus you should have only one aim that is the attainment of the pleasure of Allah عَزَّوَجَلَّ. That way, satan will fail and flee away, اِنْ شَآءَاللّٰہ عَزَّوَجَلَّ.

Du'ā of pathway to 'Arafāt

(Recite the following Du'ā after leaving Minā).

اَللّٰهُمَّ اجْعَلْهَا خَيْرَ غُدْوَةٍ غَدَوْتُهَا قَطُّ وَقَرِّبْهَا مِنْ رِضْوَانِكَ وَاَبْعِدْهَا مِنْ سَخَطِكَ ط اَللّٰهُمَّ اِلَيْكَ تَوَجَّهْتُ وَعَلَيْكَ تَوَكَّلْتُ وَوَجْهَكَ اَرَدْتُّ فَاجْعَلْ ذَنْبِيْ مَغْفُوْرًا وَّحَجِّيْ مَبْرُوْرًا وَّارْحَمْنِيْ وَلَا تُخَيِّبْنِيْ وَبَارِكْ لِيْ فِيْ سَفَرِيْ وَاقْضِ بِعَرَفَاتٍ حَاجَتِيْ اِنَّكَ عَلٰى كُلِّ شَيْءٍ قَدِيْرٌ ط

Translation: *O Allah عَزَّوَجَلَّ! Make this morning of mine the best of mornings and make it closer to Your pleasure and distance it from Your wrath. O Allah عَزَّوَجَلَّ! I have turned towards You and I have trusted You and intended Your Wajĥ-e-Karīm. Forgive my sins, accept my Hajj, have mercy on me and do not make me deprived. Bless my journey with bounties and fulfill my needs in 'Arafāt. Without doubt, You have power over all things.*

Entering 'Arafāt

You have now reached the sacred plains of 'Arafāt. Get overwhelmed and let your tears flow. Shortly, you will be entering the holy plains from where the visitors do not return empty handed. As you catch the sight of Jabal-ur-Raḥmaĥ, recite Labbayk and make Du'ā more enthusiastically, as the Du'ā made here will be accepted اِنْ شَآءَاللّٰه عَزَّوَجَلَّ. Keep your heart in control and your eyes lowered. Keep on reciting Labbayk as you enter 'Arafāt weeping.

سُبْحٰنَ اللّٰـه عَزَّوَجَلَّ! These are the holy plains where millions of Muslims have gathered, all dressed alike. The calls of Labbayk are echoing everywhere. Indeed, countless Awliyā of Allah and two Prophets of Allah عَزَّوَجَلَّ namely Sayyidunā Khiḍar and Sayyidunā Ilyās عَلَيْهِمَا السَّلَام are also present in 'Arafāt on the day of 'Arafaĥ. It shows the importance of this day. Sayyidunā Imām Ja'far Ṣādiq عَلَيْهِ رَحْمَةُ اللّٰهِ الْخَالِق has narrated, 'There are some sins whose expiation is only Wuqūf-e-'Arafāt (means they can only be removed by Wuqūf-e-'Arafāt).'

(Qūt-ul-Qulūb, vol. 2, pp. 199)

Two great virtues of the day of 'Arafaĥ

1. Allah عَزَّوَجَلَّ does not free His so many slaves from Hell on any other day as He عَزَّوَجَلَّ does on the day of 'Arafaĥ, and shows to angels that He عَزَّوَجَلَّ is proud of them. *(Muslim, pp. 703, Ḥadīš 1348)*

2. Satan was not seen as belittled, disgraced, humiliated and infuriated on any other day as was seen on the day of 'Arafaĥ because this day satan sees mercy being descended and major sins of people being forgiven by Allah عَزَّوَجَلَّ.

(Muwaṭṭā Imām Mālik, vol. 1, pp. 386, Ḥadīš 982)

Seeing women on 'Arafaĥ...

A man gazed women on the day of 'Arafaĥ, so the Noble Prophet صَلَّى اللّٰهُ تَعَالٰى عَلَيْهِ وَاٰلِهٖ وَسَلَّم said, 'Today is the day when whoever keeps his ear, eye and tongue in control, will be forgiven.'

(Shu'ab-ul-Īmān, vol. 3, pp. 461, Ḥadīš 4071)

Making stones witness in plains of 'Arafāt

Picking up seven small stones in the plains of 'Arafāt on the occasion of Hajj, Sayyidunā Ibrāhīm Wāsiṭī عَلَيْهِ رَحْمَةُ اللّٰهِ الْقَوِى said to them: O stones! Be a witness to what I say

لَآ اِلٰهَ اِلَّا اللّٰهُ وَاَنَّ مُحَمَّدًا عَبْدُهٗ وَرَسُوْلُهٗ ط

Translation: *No one is worthy to be worshipped except Allah (عَزَّوَجَلَّ) and Muhammad (صَلَّى اللّٰهُ تَعَالٰى عَلَيْهِ وَاٰلِهٖ وَسَلَّم) is His distinguished Bondman and Prophet.*

He then went to sleep and had a dream in which he saw that the Day of Judgement had taken place and accountability was going on. He was also held accountable for his deeds and ordered to be sent to Hell. The angels were now taking him towards Hell. When they reached the door of Hell one of the stones came and served as a barrier at the door. They then reached the second door, so another stone came and served as a barrier. The same thing happened at all the seven doors of Hell. The angels then took him to Divine 'Arsh. Allah عَزَّوَجَلَّ said, 'O Ibrāĥīm! You made stones witness for your faith so these lifeless stones did not waste your right; how I can waste the right of your witness!' Then Allah Almighty عَزَّوَجَلَّ commanded that he be taken to Paradise. When they reached the door of Paradise, it was closed. The witness of Kalimaĥ came and he entered Paradise. *(Durra-tun-Nāṣiḥīn, pp. 37)*

Fortunate Hajj pilgrims

When staying in the plains of 'Arafāt you also pick up seven small stones, recite the above Kalimaĥ or Kalimaĥ Shaĥādaĥ, make them witness and put them back. Furthermore, wherever you are in the world, recite Kalimaĥ near trees, mountains, rivers, canals and the drops of rain, etc. making them the witness of your faith.

9 Madanī pearls regarding ritual stay in 'Arafāt

1. Towards midday, perform Ghusl as this is Sunnat-ul-Muakkadaĥ. If not possible, make Wuḍū at least. *(Baĥār-e-Sharī'at, vol. 1, pp. 1123)*

2. The stipulated time for the ritual stay in ʻArafāt is from the commencement of the timing of Ẓuĥr of 9th Żul-Ḥijjaĥ to the commencement of the timing of Fajr of 10th Żul-Ḥijjaĥ. The Muslims entering the plains of ʻArafāt even for a moment within this duration in the state of Iḥrām will become Ḥājī. Today's stay in ʻArafāt is the main pillar of Hajj.

3. In ʻArafāt, the Ṣalāĥ of Ẓuĥr and ʻAṣr are offered together during the stipulated time of Ẓuĥr but this is subject to certain conditions[1].

4. It is Sunnaĥ for the Ḥājī not to keep fast today. Furthermore, if possible, he should keep Wuḍū all the time.

5. It is preferable to stay as close as possible to the black stone-made floor area of Jabal-ur-Raḥmaĥ.

6. Some unwise people climb Jabal-ur-Raḥmaĥ and wave their handkerchiefs from there. You should not do so; nor should you have ill feelings towards them. This is not the day to find faults with others but rather it is the day to shed tears and feel ashamed of one's own faults.

7. It is preferable not essential or Wājib to stand for Wuqūf. Wuqūf is valid even if one is sitting. For Wuqūf, it is preferable to make intention and to face Qiblaĥ.

8. It is a Sunnaĥ to perform Wuqūf instantly after Ṣalāĥ.

(Baĥār-e-Sharīʻat, vol. 1, pp. 1124)

9. If possible, one should refrain from shade of anything, even that of an umbrella in Mawqif (lodging in ʻArafāt). However,

---

[1] You should offer Ṣalāt-uẓ-Ẓuĥr in Ẓuĥr timings and Ṣalāt-ul-ʻAṣr in ʻAṣr timings with Jamāʼat inside your tent.

one who is incapable is exempted. *(ibid, pp. 1128)* If staying under an umbrella, men should take the precaution that it should not touch their heads, otherwise this may result in expiation being due.

Emphatic advice of Imām Aḥmad Razā Khān رَحْمَةُ اللهِ عَلَيْه

Unlawful gazing is always Ḥarām whether one is in Iḥrām or in Mawqif or in Masjid-ul-Ḥarām or in front of the Holy Ka'baĥ or is even doing the Ṭawāf of the Ka'baĥ. This is an occasion of your trial. The women have been ordered not to veil their faces and you have been commanded not to look at them.

Remember that these (women) are the servants of the Most Honourable King in Whose holy court, you and they, are all present at the moment. Without any comparison, when the cub of a lion is in his lap, who can dare to cast an evil look at it. These 'female-servants' of Allah عَزَّوَجَلَّ, the Omnipotent, are also present in His special court. How dreadful it would be to gaze at them.

وَ لِلّٰهِ الْمَثَلُ الْاَعْلٰى *And the glory of Allah is the highest.*

[Kanz-ul-Īmān (Translation of Quran)] (Part 14, Sūraĥ An-Naḥl, verse 60)

Be careful! Protect your faith. Protect your heart and eyes. The sacred Ḥaram is a place where even the intention of committing a sin is recorded as a sin and the punishment of committing a single sin is equal to a hundred thousand sins. May Allah عَزَّوَجَلَّ guide us towards good. (Remember that 'Arafāt is out of the limits of Ḥaram.)

(Fatāwā Razawiyyaĥ referenced, vol. 10, pp. 750)

اٰمِين بِجَاهِ النَّبِيِّ الْاَمِين صَلَّى اللهُ تَعَالٰى عَلَيْهِ وَاٰلِهٖ وَسَلَّم

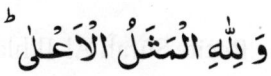

Du'ās of 'Arafāt

1. According to a Ḥadīš, the one reciting following Kalimaĥ of Tawḥīd (oneness), Sūraĥ Al-Ikhlāṣ and the below-mentioned Ṣalāt-'Alan-Nabī 100 times each, in the afternoon, in his Mawqif (allocated place in plains of 'Arafāt), he is forgiven. In addition, if he intercedes for all those present in 'Arafāt, his intercession will be recognized.

❖ Recite this Kalimaĥ of Tawḥīd 100 times:

لَآ اِلٰهَ اِلَّا اللّٰهُ وَحۡدَهٗ لَا شَرِيۡكَ لَهٗ ط لَهُ الۡمُلۡكُ وَلَهُ الۡحَمۡدُ يُحۡيٖ وَ يُمِيۡتُ وَهُوَ عَلٰى كُلِّ شَيۡءٍ قَدِيۡرٌ ط

Translation: *No one is worthy of worship except Allah* عَزَّوَجَلَّ*. He is One. He has no partner. For Him only is sovereignty and all glorifications. He gives life and death and He has power over everything.*

❖ Recite Sūraĥ Al-Ikhlāṣ 100 times.

❖ Recite this Ṣalāt-'Alan-Nabī 100 times:

اَللّٰهُمَّ صَلِّ عَلٰى (سَيِّدِنَا) مُحَمَّدٍ كَمَا صَلَّيۡتَ عَلٰى (سَيِّدِنَا) اِبۡرَاهِيۡمَ وَ عَلٰى اٰلِ (سَيِّدِنَا) اِبۡرَاهِيۡمَ اِنَّكَ حَمِيۡدٌ مَّجِيۡدٌ وَّعَلَيۡنَا مَعَهُمۡ ط

Translation: *O Allah* عَزَّوَجَلَّ *send Ṣalāt on (our Master) Muhammad* صَلَّى اللهُ تَعَالٰى عَلَيْهِ وَاٰلِهٖ وَسَلَّم *as You sent Ṣalāt on (our Master) Ibrāĥīm* عَلَيْهِ السَّلَام

and descendants of (our Master) Ibrāĥīm عَلَيْهِ السَّلَام. Indeed, You are glorified and glorious. And [send Ṣalāt] upon us as well alongwith them.

2. Recite the following three times اَللّٰهُ اَكْبَرُ وَلِلّٰهِ الْحَمْدُ. Recite Kalimaĥ of Tawḥīd once and then recite the following Du'ā thrice:

اَللّٰهُمَّ اهْدِنِىْ بِالْهُدٰى وَنَقِّنِىْ

وَاعْصِمْنِىْ بِالتَّقْوٰى وَاغْفِرْلِىْ فِى الْاٰخِرَةِ وَالْاُوْلٰى ط

***Translation:** O Allah عَزَّوَجَلَّ! Bless me with true guidance. Make me pure and grant me protection from sinning through piety and forgive me in this world and the Hereafter.*

❖ Thereafter, recite the following Du'ā once:

اَللّٰهُمَّ اجْعَلْهُ حَجًّا مَّبْرُوْرًا وَّ ذَنْبًا مَّغْفُوْرًا ط اَللّٰهُمَّ لَكَ

الْحَمْدُ كَالَّذِىْ نَقُوْلُ وَخَيْرًا مِّمَّا نَقُوْلُ ط اَللّٰهُمَّ لَكَ صَلَاتِىْ

وَنُسُكِىْ وَمَحْيَاىَ وَمَمَاتِىْ وَاِلَيْكَ مَاٰبِىْ وَلَكَ رَبِّ تُرَاثِىْ ط

اَللّٰهُمَّ اَعُوْذُبِكَ مِنْ عَذَابِ الْقَبْرِ وَوَسْوَسَةِ الصَّدْرِ وَشَتَاتِ

الْاَمْرِ ط اَللّٰهُمَّ اِنِّىْٓ اَسْئَلُكَ مِنْ خَيْرِ مَا تَجِىْٓءُ بِهِ الرِّيْحُ

وَنَعُوْذُبِكَ مِنْ شَرِّ مَا تَجِىْٓءُ بِهِ الرِّيْحُ ط اَللّٰهُمَّ اهْدِنَا

بِالْهُدٰى وَ زَيِّنَّا بِالتَّقْوٰى وَاغْفِرْلَنَا فِي الْاٰخِرَةِ وَ الْاُوْلٰى ؕ
اَللّٰهُمَّ اِنِّيْٓ اَسْئَلُكَ رِزْقًا طَيِّبًا مُّبَارَكًا ؕ اَللّٰهُمَّ اِنَّكَ اَمَرْتَ
بِالدُّعَآءِ وَقَضَيْتَ عَلٰى نَفْسِكَ بِالْاِجَابَةِ وَاِنَّكَ لَا تُخْلِفُ
الْمِيْعَادَ وَلَا تَنْكُثُ عَهْدَكَ ؕ اَللّٰهُمَّ مَا اَحْبَبْتَ مِنْ خَيْرٍ
فَحَبِّبْهُ اِلَيْنَا وَيَسِّرْهُ لَنَا وَمَا كَرِهْتَ مِنْ شَرٍّ فَكَرِّهْهُ اِلَيْنَا
وَجَنِّبْنَاهُ وَلَا تَنْزِعْ مِنَّا الْاِسْلَامَ بَعْدَ اِذْ هَدَيْتَنَا ؕ اَللّٰهُمَّ
اِنَّكَ تَرٰى مَكَانِيْ وَتَسْمَعُ كَلَامِيْ وَتَعْلَمُ سِرِّيْ وَعَلَانِيَتِيْ
وَلَا يَخْفٰى عَلَيْكَ شَيْءٌ مِّنْ اَمْرِيْ اَنَا الْبَآئِسُ الْفَقِيْرُ
الْمُسْتَغِيْثُ الْمُسْتَجِيْرُ الْوَجِلُ الْمُشْفِقُ الْمُقِرُّ الْمُعْتَرِفُ
بِذَنْبِهٖ اَسْئَلُكَ مَسْاَلَةَ الْمِسْكِيْنِ وَاَبْتَهِلُ اِلَيْكَ اِبْتِهَالَ
الْمُذْنِبِ الذَّلِيْلِ وَاَدْعُوْكَ دُعَآءَ الْخَآئِفِ الْمُضْطَرِّ دُعَآءَ
مَنْ خَضَعَتْ لَكَ رَقَبَتُهٗ وَفَاضَتْ لَكَ عَيْنَاهُ وَنَحَلَ لَكَ جَسَدُهٗ
وَرَغِمَ اَنْفُهٗ ؕ اَللّٰهُمَّ لَا تَجْعَلْنِيْ بِدُعَآئِكَ رَبِّ شَقِيًّا وَّكُنْ بِيْ
رَؤُوْفًا رَّحِيْمًا يَا خَيْرَ الْمَسْئُوْلِيْنَ وَخَيْرَ الْمُعْطِيْنَ ؕ

Translation: *O Allah عَزَّوَجَلَّ! Make this an accepted Hajj and forgive sins. O Allah عَزَّوَجَلَّ! For You are all glorifications which we express and even better than what we express. O Allah عَزَّوَجَلَّ, my Ṣalāĥ, my worship, my living and my dying are all for You and towards You is my return, and O Allah عَزَّوَجَلَّ You are my protector. O Allah عَزَّوَجَلَّ, I beg You for protection from the torment of the grave, from the whisperings of my heart and from doing evil. O Allah عَزَّوَجَلَّ, I seek the good which is brought by the wind, and I seek protection from any evil which is brought by the wind. O Allah عَزَّوَجَلَّ, guide us towards truth, beautify us with piety and forgive us in the Hereafter. O Allah عَزَّوَجَلَّ, I beg from You pure and virtuous sustenance. O Allah عَزَّوَجَلَّ, You have commanded us to make Du'ā and have taken the responsibility of fulfilling our needs and without doubt You do not go against Your word and Your promise. O Allah عَزَّوَجَلَّ, whatever is dear to You, make it dear to us and make the same available to us and whatever You dislike, make us dislike it and make us refrain from it. After You have guided us to Islam, do not make us deviate from it. O Allah عَزَّوَجَلَّ, without doubt You see my abode, You listen to my words, You are aware of my hidden being and apparent being and nothing from my affairs is hidden from You. I am Your helpless sinful slave, fearful of my sins and I admit that I am a sinner begging You for protection from all sins. I plead with You like a beggar, as a sinful and wretched person whose head is bowed in humility to You, whose eyes are tearful, whose body is weak and whose nose is in the dust. O Allah عَزَّوَجَلَّ, don't make me unfortunate and be the most kind and merciful to me. O the best One to be asked, and the best bestower of all!*

3. Sayyidunā 'Alī كَرَّمَ اللّٰهُ تَعَالٰى وَجْهَهُ الْكَرِيْم has narrated that the Holy Prophet صَلَّى اللّٰهُ تَعَالٰى عَلَيْهِ وَاٰلِهٖ وَسَلَّم has stated, 'On the day of 'Arafaĥ, the Du'ā of mine and that of other Prophets is as follows:

لَآ اِلٰهَ اِلَّا اللّٰهُ وَحْدَهٗ لَا شَرِيْكَ لَهٗ ط لَهُ الْمُلْكُ وَلَهُ الْحَمْدُ
يُحْيٖ وَيُمِيْتُ وَهُوَ عَلٰى كُلِّ شَيْءٍ قَدِيْرٌ ط اَللّٰهُمَّ اجْعَلْ فِيْ
سَمْعِيْ نُوْرًا وَّفِيْ بَصَرِيْ نُوْرًا وَّفِيْ قَلْبِيْ نُوْرًا ط اَللّٰهُمَّ اشْرَحْ
لِيْ صَدْرِيْ وَيَسِّرْ لِيْٓ اَمْرِيْ وَاَعُوْذُبِكَ مِنْ وَّسَاوِسِ الصَّدْرِ
وَتَشْتِيْتِ الْاَمْرِ وَعَذَابِ الْقَبْرِ ط اَللّٰهُمَّ اِنِّيْٓ اَعُوْذُبِكَ مِنْ
شَرِّ مَا يَلِجُ فِي اللَّيْلِ وَشَرِّ مَا يَلِجُ فِي النَّهَارِ وَشَرِّ مَا تَهُبُّ
بِهِ الرِّيْحُ وَشَرِّ بَوَآئِقِ الدَّهْرِ ط

Translation: *There is none worthy to be worshiped except Allah عَزَّوَجَلَّ, Who is one with no partners. For Him is all sovereignty and all glorification. He عَزَّوَجَلَّ is alive and will never die and He عَزَّوَجَلَّ has power over all things. O Allah عَزَّوَجَلَّ, make my hearing refulgent, my sight refulgent and fill my heart with refulgence. O Allah عَزَّوَجَلَّ, broaden my chest and make easy my affairs. I beg You for protection from the whisperings of the heart, from ill-affairs and from the torment of the grave. I beg You for protection from that which comes with the night and that which comes with the day and that which comes with the wind and from the calamity of time.*

Madanī pearl

Mentioning some Du'ās to be recited in the plains of 'Arafāt, Muftī Muhammad Amjad 'Alī A'ẓamī عَلَيْهِ رَحْمَةُ اللّٰهِ الْقَوِى stated, 'Many Du'ās to be recited at this place are mentioned in books but these are sufficient and Ṣalāt-'Alan-Nabī and the recitation of the Holy Quran are better than all Du'ās.' *(Bahār-e-Sharī'at, vol. 1, pp. 1127)*

It is Sunnaĥ to make Du'ā in 'Arafāt whilst standing

Dear Ḥujjāj! It is a Sunnaĥ to make Du'ā in 'Arafāt whilst standing. Therefore, make Du'ā to your Merciful Allah عَزَّوَجَلَّ whilst standing for as long as possible, with concentration of mind and sincerity of heart.

Imagine that it is the Day of Judgement, and you are present in the court of your Creator عَزَّوَجَلَّ for the accountability of your deeds. With utmost humbleness and humility, with eyes closed and head bowed, with hope and fear, make Du'ā whilst trembling. Raise hands towards the sky (above the head) and become lost in asking for forgiveness and repentance. During the Du'ā, recite Talbiyaĥ as often as possible, and beg for the forgiveness of yourself, your parents and the entire Ummaĥ. Make an attempt to shed at least even a single tear (as this is an indication of acceptance). If you cannot weep, at least wear a weeping look on the face, as imitating the good is also good.

Make Du'ā to Allah عَزَّوَجَلَّ with the Wasīlaĥ of the Beloved and Blessed Prophet صَلَّى اللهُ تَعَالٰى عَلَيْهِ وَاٰلِهٖ وَسَلَّم, all the other Prophets عَلَيْهِمُ السَّلَام, the Ṣaḥābaĥ Kirām رَضِىَ اللّٰهُ تَعَالٰى عَنْهُم, and the blessed family of the Holy Prophet. Make Tawassul of Sayyidunā Ghauš-e-A'ẓam, Khuwājaĥ Gharīb Nawāz and A'lā Ḥaḍrat Imām Aḥmad Razā رَحِمَهُمُ اللّٰهُ تَعَالٰى and give the Wasīlaĥ of every Walī of Allah عَزَّوَجَلَّ and of every devotee of Rasūlullāĥ. Today the doors of mercy are open; there is no possibility of deprivation for those who beseech. The mercy of Allah عَزَّوَجَلَّ is showering. The entire plains of 'Arafāt is full of mercy and blessings. Whilst making Du'ā, at times tremble due to the fear of torment from Allah عَزَّوَجَلَّ and at other times fill your sad heart with the hope of immense mercy from Allah عَزَّوَجَلَّ.

Du'ā of 'Arafāt (English)*

(Recite Labbayk and Ṣalāt-'Alan-Nabī during Du'ā now and then.)

Raise both hands up to the level of either your chest or shoulders or face; or raise them above your head making your palms facing the sky. In all these four conditions palms should be spread facing the sky because the Qiblaĥ for Du'ā is sky. Now begin Du'ā like this:

اَلْحَمْدُ لِلّٰهِ رَبِّ الْعٰلَمِيْنَ وَالصَّلٰوةُ وَالسَّلَامُ عَلٰى سَيِّدِ الْمُرْسَلِيْنَ ط

يَآ اَرْحَمَ الرّٰحِمِيْنَ يَآ اَرْحَمَ الرّٰحِمِيْنَ يَآ اَرْحَمَ الرّٰحِمِيْنَ[1]

يَا رَبَّنَا يَا رَبَّنَا يَا رَبَّنَا يَا رَبَّنَا يَا رَبَّنَا[2]

After you have made as many Māšūraĥ Du'ās[3] in Arabic as you have learnt by heart, express your feelings in your own mother tongue to Allah Almighty عَزَّوَجَلَّ with the firm belief that your Du'ās are being accepted. Make Du'ā like this.

يَا اَللّٰهُ يَا رَحْمٰنُ يَا رَحِيْمُ ط

---

* Please note that the Du'ā was originally written in Urdu by Amīr-e-Aĥl-e-Sunnat دَامَتْ بَرَكَاتُهُمُ الْعَالِيَه. [Translator's Note]

[1] The Holy Prophet صَلَّى اللهُ تَعَالٰى عَلَيْهِ وَاٰلِهٖ وَسَلَّم has said, 'Allah عَزَّوَجَلَّ has appointed an angel for the Divine name (اَرْحَمُ الرَّاحِمِيْن). Whosoever utters it three times, the angel calls out 'Ask because the 'اَرْحَمُ الرَّاحِمِيْن' has turned His divine attention towards you.' *(Aḥsan-ul-Wi'ā, pp. 70)*

[2] Sayyidunā Imām Ja'far Ṣādiq رَحْمَةُ اللهِ تَعَالٰى عَلَيْه has stated that whosoever utters (يَا رَبَّنَا) five times in helplessness, Allah عَزَّوَجَلَّ will save him from what he is afraid of and will accept his Du'ā. *(Aḥsan-ul-Wi'ā, pp. 71)*

[3] The Du'ās stated in Quran and Ḥadīš.

O Allah عَزَّوَجَلَّ! It is Your infinite favour that You have created me as a human being, made me a Muslim and privileged me to be amongst the followers of Your Beloved Prophet صَلَّى اللّٰهُ تَعَالٰى عَلَيْهِ وَاٰلِهٖ وَسَلَّم. O Allah عَزَّوَجَلَّ! O Creator of the Noble Prophet صَلَّى اللّٰهُ تَعَالٰى عَلَيْهِ وَاٰلِهٖ وَسَلَّم! How can I possibly thank You? You have granted me the opportunity to perform Hajj, and today on the day of 'Arafaĥ, You have granted me the privilege to stay on the ground of 'Arafāt.

Undoubtedly, Your Beloved and my Master صَلَّى اللّٰهُ تَعَالٰى عَلَيْهِ وَاٰلِهٖ وَسَلَّم also came here. How fortunate I am! I am present today in the same ground of 'Arafāt that had the opportunity to kiss the blessed soles of the Beloved Prophet صَلَّى اللّٰهُ تَعَالٰى عَلَيْهِ وَاٰلِهٖ وَسَلَّم. Muslims from all parts of the world have gathered here today, and certainly two of Your Prophets Sayyidunā Ilyās and Sayyidunā Khiḍar عَلَيْهِمَا السَّلَام and many Awliyā are also present. Therefore, O Creator of the Merciful Prophet صَلَّى اللّٰهُ تَعَالٰى عَلَيْهِ وَاٰلِهٖ وَسَلَّم! For the sake of the mercy which is descending upon the Prophets عَلَيْهِمُ السَّلَام and the Awliyā رَحِمَهُمُ اللّٰهُ تَعَالٰى, shower at least a tiny drop upon this sinful servant also.

يَا اَللّٰهُ يَا رَحْمٰنُ يَا حَنَّانُ يَا مَنَّانُ

(Recite Labbayk thrice with Ṣalāt-'Alan-Nabī once before and after it).

O Allah عَزَّوَجَلَّ! My inefficiency and weakness is apparent to You. I am that slave who cannot bear heat and severe cold. You also know that I cannot even bear the sting of a mosquito or bug and if even an ant bites me, I become uncomfortable. You know that if an insect gets under my garment, it makes me jump. O my Allah عَزَّوَجَلَّ! Due to sins, if I am surrounded by fire in my grave, what will I do? If snakes and scorpions clung to my shroud-wrapped body, what would I do? O my Allah Almighty عَزَّوَجَلَّ! Have mercy on me for the sake of the Beloved Prophet صَلَّى اللّٰهُ تَعَالٰى عَلَيْهِ وَاٰلِهٖ وَسَلَّم and save me from death throes and afflictions of the grave and the Judgement Day. Certainly, only one drop of the rain of Your mercy will make me successful in the worldly life as well as in the afterlife. O Allah Almighty عَزَّوَجَلَّ! Have mercy on me and be pleased with me forever. Make me among those who have earned Your favour. *(Recite Labbayk thrice with Ṣalāt-'Alan-Nabī once before and after it).*

O Creator عَزَّوَجَلَّ of Mustafa! Your Beloved Prophet صَلَّى اللهُ تَعَالٰى عَلَيْهِ وَاٰلِهٖ وَسَلَّم has told us the following words of Yours, '*O son of Ādam! As long as you keep making Du'ā to Me with hope, I will also keep forgiving your sins. O son of Ādam! Even if your sins reach the limit of the heavens, still seek forgiveness for them, I will indeed forgive. O son of Ādam! If you approach Me with all the sins of the earth, without having committed Shirk (polytheism) and Kufr (disbelief), I will come towards you with mercy and forgiveness equivalent to the earth*[1].'

O Rab عَزَّوَجَلَّ of Muhammad! I have certainly filled the earth with sins and transgression, yet I have hope for Your mercy. With the Wasīlaĥ of Ghauš-e-A'ẓam, my Khuwājaĥ Gharīb Nawāz رَحِمَهُمَا اللهُ تَعَالٰى, my Murshid, with the Wasīlaĥ of the leader of true lovers, A'lā Ḥaḍrat رَحْمَةُ اللهِ تَعَالٰى عَلَيْه, kindly forgive me, kindly forgive me, kindly forgive me. *(Recite Labbayk thrice with Ṣalāt-'Alan-Nabī once before and after it).*

O the Rab of Mustafa! I admit that I have committed major sins, yet all this is very small compared to Your mercy. O my Beloved Creator! Without doubt, Your mercy searches for the sinners, and who is a bigger sinner than me in this blessed plains of 'Arafāt. O the Rab of Mustafa! I am ashamed of my sins and have hope that Your mercy will bless me. O Allah عَزَّوَجَلَّ! With the Wasīlaĥ of the rightly guided caliphs, with the Wasīlaĥ of the blessed mothers of the believers رَضِىَ اللهُ تَعَالٰى عَنْهُنَّ, with the Wasīlaĥ of Sayyidatunā Fāṭimaĥ and Ḥasnayn

[1] Tirmiżī, vol. 5, pp. 318. Ḥadīš 3551

Karīmayn, with the Wasīlaĥ of Bilāl Ḥabshī, with the Wasīlaĥ of Oways Qarnī رضی اللہ تعالٰی عنھما, forgive me, my Murshid, my teachers, forgive my parents, my whole family, all scholars and saints of the Aĥl-e-Sunnat and the entire Ummaĥ. *(Recite Labbayk thrice with Ṣalāt-'Alan-Nabī once before and after it).*

O Allah Almighty عَزَّوَجَلَّ! Undoubtedly, You get pleased by the charity given by Muslims. Who is more needy, destitute and devoid of good deeds than me? And who is more generous than You. Therefore, bless me with the charity of forgiveness. O Allah عَزَّوَجَلَّ! You are the most Merciful, most Beneficent! For the sake of Your Beloved Prophet صَلَّى اللهُ تَعَالٰى عَلَيْهِ وَاٰلِهٖ وَسَلَّم, bless me with the charity of Your ever-lasting pleasure, freedom from Hell, forgiveness and steadiness in religion.

(Recite Labbayk thrice with Ṣalāt-'Alan-Nabī once before and after it).

O Rab عَزَّوَجَلَّ Who has made the perspiration of Mustafa, the sweetest smelling perfume! Without doubt, the greatest disease is the love of this world and greed of wealth. The worst of the sinners is standing in Your blessed court, O Curer of all diseases! I seek help from You for the cure of this disease. Bless me with cure for all diseases. With the Wasīlaĥ of Your Beloved Prophet صَلَّى اللهُ تَعَالٰى عَلَيْهِ وَاٰلِهٖ وَسَلَّم, make me pious. Bless me with deep love for Muhammad ﷺ and for Madīnaĥ. *(Recite Labbayk thrice with Ṣalāt-'Alan-Nabī once before and after it).*

O Rab of Mustafa! With the Wasīlaĥ of every Prophet عَلَيْهِ السَّلَام, every Ṣaḥābī رضی اللہ تعالٰی عنہ, every family member of the Holy Prophet صَلَّى اللهُ تَعَالٰى عَلَيْهِ وَاٰلِهٖ وَسَلَّم and every Walī, cure those who are ill. Those who are in debt, remove their debt. Those who are poor, bless them with wealth. Those who are needy, bless them with Ḥalāl and easily attainable sustenance. Those who are without children, bless them with pious children without surgery. Those who wish to marry, bless them with pious life partners. Those who have split with family let them be united. Save our Muslims from European fashion and bless Muslims with adopting the Sunnaĥ of our Beloved Prophet Muhammad صَلَّى اللهُ تَعَالٰى عَلَيْهِ وَاٰلِهٖ وَسَلَّم. Those encountering wrongful court cases, free them from this predicament. Those who are lost, make them meet their beloved ones. Those who suffer from black magic and other afflictions let them be cured. O Allah Almighty عَزَّوَجَلَّ! Save Muslims from disasters, adversities, enmities, evils, jealousy and the evil eye. *(Recite Labbayk thrice with Ṣalāt-'Alan-Nabī once before and after it).*

O Merciful Rab عَزَّوَجَلَّ! With the Wasīlaĥ of Sayyidatunā Fāṭimaĥ, Sayyidatunā Zaynab, Sayyidatunā Sakīnaĥ, Sayyidatunā Sāraĥ, Sayyidatunā Ḥawwā, Sayyidatunā Ĥājiraĥ, Sayyidatunā Āsiyaĥ and Sayyidatunā Maryam رَضِىَ اللّٰهُ تَعَالٰى عَنْهُنَّ, bless our mothers, sisters, daughters and wives with modesty. Bless them with the ability to observe Islamic veil in front of their male cousins, their brothers in law, their maternal and paternal cousins, husband of the sister of the father and that of the sister of the mother[1]. *(Recite Labbayk thrice with Ṣalāt-'Alan-Nabī once before and after it).*

O the True and Beloved Rab of the Noble Prophet! Save us from every act which is not accepted by You; from that heart which is heedless of You, from those eyes which watch dramas, films and unlawful things, from those ears which listen to music and backbiting, from those legs which move towards bad companies, from those hands which oppress people, from that tongue which speaks uselessly and abuses people, from that brain which plans evil and bad and from that heart which has grudge against Muslims.

O Allah عَزَّوَجَلَّ I implore You for the sake of Your Beloved Prophet صَلَّى اللهُ تَعَالٰى عَلَيْهِ وَاٰلِهٖ وَسَلَّم, and with the Wasīlaĥ of all Mujtaĥidīn, the four Imāms and that of the four spiritual orders, make me fully obedient

[1] Unfortunately, Islamic veiling is not observed with these relatives nowadays, whereas Sharī'aĥ has declared it mandatory to observe veiling. Unveiling and informality with them is a severe sin that can lead to Hellfire.

to You; it will be great mercy and kindness of Yours. O Allah عَزَّوَجَلَّ I implore You with the Wasīlaĥ of every devotee of the Prophet and with the Wasīlaĥ of the one You love the most from Your entire creation! Make me a true devotee of Your Prophet. Bless me with a heart that remembers him and eyes that shed tears in his remembrance. Make my empty heart an abode of love for the Prophet Muhammad صَلَّى اللهُ تَعَالٰى عَلَيْهِ وَاٰلِهٖ وَسَلَّم. Illuminate my night and day with the spiritual light of the Prophet Muhammad صَلَّى اللهُ تَعَالٰى عَلَيْهِ وَاٰلِهٖ وَسَلَّم. Make me a true devotee of the Holy Prophet. *(Recite Labbayk thrice with Ṣalāt-'Alan-Nabī once before and after it).* O Allah Almighty عَزَّوَجَلَّ! For the sake of Ka'baĥ and the Green Dome, accept my Hajj, visit to holy places and my permissible Du'ās which are in my interest. Make me Mustajāb-ud-Da'wāt [one whose Du'ā is accepted]. Forgive me and every Ḥājī present in the plains of 'Arafāt and bless me with the opportunity of performing Hajj and paying a visit to Madīnaĥ every year, martyrdom in Madīnaĥ under the Green Dome whilst I am beholding the Holy Prophet صَلَّى اللهُ تَعَالٰى عَلَيْهِ وَاٰلِهٖ وَسَلَّم, burial in Jannat-ul-Baqī' and the neighbourhood of the Beloved Prophet صَلَّى اللهُ تَعَالٰى عَلَيْهِ وَاٰلِهٖ وَسَلَّم in Jannat-ul-Firdaus. O Allah Almighty عَزَّوَجَلَّ! Accept the permissible Du'ās of those Islamic brothers and sisters who have asked me for Du'ā and forgive all of them.

اٰمِيْن بِجَاهِ النَّبِيِّ الْاَمِيْن صَلَّى اللهُ تَعَالٰى عَلَيْهِ وَاٰلِهٖ وَسَلَّم

(Recite Labbayk thrice with Ṣalāt-'Alan-Nabī once before and after it).

Continue to make Du'ā even after sunset

You should continue to make Du'ā in this manner until full sunset takes place and some part of night passes. Moving away earlier than this time from where you are stationed is forbidden. Leaving the plains of 'Arafāt prior to sunset is Ḥarām. If one does so, *Dam* will become Wājib. If you enter the plains of 'Arafāt before the sunset, *Dam* will become void.

Remember! You do not have to offer Ṣalāt-ul-Maghrib here. Instead, both Maghrib and 'Ishā will be offered in combination in Muzdalifaĥ within the stipulated time of 'Ishā.

Freed from sins

Beloved Ḥujjāj! Trusting Allah's promise, it is necessary for you to believe that you have been as cleansed of sins as you were on the day of your birth. Therefore, you should now strive to refrain from committing any sins in the future. Do not be lazy in carrying out worship like Ṣalāĥ, fasts, Zakāĥ etc. Do not fall into the trap of satan by watching movies, dramas, listening to music, acquiring unlawful earnings, shaving your beards or trimming it less than a fist-length, hurting parents etc.

صَلُّوْا عَلَى الْحَبِيْب   صَلَّى اللّٰهُ تَعَالٰى عَلٰى مُحَمَّد

Departure for Muzdalifaĥ

When it is sure that the sun has set completely, move from 'Arafāt to Muzdalifaĥ. Keep doing Żikr and reciting Ṣalāt-'Alan-Nabī and Labbayk tearfully all the way. Yesterday, the rights of Allah عَزَّوَجَلَّ were forgiven, forgiveness for the rights of people is promised here (in Muzdalifaĥ). *(Baĥār-e-Sharī'at, vol. 1, pp. 1131, 1133)*

You have now arrived in the blessed plains of Muzdalifaĥ which will be busy with crowds of people. There is a huge crowd at the start of Muzdalifaĥ. You continue to go ahead; you will find enough space in the farther part of Muzdalifaĥ but take care not to enter Minā. It is a suggestion that the pedestrians make Istinjā and Wuḍū etc. before they enter Muzdalifaĥ. Otherwise, they may face severe difficulty in the crowd.

Method of offering Maghrib and 'Ishā Ṣalāĥ in combination

Here (in Muzdalifaĥ), you have to offer both Ṣalāĥs with a single Ażān and a single Iqāmaĥ. Therefore, after Ażān and Iqāmaĥ, first offer three Farḍ Rak'āt of Ṣalāt-ul-Maghrib. Then, right after performing the Salām of Ṣalāt-ul-Maghrib, offer Farḍ of Ṣalāt-ul-'Ishā. Thereafter, offer Sunan, Nafl (Awwābīn) of Maghrib and then offer Sunan, Nafl and Witr of 'Ishā. *(Bahār-e-Sharī'at, vol. 1, pp. 1132)*

Collect stones

Some great Islamic scholars are of the opinion that the night of the stay in Muzdalifaĥ is superior to even Layla-tul-Qadr. Therefore, one should not waste time in useless conversation and heedlessness. If possible, spend the entire night doing Żikr and reciting Ṣalāt-'Alan-Nabī and Talbiyaĥ. Collect 49 date-seed-sized stones within the night in order to pelt satan. It is better that some extra stones be collected so that they could be used in case the target is missed. It is preferable to wash these stones thrice. Do not break down big stones to get smaller ones. Do not pick up stones from an unclean place or a Masjid or from near Jamraĥ.

An important caution

Although it is preferable to offer Ṣalāt-ul-Fajr today in its initial timing, ensure that you offer Ṣalāt-ul-Fajr after the commencement of the time of Ṣubḥ-e-Ṣādiq. It has also been noticed that Mu'allim's representatives start awaking people very early shouting '*Ṣalāĥ Ṣalāĥ*' and announcing that the time of Fajr has begun. Some Ḥujjāj offer the Fajr Ṣalāĥ before its stipulated time. You do not do that but rather, calling them towards righteousness, explain to them politely that the time of Ṣalāĥ has not yet started, and inform them that the sound of cannon fire[1] will be heard after the time of Fajr begins.

---

[1] A cannon is customarily fired to indicate to the Ḥujjāj that Fajr time has begun.

Ritual stay in Muzdalifaĥ

It is Sunnat-ul-Muakkadaĥ to spend night in Muzdalifaĥ but it is Wājib to stay over there at least for a moment. The stipulated time for stay at Muzdalifaĥ is from Ṣubḥ-e-Ṣādiq up to sunrise. If one spends even a single moment in Muzdalifaĥ within the described duration, his stay in Muzdalifaĥ will be valid.

Obviously, the one who offers Ṣalāt-ul-Fajr within Fajr timings in Muzdalifaĥ, his stay is valid. If he leaves before Ṣubḥ-e-Ṣādiq, it will become Wājib for him to pay *Dam* as expiation. However, if a woman, an ill person, an old or a weak person leaves early for fear of being harmed due to crowd, there is no expiation for them. *(Baĥār-e-Sharī'at, vol. 1, pp. 1135)*

Try to stay at the mount Mash'ar-ul-Ḥarām. If not possible, stay anywhere in whole Muzdalifaĥ except the valley of Muḥassir[1] as it is impermissible to stay over there. Like the ritual stay in 'Arafāt remain busy with worship during the stay in Muzdalifaĥ as well. Keep doing Żikr and reciting Ṣalāt-'Alan-Nabī, Du'ā and Talbiyaĥ in abundance. *(ibid, pp. 1133)*

Make Du'ā as every (permissible) Du'ā will be accepted here. The rights of Allah عَزَّوَجَلَّ were forgiven in 'Arafāt, forgiveness for the rights of people is promised here, (in Muzdalifaĥ). (Details of the rights of people are given on page xiv.) If you leave Muzdalifaĥ without offering Ṣalāt-ul-Fajr after the time of Ṣalāt-ul-Fajr has started, it is disliked but *Dam* will not be Wājib. *(ibid)*

---

[1] This is situated between Minā and Muzdalifaĥ. This starts with the peak of a mountain and has extended almost 272.5 yards. One can see this mountain at the left side while going from Muzdalifaĥ to Minā. This valley lies out of the limits of both Muzdalifaĥ and Minā. The people of Fīl stayed here and were inflicted with the torment of the flocks of birds. It is not permissible to stay here. One should cross it quickly whilst seeking security from Divine torment.

Du'ā to be recited on the way from Muzdalifaĥ to Minā

Head for Minā when as much time as two Rak'āt Ṣalāĥ can be offered is left in sunrise. Keep making Żikr, reciting Ṣalāt and Labbayk throughout the way. Recite the following Du'ā as well:

اَللّٰهُمَّ اِلَيْكَ اَفَضْتُ وَمِنْ عَذَابِكَ اَشْفَقْتُ وَاِلَيْكَ رَجَعْتُ

وَمِنْكَ رَهِبْتُ فَاقْبَلْ نُسُكِيْ وَعَظِّمْ اَجْرِيْ وَارْحَمْ تَضَرُّعِيْ

وَاقْبَلْ تَوْبَتِيْ وَاسْتَجِبْ دُعَآئِيْ ط

Translation: *O Allah* عَزَّوَجَلَّ*! I have returned to You and have feared torment from You and repented to You and have had fear of You. Accept my worship and increase my reward and have mercy on my incapacity and accept my repentance and Du'ā.*

Recite this Du'ā on seeing Minā

When Minā appears, recite the same Du'ā, with Ṣalāt-'Alan-Nabī once before and after it, which you had recited on reaching Minā from Makkaĥ. The Du'ā is as follows:

اَللّٰهُمَّ هٰذِهٖ مِنًى فَامْنُنْ عَلَيَّ بِمَا مَنَنْتَ بِهٖ عَلٰٓى اَوْلِيَآئِكَ

Translation: *O Allah* عَزَّوَجَلَّ*! This is Minā. Bless me with the boon that You bestowed upon Your Awliyā (beloveds).*

***

Ramī; first rite of 10th Żul-Ḥijjaĥ

On returning to Minā from Muzdalifaĥ, come straight towards Jamra-tul-'Aqabaĥ (the big satan). Today (i.e., 10th Żul-Ḥijjaĥ), only the big satan is to be pelted with stones. First find out the direction of the Ka'baĥ. Stand at least 5 'hand-length' (i.e. almost two and a half yards) or more away from the Jamarāt facing it such that Minā is on your right hand side and the Ka'baĥ on your left. Keep seven or more than seven stones[1] in your left hand. Then holding one stone between your right hand index finger and thumb, raise your right arm as high as possible, revealing the armpit, and throw the stone at the Jamarāt whilst reciting بِسْمِ اللّٰهِ اَللّٰهُ اَكْبَرْ.

In this way throw seven stones one by one such that they reach the Jamarāt or fall within the distance of 3 'hand-length' from it. Stop reciting Talbiyaĥ as soon as you throw the first stone. After throwing seven stones in such a way that meets the above conditions, do not stay over there any longer. Neither go straight nor turn right nor left; rather, turn around and return to your camp immediately making Żikr and Du'ā. *(Bahār-e-Sharī'at, vol. 1, pp. 1193)*

(The Sunnaĥ is to return instantly but it is not possible to do so these days due to new constructions. Therefore, go ahead a little after you have thrown stones and then return.)

5 Madanī pearls of precautions about Ramī

Fortunate Ḥujjāj! Be aware that there is a huge crowd at the Jamarāt, especially in the morning of the 10th Żul-Ḥijjaĥ. At times, people are trampled to death due to crowd or stampede. During the Hajj of 1400 A.H. I personally witnessed a heart rending scene when dead

[1] If only we would make the intention in our heart whilst throwing stones that we are driving off the Satan imposed on us.

bodies were being laid in a row. But the space has now been greatly extended. Four more storeys have been built besides the ground floor so that all the people would not have to gather at one place only, definitely reducing the crowd. Here are some precautions:

1. There is a large crowd on the 10th of Żul-Ḥijjaĥ in the morning. The crowd reduces around 3 or 4 o'clock in the afternoon. Now accompanying Islamic sisters can also perform Ramī without much difficulty. If you perform Ramī from any upper floor you will find a relatively small crowd and will also be enjoying fresh air.

2. Do not carry a stick, an umbrella and any other luggage with you. The authorities will seize these things and it will be difficult for you to get them back. Sometimes they allow a small school bag hanging behind the back but it is still better not to take even this type of bag on 10th Żul-Ḥijjaĥ. If you are prevented, you will get into trouble. On the 11th and 12th of Żul-Ḥijjaĥ, authorities show a little leniency for those carrying small things.

3. The appropriate time for the wheelchair users is to perform Ramī after Ṣalāt-ul-'Aṣr all three days.

4. Never bend down if anything falls from your hand or your slipper slips from your foot when throwing stones in the crowd.

5. In case of performing Ramī in the form of a group, fix a meeting point up in advance to avoid getting lost. If anyone gets lost it can cause untold problems. I have seen some old male and female Ḥujjāj who had got lost and did not even know the name of their Mu'allim. Such people are seen facing a lot of terrible troubles, اَلْاَمَانْ وَالْحَفِيظ.

Eight Madanī pearls regarding Ramī

Two sayings of the Beloved Prophet صَلَّى اللهُ تَعَالٰى عَلَيْهِ وَاٰلِهٖ وَسَلَّم:

1. Someone humbly asked the Holy Prophet صَلَّى اللهُ تَعَالٰى عَلَيْهِ وَاٰلِهٖ وَسَلَّم: What is the reward of Ramī of Jamarāt? He صَلَّى اللهُ تَعَالٰى عَلَيْهِ وَاٰلِهٖ وَسَلَّم replied, 'You will be granted its reward before your Rab عَزَّوَجَلَّ when you really need it.' *(Al-Mu'jam-ul-Awsaṭ, vol. 3, pp. 150, Ḥadīš 4147)*

2. Performing Ramī of Jamarāt will be a Nūr for you on the Day of Judgement. *(Attarghīb Wattarĥīb, vol. 2, pp. 134, Ḥadīš 3)*

3. Throwing less than seven stones is not permissible. If you have thrown only three stones or have not performed Ramī at all, *Dam* will be Wājib. If you have thrown four stones, you have to give one Ṣadaqaĥ for each stone not thrown. *(Rad-dul-Muḥtār, vol. 3, pp. 608)*

4. If all the stones are thrown at once, it will be considered a single stone. *(ibid, pp. 607)*

5. It is necessary that the stones be earthen such as granite, stone, sand-stone, earth and lime. If animal droppings are thrown, Ramī will not be valid. *(Durr-e-Mukhtār, Rad-dul-Muḥtār, vol. 3, pp. 608)*

6. Some people throw sandals, shoes, tin boxes etc. This is not Sunnaĥ and Ramī will not be valid in this case.

7. It is more appropriate that the stones for Ramī be taken from Muzdalifaĥ. However, this is not essential. Stones from any part of the world may be used. Ramī will be valid.

8. Performing Ramī on 10th Żul-Ḥijjaĥ from sunrise to the time when the sun begins to decline (i.e. up to Shar'ī midday) is Sunnaĥ. Performing it from the time of sun-declining to sunset

is permissible while performing it from sunset to Ṣubḥ-e-Ṣādiq is Makruĥ. However, if there is some valid reason, it will not be Makruĥ. For example, a shepherd may perform Ramī at night. *(ibid, pp. 610)*

Ramī by Islamic sisters

It is seen that Islamic brothers perform Ramī on behalf of women without any valid reason. In this way, Islamic sisters remain deprived of this important act. Further, since Ramī is Wājib, *Dam* also becomes Wājib for them due to missing a Wājib. Therefore, Islamic sisters should perform Ramī with their own hands.

Ramī by the ill

Some Ḥujjāj are seen roaming around everywhere freely, but when it comes to performing Ramī, they use some minor ailment as an excuse to nominate someone else to perform it on their behalf.

Ramī on behalf of the ill Hajj pilgrims

Ṣadr-ush-Sharī'aĥ, Badr-uṭ-Ṭarīqaĥ, 'Allāmaĥ Maulānā Muftī Muhammad Amjad 'Alī A'ẓamī عَلَیْہِ رَحْمَۃُ اللّٰہِ الْقَوِی has stated: If a person whether male or female is so ill that he/she cannot get to the Jamarāt even by conveyance, he/she is allowed to depute someone else to perform Ramī on his/her behalf.

If the deputed person has not yet performed his own Ramī he should first perform his own Ramī and then perform the Ramī of the ill person who has deputed him. If he performs Ramī seven times in such a manner that he throws one stone for his own Ramī and one for the ill person, this is Makrūĥ. If he performs Ramī on behalf of a patient without his authorization, Ramī will not be valid. If the patient is so weak that he cannot perform Ramī, it is better that his companion places the stone onto the hand of the patient and make him perform Ramī. Likewise, the companions of an unconscious or mad or immature person should perform Ramī on his behalf but it is still better to place the stone onto his hand and make him perform Ramī. *(Bahār-e-Sharī'at, vol. 1, pp. 1148)*

Seven Madanī pearls of ritual sacrifice of Hajj

1. After throwing stones at the big satan on 10th Żul-Ḥijjaĥ, come to the slaughter area and perform Qurbānī (sacrifice of animal). This is not the sacrifice that is performed on Eid-ul-Aḍḥā. Rather, it is the sacrifice which is Wājib for a Qārin and a Mutamatte' in gratefulness to Hajj even if he is Faqīr (poor). This Qurbānī is Mustaḥab for a Mufrid even if he is wealthy.

2. The qualities of animal required for the ritual sacrifice of Eid-ul-Aḍḥā are also required for this sacrifice. *(Bahār-e-Sharī'at, vol. 1, pp. 1140)* For example, goat (including nanny goat, ram, ewe and sheep (male/female both) must be of one year. If an animal is younger than the described age, it is impermissible to sacrifice it (for Qurbānī). If the animal is older than the described age, the sacrifice is not only permissible but also preferable. However, if a six-month old lamb is so big that it appears to be one year of age when seen from some distance, its sacrifice is permissible. *(Durr-e-Mukhtār, vol. 9, pp. 533)*

   Remember! Basically, the sacrifice of a six-months-old lamb is not permissible; its sacrifice is permissible provided it is so healthy and tall that it seems to be one year of age when seen from distance. If a six-month-old lamb or even the one short of just one day in a year does not appear to be one year of age on being seen from distance, its sacrifice will not be permissible.

3. If more than one-third of the ear of the animal is severed, the sacrifice will not be valid. If one-third or less than one-third is severed or torn, or there is a hole in one ear, or there is any similar minor fault, though the sacrifice will be valid in this case, it will be Makrūĥ (Tanzīĥī).

4. If possible, sacrifice the animal with your own hands as this is Sunnaĥ or alternatively remain present at the time of slaughter. *(Baĥār-e-Sharī'at, vol. 1, pp. 1141)* However, you may also authorize someone else to perform the sacrifice on your behalf[1].

5. The sacrifice of a camel is preferable as the Beloved Prophet صَلَّى اللّٰهُ تَعَالٰى عَلَيْهِ وَاٰلِهٖ وَسَلَّم also sacrificed 63 camels with his own blessed hands, employing the method of Naḥr, on the occasion of the farewell Hajj. And the rest of the camels were sacrificed with the method of Naḥr by Sayyidunā Maulā 'Alī كَرَّمَ اللّٰهُ تَعَالٰى وَجْهَهُ الْكَرِيْم with the consent of the Noble Prophet صَلَّى اللّٰهُ تَعَالٰى عَلَيْهِ وَاٰلِهٖ وَسَلَّم. *(Muslim, pp. 634, Ḥadīš 1218)* It is also narrated that five or six camels were brought to the Beloved Prophet صَلَّى اللّٰهُ تَعَالٰى عَلَيْهِ وَاٰلِهٖ وَسَلَّم. It is as if they were all in ecstasy, and each one of them was moving forward to be slaughtered first. *(Abū Dāwūd, vol. 2, pp. 211, Ḥadīš 1765)*

6. It is better to tie both front legs and one back leg of the animal. Untie them after the animal is slaughtered. Make Du'ā for the acceptance of your Hajj and ritual sacrifice and those of all other Muslims. *(Baĥār-e-Sharī'at, vol. 1, pp. 1141)*

7. It is better to perform sacrifice on 10th Żul-Ḥijjaĥ, however, it may be performed on the 11th and 12th as well. After the sunset of the 12th, the time for this sacrifice ends.

---

[1] For detailed information about the rulings of ritual sacrifice, study from page 327 to 353 of the 3rd volume of *Baĥār-e-Sharī'at* and Maktaba-tul-Madīnaĥ's published booklet '*Piebald Horse Rider*'.

Ḥājī and the ritual sacrifice of Eid-ul-Aḍḥā

Question: Is ritual sacrifice of Eid-ul-Aḍḥā Wājib for Ḥājī or not?

Answer: It is Wājib for a wealthy Ḥājī who is resident. It is not Wājib for a travelling Ḥājī even if he is wealthy. It is not necessary to perform the ritual sacrifice of Eid-ul-Aḍḥā in Ḥaram. It can be performed even in one's own country through someone else. But in that case one should be cautious about the days of ritual sacrifice i.e. the sacrifice should be performed on such a day when the days of sacrifice are continuing at the place where the sacrifice is being performed as well as the place where the person for whom sacrifice is being performed is present.

It is stated in '*Al-Baḥr-ur-Rāiq*' regarding this Wājib of ritual sacrifice on a resident Ḥājī: If the Ḥājī is non-resident, ritual sacrifice is not Wājib for him. If he is resident, he is like the inhabitants of Makkaĥ and ritual sacrifice is Wājib for him (provided he is wealthy). *(Al-Baḥr-ur-Rāiq, vol. 2, pp. 606)*

The verdict of Islamic scholars that ritual sacrifice is not Wājib for Ḥājī actually applies to a non-resident Ḥājī. It is stated in '*Mabsūṭ*': Except for Ḥujjāj, ritual sacrifice is Wājib for urban inhabitants. Here Ḥujjāj means non-residents and urban inhabitants mean residents. Sacrifice is Wājib for the inhabitants of Makkaĥ even if they perform Hajj. *(Al-Mabsūṭ lil-Sarkhasī, vol. 6, Al-Juz-uš-Šānī 'Ashr, pp. 24)*

Tokens for animal sacrifice

These days, a lot of Ḥujjāj deposit their money for Qurbānī in the Islamic development bank accounts and receive tokens in return. Please refrain from doing so.

Performing Qurbānī via this system is extremely risky because a Mutamatte' and a Qārin are to perform Ramī, sacrifice and Ḥalq or Taqṣīr in sequence (first Ramī, then sacrifice and then Ḥalq or Taqṣīr). If these rites were not performed in the described sequence *Dam* would become Wājib.

If someone deposits his money in this bank account, it will be very difficult for him to know with certainty whether or not his Qurbānī has been performed at the time specified by the bank. If he gets Ḥalq or Qaṣr done before Qurbānī, *Dam* will be Wājib.

This institution also makes an offer, allowing people to see their animals being sacrificed. They ask for a representative to be nominated for a group of 30 Ḥujjāj. The representative is given a special pass whereby he can go and personally see the animals being sacrificed. Although the institution makes this offer to satisfy the Ḥujjāj, there is still a great risk in it. Thousands of animals are purchased by this institution. It is almost impossible that each and every animal is free of defects. Most of caravan-organizers also arrange for collective sacrifice but some of them have also been reported to have been involved in corrupt acts. Therefore, it seems safer that you perform sacrifice yourself.

17 Madanī pearls regarding Ḥalq and Taqṣīr

Read 2 sayings of the Holy Prophet صَلَّى اللهُ تَعَالٰى عَلَيْهِ وَاٰلِهٖ وَسَلَّم about getting the head shaved after taking off the Iḥrām of Hajj and 'Umraĥ:

1. There is one virtue for every hair when the head is shaved, and one sin is removed. *(Attarghīb Wattarĥīb, vol. 2, pp. 135, Ḥadīš 3)*

2. Whilst shaving the head, the hair falling on the ground will become a Nūr for you on the Day of Judgement. *(ibid)*

3. After having performed the Qurbānī, males whilst facing the Qiblaĥ should do Ḥalq (i.e. shaving the head completely) or Taqṣīr (i.e. trimming each hair of a quarter (¼) of the head equal to a finger digit in length). Trimming just a few hair from two or three places with a pair of scissors will not suffice.

4. Begin trimming hair from the right side whether doing Ḥalq or Taqṣīr.

5. Islamic sisters should only get Taqṣīr done i.e. get trimmed each hair of a quarter of the head equal to a finger digit in length or do it themselves using a pair of scissors. For them to have the head shaved is Ḥarām. *(Bahār-e-Sharī'at, vol. 1, pp. 1142)* Remember! It is even impermissible for a woman to show her hair to a non-Maḥram, let alone having him cut her hair.

6. As hair is of different lengths, some are long while some are short; it is safer to get hair cut more than the length of a finger digit so that not even a single hair is left from being cut equal to the length of a finger digit.

7. When the time of removing Iḥrām has arrived, the Muḥrim can shave his own head and that of any other person even though the other person is also a Muḥrim.

8. Prior to Ḥalq or Taqṣīr, the Muḥrim can neither cut nails nor trim his beard. If he does so, expiation will become due. After the head is shaved, it is Mustaḥab to trim the moustache and to remove pubic hair.

9. The stipulated time for Ḥalq or Taqṣīr is from 10th to 12th Żul-Ḥijjaĥ. However, it is preferable to perform Ḥalq or Taqṣīr on 10th Żul-Ḥijjaĥ. If Ḥalq or Taqṣīr is not done by the sunset of 12th of Żul-Ḥijjaĥ, *Dam* will become due.

('Ālamgīrī, vol. 1, pp. 231; Rad-dul-Muḥtār, vol. 3, pp. 616)

10. If a Muḥrim is naturally bald, it is still Wājib for him to run a razor on his head. *('Ālamgīrī, vol. 1, pp. 231)*

11. If the head of a Muḥrim cannot be shaved due to sores or wounds on his head, nor does he have hair long enough to be cut, he is no longer required to get his hair shaved or trimmed on account of this compulsion. He will be considered to have been out of the restrictions of Iḥrām like those who have got their hair shaved or trimmed. However, it is still better for him to remain in the state of Iḥrām till the days of sacrifice end. *(ibid)*

12. It is Sunnaĥ to do Ḥalq or Qaṣr in Minā, whereas it is Wājib to do it within Ḥaram. If it is done out of the limits of Ḥaram, *Dam* will become Wājib.

13. Keep reciting the following Takbīr during Ḥalq or Taqṣīr. Recite it also after the Ḥalq or Taqṣīr.

اَللّٰهُ اَكْبَرُ ط اَللّٰهُ اَكْبَرُ ط

لَآ اِلٰهَ اِلَّا اللّٰهُ وَاللّٰهُ اَكْبَرُ ط اَللّٰهُ اَكْبَرُ ط وَلِلّٰهِ الْحَمْدُ ط

14. After the Ḥalq or Taqṣīr is done, recite the following Du'ā with Ṣalāt-'Alan-Nabī once before and after it.

اَللّٰهُمَّ اَثْبِتْ لِیْ لِكُلِّ شَعْرَةٍ حَسَنَةً وَّامْحُ عَنِّیْ بِهَا سَيِّئَةً وَّارْفَعْ لِیْ بِهَا عِنْدَكَ دَرَجَةً ط

***Translation:** O Allah عَزَّوَجَلَّ! Record one virtue for me for every hair and remove one sin, and raise one rank of mine in Your court.*

(Ihyā-ul-'Ulūm, vol. 1, pp. 343)

Make also the Du'ā of forgiveness for the entire Ummaĥ.

15. If a Mufrid wants to perform sacrifice, it is Mustaḥab for him to do it before Ḥalq or Taqṣīr. Even if he performs sacrifice after the Ḥalq, there is still no harm in it. However, it is Wājib for a Mutamatte and a Qārin to have sacrifice performed after the Ḥalq or Taqṣīr has been done. If they perform Ḥalq or Taqṣīr before sacrifice, *Dam* will become Wājib.

(Baĥār-e-Sharī'at, vol. 1, pp. 1142)

16. Bury the hair and all other things that are separated from the body e.g. hair, nails or skin. *(ibid, pp. 1144)*

17. After a Muḥrim has done Ḥalq or Taqṣīr, he is allowed to do all such acts declared Ḥarām by Iḥrām except for having intercourse, touching the wife lustfully, kissing her and seeing her private parts. *(ibid)*

صَلُّوْا عَلَى الْحَبِيْب صَلَّى اللّٰهُ تَعَالٰى عَلٰى مُحَمَّد

10 Madanī pearls regarding Ṭawāf-uz-Ziyāraĥ

1. Ṭawāf-uz-Ziyāraĥ is also called Ṭawāf-e-Ifāḍaĥ. It is the second pillar of Hajj. Its time begins from the Ṣubḥ-e-Ṣādiq of the 10th Żul-Ḥijjaĥ. It cannot be performed before this time. It is Farḍ to perform its four rounds. Without them Ṭawāf will not be valid and Hajj will be also invalid. To perform all the seven rounds is Wājib.

2. It is preferable to perform Ṭawāf-uz-Ziyāraĥ on 10th Żul-Ḥijjaĥ. After performing the Ramī of Jamra-tul-'Aqabaĥ, Qurbānī and Ḥalq or Taqṣīr, one should first consume a little Qurbānī meat and then walk to Makkaĥ as it is preferable. Likewise, it is also preferable to enter Masjid-ul-Ḥarām through Bāb-us-Salām and then perform Ṭawāf-uz-Ziyāraĥ.

3. Although it is preferable to perform Ṭawāf-uz-Ziyāraĥ on 10th Żul-Ḥijjaĥ, it can also be performed on any of the three days by the sunset of 12th Żul-Ḥijjaĥ. As there is too much rush on 10th Żul-Ḥijjaĥ it is better to perform it on a convenient day. In this way, one can avoid facing troubles and causing troubles to others in some cases, intermingling with women, bumping against them and many other sins committed under the provocation of satan and Nafs.

4. Perform Ṭawāf in the state of Wuḍū with Satr-e-'Awrat[1] fully concealed.

5. If a Qārin and a Mufrid have already performed Raml and Sa'ī for Hajj during Ṭawāf-ul-Qudūm, they are no longer required to perform them during Ṭawāf-uz-Ziyāraĥ. There is the same ruling for a Mutamatte' if he has also performed Raml and Sa'ī for Hajj during a Nafl Ṭawāf after putting on the Iḥrām of Hajj.

6. If one has not already performed Raml and Sa'ī for Hajj, he now can perform them in sewn dress. However, Iḍṭibā' will not be performed as it is no longer possible because of being in sewn dress.

7. Whoever has not performed Ṭawāf on 11th Żul-Ḥijjaĥ can perform it on 12th Żul-Ḥijjaĥ. To delay Ṭawāf-uz-Ziyāraĥ without any Shar'ī reason so much that 12th Żul-Ḥijjaĥ has passed is a sin and the one delaying it will have to slaughter animal sacrifice as expiation. However, for example, if a woman suffers menses or post-natal bleeding so she will have to perform Ṭawāf after the menses have stopped. But if the menses or

[1] The forearms of most of women are exposed during Ṭawāf. If a woman performed four or more than four rounds of Ṭawāf-uz-Ziyāraĥ with one quarter of her forearm or the hair of one quarter of her head uncovered, *Dam* would become Wājib for her. However, if she repeats the Ṭawāf with her Satr covered the expiation will become void.

post-natal bleeding stops at a time when she can perform four rounds after taking ritual bath before the sunset of the 12th Żul-Ḥijjaĥ, it is Wājib for her to perform Ṭawāf. If she does not perform Ṭawāf, she will be sinner. In the same way, if she had sufficient time to perform Ṭawāf but she delayed it and then suffered menses or post-natal bleeding, she will be sinner. *(Baĥār-e-Sharī'at, vol. 1, pp. 1145)*

8. As long as Ṭawāf-uz-Ziyāraĥ remains unperformed, conjugal relations with the wife will not be Ḥalāl (lawful), even if many years have elapsed. *('Ālamgīrī, vol. 1, pp. 232)* In the same manner, if the wife has not performed Ṭawāf-uz-Ziyāraĥ, the husband will not be Ḥalāl for her.

9. After finishing Ṭawāf, perform two Rak'āt Ṣalāĥ as 'Wājib-uṭ-Ṭawāf.' Now come at Multazam and embrace it. Then drink as much Zam Zam as you possibly can.

10. اَلْحَمْدُ لِلّٰہ عَزَّوَجَلَّ! (After the fulfilment of these rites), Hajj has been completed, rendering conjugal relations with wives Ḥalāl.

صَلُّوْا عَلَى الْحَبِيْب   صَلَّى اللّٰهُ تَعَالٰى عَلٰى مُحَمَّد

18 Madanī pearls regarding Ramī of 11th and 12th Żul-Ḥijjaĥ

1. On 11th and 12th of Żul-Ḥijjaĥ, stones are to be thrown at all the three satans. Its sequence is as follows: First throw stones at Jamra-tul-Aūlā (the small satan), then Jamra-tul-Wusṭā (the middle satan) and finally Jamra-tul-'Aqabaĥ (the big satan).

2. After midday, approach Jamra-tul-Aūlā (the small satan) and throw seven stones with face towards the Qiblaĥ. (The method

of holding stones and throwing them are described on the page 126 of this book.) After throwing stones, move ahead a little, shift towards the left a bit and, whilst facing the Qiblaĥ, lift hands up to shoulders with palms not facing the sky but Qiblaĥ[1] and remain busy with Du'ā and Istighfār for as long as 20 (Quranic) verses can be recited.

3. Perform Ramī at Jamra-tul-Wusṭā in the same way.

4. Finally, perform Ramī at Jamra-tul-'Aqabaĥ as you did on the 10th of Żul-Ḥijjaĥ. Remember that you don't have to stay there after the Ramī of Jamra-tul-'Aqabaĥ. Instead, you are to return immediately making Du'ā. (This is the correct method but now it is not possible to return instantly. Therefore, move ahead somewhat after you have thrown stones and then take a U-turn.)

5. Perform Ramī at all the three satans in the same way on 12th Żul-Ḥijjaĥ.

6. The time for the Ramī of 11th and 12th Żul-Ḥijjaĥ starts from the declining of the sun (i.e. right after the commencement of the timings of Ṣalāt-uẓ-Ẓuĥr). So the Ramī of the 11th of Żul-Ḥijjaĥ and 12th Żul-Ḥijjaĥ is not valid at all before the commencement of the timing of Ṣalāt-uẓ-Ẓuĥr. *(Bahār-e-Sharī'at, vol. 1, pp. 1148)*

7. It is Sunnaĥ to spend nights (more than half of the night-time) of the 10th, 11th, and 12th of Żul-Ḥijjaĥ in Minā.

8. After performing Ramī on 12th Żul-Ḥijjaĥ, you are at liberty to move to Makkaĥ before sunset. If the sun sets whilst you were

[1] During the Du'ā made after the Ramī of Jamarāt, palms should face the Qiblaĥ. Similarly, palms should face Ḥajar-ul-Aswad at the time of standing in front of it. On other occasions, palms should face the sky.

still within Minā, it is then not good to leave Minā. What you should do now is to stay in Minā that night, perform Ramī at all the three satans after the declining of the sun as usual on 13th Żul-Ḥijjaĥ and then proceed to Makkaĥ as it is preferable to do so.

9. If the Ṣubḥ-e-Ṣādiq of 13th Żul-Ḥijjaĥ takes place whilst a Ḥājī is still within the limits of Minā, performing the Ramī of 13th will become Wājib for him. If he went without performing Ramī, *Dam* would become Wājib for him.

10. Although the time for the Ramī of 11th and 12th Żul-Ḥijjaĥ is from the declining of the sun to Ṣubḥ-e-Ṣādiq, doing Ramī after sunset without a valid reason is Makrūĥ.

11. The time for the Ramī of 13th Żul-Ḥijjaĥ is from the Ṣubḥ-e-Ṣādiq until sunset. To perform Ramī from Ṣubḥ-e-Ṣādiq till the commencement of Ẓuĥr timing is Makrūĥ. It is Sunnaĥ to perform Ramī after the commencement of Ẓuĥr timing.

12. If some day's Ramī is missed, make Qaḍā for it the next day, and pay *Dam* as well. The cut off time for performing any missed Ramī (Qaḍā Ramī) is up to the sunset of 13th Żul-Ḥijjaĥ.

13. If one day's Ramī is missed, one *Dam* is Wājib regardless of whether or not its Qaḍā is made by the sunset of 13th Żul-Ḥijjaĥ. Similarly, if more than one day's Ramī is missed or even if the Ramī is not performed at all, only one *Dam* is Wājib in these cases.

14. The remaining stones may be given to someone who needs them or may be placed at some clean place. It is Makruĥ to throw them at Jamarāt.

15. Whilst stoning the Jamraĥ, if the stone bounced off someone's head and then hit the Jamraĥ or it fell within the distance of at least 3 hands[1] from the Jamraĥ, it would be valid.

16. If you threw a stone which fell onto someone who jerked his hand etc., causing it to reach the Jamraĥ, this stoning will not be valid. Throw another stone in place of it.

17. Whilst stoning the Jamraĥ from the upper floor, if the stone fell within the boundary made around the Jamraĥ, the stoning would be valid as it will roll from the boundary and either hit the Jamraĥ or fall within the distance of three hands' from the Jamraĥ.

18. If you have any doubts on whether or not any stone has reached the Jamraĥ, throw another stone. *(Baĥār-e-Sharī'at, vol. 1, pp. 1146, 1148)*

12 Makrūĥ acts in Ramī

(The cases given in number 1 and 2 are Isā-at due to abandoning Sunnat-ul-Muakkadaĥ, whereas the remaining acts are Makrūĥ Tanzīĥī.)

1. To perform Ramī of 10th Żul-Ḥijjaĥ after sunset without a valid reason. (It is Isā-at as it is contrary to Sunnat-ul-Muakkadaĥ.)
2. To stone the Jamarāt in wrong sequence
3. To perform Ramī before the time of Ẓuĥr on 13th Żul-Ḥijjaĥ.
4. To throw large stones
5. To make small stones by breaking a large one
6. To use stones from a Masjid
7. To use stones lying around the Jamraĥ. These are the unaccepted stones. The accepted ones are picked up and will be placed onto

[1] 'Hand' here refers to the length from fingers up to the elbow of the arm.

the pan of the good deeds of the weighing-scale on the Day of Judgement.

8. To deliberately throw more than seven stones at the Jamraĥ

9. To use impure stones

10. To face a wrong direction when stoning

11. To stand less than 5 hands away from any of the Jamraĥ. There is no problem in standing more distance away. (However, it is necessary to throw stone even if one is standing closer to the Jamraĥ. Do not just place stone at the Jamraĥ.)

12. To put stone near the Jamraĥ instead of throwing it.

(Baĥār-e-Sharī'at, vol. 1, pp. 1148, 1149)

صَلُّوْا عَلَى الْحَبِيْب   صَلَّى اللّٰهُ تَعَالٰى عَلٰى مُحَمَّد

19 Madanī pearls about Ṭawāf-ur-Rukhṣat

1. After performing Hajj, when an Āfāqī Ḥājī intends to return back to his country, Ṭawāf-ur-Rukhṣat (i.e. farewell Ṭawāf) becomes Wājib for him. If he does not perform it, *Dam* will become Wājib for him. It is also called Ṭawāf-e-Wadā' and Ṭawāf-e-Ṣadr.

2. Ṭawāf-ur-Rukhṣat does not require Iḍṭibā', Raml and Sa'ī.

3. Ṭawāf-ur-Rukhṣat is not Wājib for those performing 'Umraĥ only.

4. If the seat for the return flight of a woman experiencing menses or post-natal bleeding is already booked, she may return. This Ṭawāf is no longer Wājib for her. There is no *Dam* for it either.

5. There is no specific intention to be made for Ṭawāf-ur-Rukhṣat. Just making the intention of performing a Ṭawāf is sufficient. It is not necessary to include the term Wājib, farewell Ṭawāf or the Ṭawāf being performed within the stipulated time, etc. in the intention. Even if the intention for a Nafl Ṭawāf is made at this stage, the Wājib will get offered.

6. After performing Ṭawāf-ur-Rukhṣat, if a Ḥājī had the intention of departing but he had to stay due to some reason like delay in conveyance, and he has not made the intention of stay either, he does not need to perform Ṭawāf-ur-Rukhṣat again; the previously performed Ṭawāf is sufficient. There is no harm for him in going to Masjid-ul-Ḥarām for offering Ṣalāĥ etc. However, it is Mustaḥab for him to perform the Ṭawāf again so that the last act of him is Ṭawāf.

7. The very first Ṭawāf performed after Ṭawāf-uz-Ziyāraĥ is considered Ṭawāf-ur-Rukhṣat.

8. The one who has left without performing Ṭawāf-ur-Rukhṣat and has not yet crossed the limit of Mīqāt should return and perform the Ṭawāf.

9. If the one who had missed Ṭawāf-ur-Rukhṣat recalls it having gone out of the limits of Mīqāt, it is not necessary for him to return. Instead, he should send an animal to Ḥaram for paying *Dam*. If he wishes to return, he may do so but after putting on Iḥrām for 'Umraĥ. He is required to perform 'Umraĥ first and then Ṭawāf-ur-Rukhṣat. In this case, *Dam* will become void.

10. If someone missed three rounds of Ṭawāf-ur-Rukhṣat, he has to pay one Ṣadaqaĥ for each missed round. If he missed four or more than four rounds, he will have to pay *Dam*.

11. If possible, perform Ṭawāf-ur-Rukhṣat with tearful eyes and broken heart as one does not know as to whether or not he will be able to get this privilege again in his life.

12. After performing the Ṭawāf, offer two Rak'āt Ṣalāĥ as Wājib-uṭ-Ṭawāf.

13. After performing Ṭawāf-ur-Rukhṣat, drink as much Zam Zam water as possible and pour a little of it over the body.

14. Then, approach the blessed door of the Holy Ka'baĥ and kiss it, if possible. Make Du'ā for the acceptance of Hajj and for the privilege of repeatedly visiting this holy land. Make this comprehensive Du'ā (i.e. رَبَّنَا اٰتِنَا) or the following Du'ā:

اَلسَّآئِلُ بِبَابِكَ يَسْأَلُكَ مِنْ فَضْلِكَ وَمَعْرُوْفِكَ وَيَرْجُوْ رَحْمَتَكَ

Translation: *The beggar is present on Your doorstep begging for Your Benevolence and Favour, and is hopeful for Your Mercy.*

(Baĥār-e-Sharī'at, vol. 1, pp. 1152)

15. Come to Multazam doing Żikr and reciting Ṣalāt-'Alan-Nabī and Du'ā abundantly. Cling onto the cover of the Ka'baĥ.

16. If possible, kiss Ḥajar-ul-Aswad and shed tears.

17. Whilst leaving, turn around and look at the Holy Ka'baĥ repeatedly with deep regret and sorrow. The thought of separation should move you to tears. If you cannot weep at least wear a weeping look on the face. Whilst exiting the Masjid, step left foot out first and recite the Du'ā of leaving the Masjid.

18. The Islamic sisters experiencing menses or post-natal bleeding should stand at the door of the Masjid and look at the Holy Ka'baĥ desperately. They should make Du'ā with tears in eyes as they depart.

19. Afterwards, give as much charity and alms as possible to the poor and the needy in this blessed city.

(Baĥār-e-Sharī'at, vol. 1, pp. 1151, 1153)

صَلُّوْا عَلَى الْحَبِيْب صَلَّى اللّٰهُ تَعَالٰى عَلٰى مُحَمَّد

Hajj Badal

There are certain conditions for the Hajj performed on behalf of the one for whom Hajj is Farḍ. As for a Nafl Hajj, there is no condition as a Nafl Hajj is a form of Īṣāl-e-Šawāb that may be made by any virtuous deed like Farḍ Ṣalāĥ, fasting, Hajj, Zakāĥ, charity, alms etc. Therefore, if someone wishes to perform Hajj on behalf of his deceased parents for whom Hajj was not Farḍ, nor had they made any will in this regard, there is no condition for it. What he has to do is to simply put on Iḥrām for Hajj with the intention of performing it on behalf of his father or mother and carry out the rites of Hajj.

Its benefit is that the one on whose behalf Hajj is performed will be given the reward of one Hajj but the performer of this Hajj will be given the reward of ten Hajj, as described in Ḥadīš. *(Dār Quṭnī, vol. 2, pp. 329, Ḥadīš 2587)* Therefore, whenever someone gets the privilege of performing a Nafl Hajj, it is more virtuous for him to perform it on behalf of his father or mother.

Remember! Ritual sacrifice is Wājib for Hajj Tamattu' and Qirān performed for the sake of Īṣāl-e-Šawāb. The Ḥājī should perform it with his own intention and then make its Īṣāl-e-Šawāb.

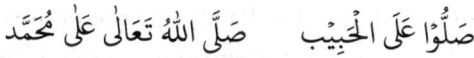

17 Pre-conditions of Hajj Badal

Here are conditions for the Hajj Badal of those for whom Hajj is Farḍ:

1. It is a condition that Hajj is Farḍ for the person who is having Hajj Badal performed on his behalf. If Hajj is not Farḍ for him and he makes someone perform Hajj Badal on his behalf, Farḍ Hajj will not get performed. That is, if Hajj becomes Farḍ for him later on, the previously performed Hajj will not suffice.

2. The person for whom Hajj Badal is being performed has to be in a state where he cannot perform it himself. If he can perform Hajj himself, Hajj Badal cannot be performed on his behalf.

3. The valid reason for getting Hajj Badal done has to remain from the time of the performance of Hajj till his death. In other words, if he regains the ability to perform Hajj himself anytime before his death, the previously performed Hajj Badal will no longer remain sufficient.

4. However, if the reason was such that there was no possibility of cure e.g. he was blind but gained his eyesight amazingly, the Hajj Badal performed on his behalf would still be valid in this case.

5. It is a condition that the person on behalf of whom Hajj is to be performed gives formal permission for it. Hajj Badal cannot be performed on his behalf without his prior permission.

6. However, if the legatee (i.e. the inheritor) performs Hajj Badal on behalf of the legator there is no need for permission in this case.

7. All expenses or at least most of them should be given by the sender. *(Mulakhkhaṣ az: Bahār-e-Sharī'at, vol. 1, pp. 1201, 1202)*

8. If the deceased had made the will that the expenses for Hajj Badal be paid from his money, yet the inheritor paid from his own wealth, Hajj Badal would remain unperformed.

However, if the inheritor paid money with the intention of getting it back from the inheritance left by the deceased, the Hajj Badal would be valid. If the inheritor does not have the intention of getting it back, Hajj Badal will remain unperformed. If a stranger (who is not the inheritor) pays the expenses for Hajj Badal of someone, Hajj Badal will remain unperformed even if he has the intention of getting the money back and, even if the deceased had also asked that person to perform his Hajj.
(Rad-dul-Muḥtār, vol. 4, pp. 28)

9. If the deceased had made the will that Hajj Badal be performed on his behalf without indicating whether its expenses be paid from his wealth, and then his inheritors paid the expenses without the intention of taking their money back, the Hajj Badal would be valid. *(ibid)*

10. Hajj Badal may be performed only by the person who has been nominated to do so. If the nominated person makes someone else perform Hajj Badal, it would remain unperformed.
(Bahâr-e-Sharī'at, vol. 1, pp. 1202)

11. If the person nominated by the deceased in his will passes away, or if the nominated person is not prepared to perform Hajj Badal, someone else may be made to perform Hajj Badal in this case. It is permissible. *(Rad-dul-Muḥtār, vol. 4, pp. 19)*

12. The person doing Hajj Badal must travel most of the distance on conveyance, otherwise Hajj will not be valid and the expense will have to be afforded by the sender. However, if money is short, he may travel on foot. *(Bahâr-e-Sharī'at, vol. 1, pp. 1203)*

13. It is necessary for the person performing Hajj Badal to go on Hajj-pilgrimage from the town of the sender. *(ibid)*

14. If a person nominates and asks someone to perform Hajj Badal on his behalf but the nominated person performs Hajj Tamattu', he has to return the expenses in this case *(Fatāwā Razawiyyah referenced, vol. 10, pp. 660)* because the Iḥrām for Hajj Tamattu' will not commence from the Mīqāt of the sender, instead it will be put on from the Ḥaram border. However, if Hajj Tamattu' was performed with the consent of the one on whose behalf Hajj was performed, there is no harm in it.

15. If the one to whom the deceased made the will to get Hajj Badal done on his behalf sends someone from any other place to perform Hajj Badal despite having one third part of the deceased's wealth which is sufficient to send someone from the deceased's own town, Hajj Badal will not be valid in this case.

    However, if that town is so near to the deceased's town that one can go and return within the same day before night falls, Hajj Badal would be valid in this case. Otherwise, he (i.e. the one to whom will was made) should arrange to repeat Hajj Badal on behalf of the deceased from his own money.

    ('Ālamgīrī, vol. 1, pp. 259; Rad-dul-Muḥtār, vol. 4, pp. 27)

16. The intention of the performer of Hajj Badal has to be the same as that of the one who has commanded him. It is even better to say لَبَّيْك عَنْ فُلان[1] (i.e. *I am in attendance on behalf of so and so person*). If he has forgotten the name of that person, he should make the intention that he is performing Hajj on behalf of the one for whom he has been sent. *(Rad-dul-Muḥtār, vol. 4, pp. 20)*

---

[1] The performer of Hajj Badal should mention the name of the one on whose behalf he is performing Hajj in lieu of saying 'so and so person'. For instance, he should say 'لَبَّيْك عَنْ عَبْدِالرَّحْـمٰنِ اَللّٰهُمَّ لَبَّيْك'.

17. If one performing Hajj Badal forgot to make intention while putting on Iḥrām, he can make it before the commencement of Hajj-rites. *(ibid, pp. 18)*

9 Miscellaneous Madanī pearls regarding Hajj Badal

1. If the one to whom the will was made nominates someone to perform Hajj Badal but the nominated person performs Hajj Badal the next year instead of performing it the year he was asked, the Hajj Badal would still be valid. There is no penalty on the nominated person. *('Ālamgīrī, vol. 1, pp. 260)*

2. It is necessary for the performer of Hajj Badal to return any remaining money even if it is a small amount. It is not permissible for him to keep it. Even if he had made a deal that he would not return the remaining money, he would still have to return as such a deal is invalid. However, he may use the money in two cases:

    i. The sender had already designated him as his attorney to gift the remaining money to himself and take it in his custody.

    ii. If the sender is on death bed and makes will to the performer of Hajj to keep the remaining money, so he may keep money in these cases. *(Mulakhkhaṣ az: Bahār-e-Sharī'at, vol. 1, pp. 1210; Durr-e-Mukhtār, Rad-dul-Muḥtār, vol. 4, pp. 38)*

3. It is better to send such a person for Hajj Badal who has already performed his Farḍ Hajj. However, if the one who has not performed his Hajj is sent for Hajj Badal, it will still be valid. *('Ālamgīrī, vol. 1, pp. 257)* It is Makrūh Taḥrīmī to send such a person for Hajj Badal who has not yet performed his own Hajj despite it being Farḍ for him. *(Al-Maslak-ul-Mutaqassiṭ lil-Qārī, pp. 453)*

4. It is also better to send such a person for Hajj Badal who is well-aware of the method and rites of Hajj. However, if an adolescent boy is made to perform Hajj Badal, it will still be valid. *(Bahār-e-Sharī'at, vol. 1, pp. 1204; Durr-e-Mukhtār, vol. 4, pp. 25)*

5. The performer of Hajj Badal cannot spend the money given by the sender on feeding anyone, nor can he give any such money to any beggar. However, if the sender had already given him permission to do so, there is no harm in it. *(Bahār-e-Sharī'at, vol. 1, pp. 1210; Lubāb-ul-Manāsik, pp. 457)*

6. The *Dams* for all the intentional offences have to be paid by the performer of Hajj Badal himself, not by the sender.

7. If somebody who has not performed Hajj passed away without making will to his inheritor for Hajj Badal, and the inheritor performed Hajj Badal himself on behalf of the deceased or made someone else do so, it is hoped that the Hajj will get performed on behalf of the deceased اِنۡ شَآءَاللّٰہ عَزَّوَجَلّ. *('Ālamgīrī, vol. 1, pp. 258)*

8. If the performer of Hajj Badal settles in Makkah, it is permissible, but it is better that he returns. The expenses of both going and returning are to be paid by the sender. *(ibid)*

9. The person performing Hajj Badal can visit Madīnah only once with the expenses of the person who has sent him for Hajj Badal. He cannot spent the money on visiting the holy sites of Makkah and Madīnah. He should eat less expensive food which includes meat as well. However, he should not eat delicious food such as grilled kebab and roast chicken, sweets, cold drinks, fruit etc. Further, he is not allowed to bring dates, rosaries and sacred things.

(For further detail of Hajj Badal, study from page 1199 to 1211 of *Bahār-e-Sharī'at* 1st volume published by Maktaba-tul-Madīnah).

اَلْحَمْدُ لِلّٰهِ رَبِّ الْعٰلَمِيْنَ وَ الصَّلٰوةُ وَالسَّلَامُ عَلٰى سَيِّدِ الْمُرْسَلِيْنَ

اَمَّا بَعْدُ فَاَعُوْذُ بِاللّٰهِ مِنَ الشَّيْطٰنِ الرَّجِيْمِ ؕ بِسْمِ اللّٰهِ الرَّحْمٰنِ الرَّحِيْمِ ؕ

Journey to Madīna-tul-Munawwarah̄

◈

Ḥasan Hajj kar liyā Ka'bay say ānkĥaun nay ẓiyā pāyī

Chalo daykĥayn woĥ bastī jis kā rastaĥ dil kay andar ĥay

O Ḥasan! We have performed Ḥajj, blessing our eyes with the vision of the Holy Ka'bah̄

Let's now behold the sacred and beloved city that has its attachment to our heart

Method of enhancing fervour

Congratulations on the blessed journey to Madīnah̄! Those travelling to the sacred city of Madīna-tul-Munawwarah̄ should keep on reciting Na'at and Ṣalāt-'Alan-Nabī throughout the journey. You may also listen to inspiring Na'ats via cassette player. اِنْ شَآءَاللّٰه عَزَّوَجَلَّ! This will be a means of enhancing your fervour. Keep pondering on the sacredness and holiness of this city[1]. This will further augment enthusiasm in your heart, اِنْ شَآءَاللّٰه عَزَّوَجَلَّ!

صَلُّوْا عَلَى الْحَبِيْب   صَلَّى اللّٰهُ تَعَالٰى عَلٰى مُحَمَّد

---

[1] During stay in Makkah̄ and Madīnah̄ you should read books regarding the excellence of these sacred cities for enhancing your fervour and enthusiasm. In order to enhance devotion to the Beloved Prophet صَلَّى اللّٰه تَعَالٰى عَلَيْهِ وَاٰلِهٖ وَسَلَّم, go through Na'at books such as *Ḥadāiq-e-Bakhshish* by Imām Aḥmad Razā Khān عَلَيْهِ رَحْمَةُ الرَّحْمٰن and *Żauq-e-Na'at* by Maulānā Ḥasan Razā Khān عَلَيْهِ رَحْمَةُ الرَّحْمٰن.

How long will it take to get to Madīnaĥ?

The distance between Makka-tul-Mukarramaĥ and Madīna-tul-Munawwaraĥ is almost 425 kilometres that is usually covered by bus within almost 5 hours. During Hajj season, however, it takes almost 8 to 10 hours to cover this distance because of slow and safe driving and some other reasons. The bus halts at the 'Markaz for welcoming Ḥujjāj' where passports are submitted and cards are issued which Ḥujjāj should keep safely. The official formalities here sometimes take many hours to be completed. Remain cool, calm and collected as the fruit of patience is very sweet.

Soon you will joyfully be wandering around the beautiful streets of Madīnaĥ and beholding the Grand Green Dome! As soon as your eye falls on the luminous minaret of Masjid-un-Nabawī and the Green Dome from afar, you would feel your heart pounding with excitement and tears would spontaneously well up in your eyes.

The breeze of Madīnaĥ will be refreshing your senses, making you feel a spiritual revitalization. If possible, enter this sanctified city barefoot with tears in eyes.

Jūtay utār lo chalo bā-ĥosh bā-adab
Daykĥo Madīnay kā ḥasīn gulzār ā gayā

Take off shoes and proceed rationally and reverently
Behold! The beautiful garden of Madīnaĥ has approached

صَلُّوْا عَلَى الْحَبِيْب صَلَّى اللّٰهُ تَعَالٰى عَلٰى مُحَمَّد

Quranic proof for remaining barefoot

Staying barefoot here is not contrary to Sharī'aĥ. Rather it is an act of displaying reverence to the holy place. When Sayyidunā Prophet

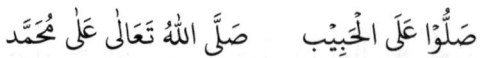

Mūsā عَلَيْهِ السَّلَام was blessed with the privilege of conversation with Allah عَزَّوَجَلَّ, he عَلَيْهِ السَّلَام was commanded by Allah عَزَّوَجَلَّ:

فَاخْلَعْ نَعْلَيْكَ ۚ اِنَّكَ بِالْوَادِ الْمُقَدَّسِ طُوًى ﴿۱۲﴾

Take off your shoes. Verily, you are in Ṭuwā, the sacred valley.

[Kanz-ul-Īmān (Translation of Quran)] (Part 16, Sūraĥ Ṭāḥā, verse 12)

سُبْحٰنَ اللّٰه عَزَّوَجَلَّ! If this is the high status accorded to the mount Sīnā that Allah عَزَّوَجَلَّ ordered Sayyidunā Mūsā عَلَيْهِ السَّلَام to remain barefoot, then imagine how greatly one would be required to display reverence in Madīnaĥ! The spiritual guide of millions of followers, a renowned devotee of Rasūl Sayyidunā Imām Mālik عَلَيْهِ رَحْمَةُ اللّٰهِ الْخَالِق never wore shoes in this blessed city. *(At-Ṭabaqāt-ul-Kubrā lish-Sha'rānī, vol. 1, pp. 76)* He رَحْمَةُ اللّٰهِ تَعَالٰى عَلَيْه never rode a horse in Madīna-tul-Munawwaraĥ. He رَحْمَةُ اللّٰهِ تَعَالٰى عَلَيْه has said: I feel shyness from Allah عَزَّوَجَلَّ to ride my horse over the land under which His Prophet صَلَّى اللّٰهُ تَعَالٰى عَلَيْهِ وَاٰلِهٖ وَسَلَّم rests (i.e. under which his blessed Rauḍaĥ is). *(Iḥyā-ul-'Ulūm, vol. 1, pp. 48)*

Preparation for the visit

Prior to visiting the sacred mausoleum of the Beloved and Blessed Prophet صَلَّى اللّٰهُ تَعَالٰى عَلَيْهِ وَاٰلِهٖ وَسَلَّم, make arrangements for your accommodation etc. If you are hungry or thirsty, eat/drink something. In short, free yourself of every such thing that may affect your concentration. Make Wuḍū and do use a Miswāk or, better still, perform Ghusl. Wear clean white clothes or new ones with a new turban, if possible. Apply kohl and fragrance preferably musk, and head towards the blessed court with tears in eyes. *(Baĥār-e-Sharī'at, vol. 1, pp. 1223)*

Grand Green Dome appears

The Green Dome that you used to see in pictures and kiss in imagination is now in front of your eyes. A sight that stirs devotees of Rasūl and brings tears to their eyes! By Allah عَزَّوَجَلَّ, the beauty of Rauḍaĥ-e-Rasūl (the blessed resting place of our Beloved Prophet صَلَّى اللهُ تَعَالٰى عَلَيْهِ وَاٰلِهٖ وَسَلَّم is matchless on the earth and even in the Paradise).

Firdaus kī bulandī bĥī cĥū sakay na is ko
Khuld-e-Barīn say aūnchā mīṫĥay Nabī kā rauḍaĥ

Even the loftiness of Firdaus cannot touch it
Rauḍaĥ of Prophet is higher than even Khuld-e-Barīn

(Wasāil-e-Bakhshish, pp. 298)

It is stated in a footnote added on page 298 of the book '*Wasāil-e-Bakhshish*' published by Maktaba-tul-Madīnaĥ, the publishing department of Dawat-e-Islami: The Arabic word رَوْضَه [Rauḍaĥ] literally means a 'garden'. The word Rauḍaĥ used in the foregoing couplet refers to the piece of land on which the blessed body of the Holy Prophet صَلَّى اللهُ تَعَالٰى عَلَيْهِ وَاٰلِهٖ وَسَلَّم rests. Describing its sanctity, Islamic jurists رَحِمَهُمُ اللهُ تَعَالٰى have stated: The piece of the land that is in contact with the blessed body of the Holy Prophet صَلَّى اللهُ تَعَالٰى عَلَيْهِ وَاٰلِهٖ وَسَلَّم is more sacred than even the Holy Ka'baĥ, 'Arsh and Kursī.

(Durr-e-Mukhtār, vol. 4, pp. 62)

Enter via Bāb-ul-Baqī'

Now come at Bāb-ul-Baqī'[1] reverentially and rationally, with tears in eyes. If you cannot weep, at least wear a weeping look on the face. Now recite اَلصَّلٰوةُ وَالسَّلَامُ عَلَيْكَ يَـا رَسُوْلَ الله and then halt a bit as if

[1] This is situated at the eastern side of Masjid-un-Nabawī. Usually, the guards deputed there do not allow people to enter through Bāb-ul-Baqī'. Therefore, people enter through Bāb-us-Salām. In this manner, they enter from the direction of the blessed head of the Holy Prophet صَلَّى اللهُ تَعَالٰى عَلَيْهِ وَاٰلِهٖ وَسَلَّم, which is contrary to Islamic manners as one should enter the mausoleum of the saints from the direction of their feet. If it is not possible to enter through Bāb-ul-Baqī', then there is no harm in entering through Bāb-us-Salām. If there is no crowd etc. try to enter through Bāb-ul-Baqī'.

you are asking permission from the Noble Prophet صَلَّى اللهُ تَعَالٰى عَلَيْهِ وَاٰلِهٖ وَسَلَّم to enter his majestic court. Now recite بِسْمِ اللّٰهِ الرَّحْمٰنِ الرَّحِيْم, place your right foot into the Masjid and enter Masjid-e-Nabawī extremely reverentially. The heart of every true Muslim is aware of the utmost reverence and veneration that is Farḍ on this occasion. Keep your hands, feet, eyes, tongue and heart free from engaging in anything else and move ahead weeping. Do not look here and there. Do not look at decors and carvings of the Masjid. Just one thought and only one will and wish should preoccupy you that an absconded culprit is going to enter the merciful court of his Master صَلَّى اللهُ تَعَالٰى عَلَيْهِ وَاٰلِهٖ وَسَلَّم.

Ṣalāĥ in gratitude

If it is not a Makrūĥ time (for Ṣalāĥ) and your overwhelming sentiments also permit you, offer two Rak'āt Ṣalāĥ each for Taḥiyya-tul-Masjid and in gratitude to your presence at the blessed court. After reciting Sūraĥ Al-Fātiḥaĥ, recite Sūraĥ Al-Kāfirūn and Sūraĥ Al-Ikhlāṣ in the first and the second Rak'at respectively.

Appearing before Golden Grille

Now, with immense reverence and devotion, come at the sacred Muwājaĥaĥ[1] from the direction of the blessed feet[2], facing the Golden Grille, lowering head and eyes, perspiring, weeping and trembling with shame of sins but having hope of mercy and blessing from the Prophet of Raḥmaĥ, the Intercessor of Ummaĥ صَلَّى اللهُ تَعَالٰى عَلَيْهِ وَاٰلِهٖ وَسَلَّم.

The Holy Prophet صَلَّى اللهُ تَعَالٰى عَلَيْهِ وَاٰلِهٖ وَسَلَّم is facing the Qiblaĥ inside his sacred tomb. If you come at the sacred Muwājaĥaĥ from the direction of the blessed feet, the sight of the Noble Prophet صَلَّى اللهُ تَعَالٰى عَلَيْهِ وَاٰلِهٖ وَسَلَّم

[1] The direction in front of the blessed face.

[2] In case of entering through Bāb-ul-Baqī', one will enter from the direction of the blessed feet but if he enters through Bāb-us-Salām, he will enter from the direction of the blessed head.

will directly be towards you, which is a means of acquiring success in the world as well as in the Hereafter, وَالْحَمْدُلِله.

(Baĥār-e-Sharī'at, vol. 1, pp. 1224)

Presence at the sacred Muwājaĥaĥ*

Now with utmost respect, face the Golden Grille standing under the large chandelier directly facing the direction of the silver nails driven upwards into the eastern side of the blessed golden door, with your back towards the Qiblaĥ. Stand at about two yards distance with utmost respect facing the blessed face of the Beloved and Blessed Rasūl صَلَّى اللهُ تَعَالٰى عَلَيْهِ وَاٰلِهٖ وَسَلَّم like you stand in Ṣalāĥ. In *Fatāwā 'Ālamgīrī* and various other books of Fiqĥ it is mentioned يَقِفُ كَمَا يَقِفُ فِي الصَّلَاةِ, i.e. stand in the court of the Holy Prophet صَلَّى اللهُ تَعَالٰى عَلَيْهِ وَاٰلِهٖ وَسَلَّم as one stands in Ṣalāĥ.

Remember! The Prophet of Raḥmaĥ, the Intercessor of Ummaĥ, the Owner of Jannaĥ صَلَّى اللهُ تَعَالٰى عَلَيْهِ وَاٰلِهٖ وَسَلَّم is alive with his true, real, worldly and bodily life in his sacred mausoleum as he صَلَّى اللهُ تَعَالٰى عَلَيْهِ وَاٰلِهٖ وَسَلَّم was before his sacred demise. He صَلَّى اللهُ تَعَالٰى عَلَيْهِ وَاٰلِهٖ وَسَلَّم is seeing you and is aware of even the thoughts of your heart.

Beware! Avoid kissing and touching the Golden Grille as it is contrary to manners because our hands are not worthy of touching the Grille. Hence stand 2 yards away. Isn't it a great privilege that the Most Beloved Prophet صَلَّى اللهُ تَعَالٰى عَلَيْهِ وَاٰلِهٖ وَسَلَّم has let you come closer to his resting place and his merciful sight which was though already towards you no matter wherever you were, is now particularly towards you with immense closeness! *(Baĥār-e-Sharī'at, vol. 1, pp. 1224-1225)*

---

* People usually are under the impression that the blessed face of the Beloved Prophet صَلَّى اللهُ تَعَالٰى عَلَيْهِ وَاٰلِهٖ وَسَلَّم is in the direction of the large opening on the Golden Grille. The same is stated in many Urdu books. However, I have pointed out the direction of the blessed face on the basis of the research carried out by A'lā Ḥaḍrat رَحْمَةُ اللهِ تَعَالٰى عَلَيْه. [Sag-e-Madīnaĥ]

Direction of the Blessed Countenance

Direction of the Blessed Countenance

An ancient memorable image of the Green Dome

Make Salām to Holy Prophet ﷺ

Now, with immense reverence and devotion, say Salām in the following words in melancholic and moderate voice. Beware your voice should not be loud and harsh lest all the good deeds are ruined. The voice should not also be too low as it is also contrary to Sunnaĥ.

اَلسَّلَامُ عَلَيْكَ اَيُّهَا النَّبِيُّ وَرَحْمَةُ اللّٰهِ وَبَرَكَاتُهٗ ط اَلسَّلَامُ عَلَيْكَ يَا رَسُوْلَ اللّٰهِ ط اَلسَّلَامُ عَلَيْكَ يَا خَيْرَ خَلْقِ اللّٰهِ ط اَلسَّلَامُ عَلَيْكَ يَا شَفِيْعَ الْمُذْنِبِيْنَ ط اَلسَّلَامُ عَلَيْكَ وَعَلٰى اٰلِكَ وَاَصْحٰبِكَ وَ اُمَّتِكَ اَجْمَعِيْنَ ط

Salām be upon you O Prophet صَلَّى اللهُ تَعَالٰى عَلَيْهِ وَاٰلِهٖ وَسَلَّم *and Allah's mercy and blessings! Salām be upon you O Rasūl of Allah* صَلَّى اللهُ تَعَالٰى عَلَيْهِ وَاٰلِهٖ وَسَلَّم*! Salām be upon you O the best of Allah's creation! Salām be upon you O the one who will intercede for the sinners! Salām be upon you, upon your family, upon your companions and upon your entire Ummaĥ!*

Continue to say Salām with different titles for as long as you can do with full concentration. If you have not learnt titles by heart, then continue to recite اَلصَّلٰوةُ وَالسَّلَامُ عَلَيْكَ يَا رَسُوْلَ اللّٰهِ. You should then convey Salām on behalf of all those who have requested you to do so. It is my (the author's) humble request to all those Islamic brothers and sisters reading this book to convey my Salām as well. You will be doing a great favour to me, the biggest sinner. Continue to make as much Du'ā as possible and go on begging him for intercession in these words: اَسْئَلُكَ الشَّفَاعَةَ يَا رَسُوْلَ اللّٰهِ, i.e. *I am begging you for intercession, Yā Rasūlallāĥ* صَلَّى اللهُ تَعَالٰى عَلَيْهِ وَاٰلِهٖ وَسَلَّم.

Make Salām to Ṣiddīq Akbar رَضِیَ اللّٰہُ عَنۡہُ

Then moving slightly eastward (i.e. towards your right) for about half a yard, stand respectfully towards the small opening in front of the blessed face of Sayyidunā Abū Bakr Ṣiddīq رَضِیَ اللّٰہُ تَعَالٰی عَنۡہُ with your hands folded and say Salām to him in these words.

اَلسَّلَامُ عَلَيْكَ يَا خَلِيْفَةَ رَسُوْلِ اللّٰهِ ؕ اَلسَّلَامُ عَلَيْكَ يَا وَزِيْرَ رَسُوْلِ اللّٰهِ ؕ اَلسَّلَامُ عَلَيْكَ يَا صَاحِبَ رَسُوْلِ اللّٰهِ فِى الْغَارِ وَرَحْمَةُ اللّٰهِ وَ بَرَكَاتُهٗ ؕ

Salām be upon you, O the successor of the Holy Prophet! Salām be upon you, O the vicegerent of the Holy Prophet! Salām be upon you, O the companion of the Holy Prophet in the cave Šaur! May mercies and blessings from Allah عَزَّوَجَلَّ be upon you!

Make Salām to Fārūq A'ẓam رَضِیَ اللّٰہُ عَنۡہُ

Then shift slightly eastwards (i.e. towards your right) for about half a yard. Stand facing the last opening of the Golden Grille and say Salām to Sayyidunā Fārūq A'ẓam رَضِیَ اللّٰہُ تَعَالٰی عَنۡہُ.

اَلسَّلَامُ عَلَيْكَ يَا اَمِيْرَ الْمُؤْمِنِيْنَ ؕ اَلسَّلَامُ عَلَيْكَ يَا مُتَمِّمَ الْاَرْبَعِيْنَ ؕ اَلسَّلَامُ عَلَيْكَ يَا عِزَّ الْاِسْلَامِ وَالْمُسْلِمِيْنَ وَرَحْمَةُ اللّٰهِ وَ بَرَكَاتُهٗ ؕ

Salām be upon you, O the chief of the believers! Salām be upon you, O the one who completes the forty! O the one who is the dignity of Islam and the Muslims! May Salām, Allah's mercy and blessings be upon you!

Make Salām to Shaykhayn رَضِىَ اللّٰهُ عَنْهُمَا together

Then, move westwards (i.e. towards your left side) by a span[1], stand in front of the space between the two small openings with your face towards the Golden Grille and say Salām jointly in the courts of Ṣiddīq Akbar and Fārūq A'ẓam رَضِىَ اللّٰهُ تَعَالٰى عَنْهُمَا.

اَلسَّلَامُ عَلَيْكُمَا يَا خَلِيْفَتَىْ رَسُوْلِ اللّٰهِ ط اَلسَّلَامُ عَلَيْكُمَا يَا وَزِيْرَىْ رَسُوْلِ اللّٰهِ ط اَلسَّلَامُ عَلَيْكُمَا يَا ضَجِيْعَىْ رَسُوْلِ اللّٰهِ وَرَحْمَةُ اللّٰهِ وَبَرَكَاتُهٗ ط اَسْئَلُكُمَا الشَّفَاعَةَ عِنْدَ رَسُوْلِ اللّٰهِ صَلَّى اللّٰهُ تَعَالٰى عَلَيْهِ وَعَلَيْكُمَا وَبَارَكَ وَسَلَّمَ ط

Salām be upon both of you, O the successors of the Holy Prophet! Salām be upon both of you, O the vicegerents of the Holy Prophet! Salām, Allah's mercy and blessings be upon both of you who are resting beside the Holy Prophet صَلَّى اللّٰهُ تَعَالٰى عَلَيْهِ وَاٰلِهٖ وَسَلَّم*! May the mercies and blessings of Allah* عَزَّوَجَلَّ *be upon both of you. I beg both of you to intercede with the Holy Prophet* صَلَّى اللّٰهُ تَعَالٰى عَلَيْهِ وَاٰلِهٖ وَسَلَّم *for me. May Allah* عَزَّوَجَلَّ *send Ṣalāt, Salām and blessings upon him and both of you!*

***

[1] The word 'span' here implies the distance between the tip of the thumb and that of the little finger when the hand is fully extended.

Make following Du'ās

All these courts are sacred places where one's Du'ā is accepted. Make Du'ā for the betterment of your worldly life as well as for afterlife. Make Du'ā of forgiveness for your parents, your spiritual guide, your teachers, children, friends, family, relatives and the entire Ummaĥ. Seek intercession from the Prophet of Raḥmaĥ, the Intercessor of Ummaĥ صَلَّى اللهُ تَعَالٰى عَلَيْهِ وَاٰلِهٖ وَسَلَّم. Recite couplets of Na'at, in particular, at the sacred Muwājaĥaĥ. If you are able to recite the following couplet of Sag-e-Madīnaĥ 12 times at the blessed Muwājaĥaĥ, you will be doing me a great favour.

Pařausī khuld mayn 'Aṭṭār ko apnā banā lī-jiye
Jaĥān ĥayn itnay iḥsān aur iḥsān Yā Rasūlallāĥ

Make 'Aṭṭār your neighbour in Paradise,
With all your favours, make this favour as well, Yā Rasūlallāĥ

12 Madanī pearls

1. Make Du'ā near the blessed Mimbar (i.e. a pulpit-like raised structure).
2. Come to the orchard of Paradise and offer two Rak'āt Nafl Ṣalāĥ over there provided the time is not Makrūĥ. Make Du'ā afterwards. (The space between the blessed Mimbar and the sacred Ḥujraĥ [i.e. blessed room of the Holy Prophet صَلَّى اللهُ تَعَالٰى عَلَيْهِ وَاٰلِهٖ وَسَلَّم] is referred to as an orchard of Paradise in a Ḥadīš.)
3. Do not waste even a single moment for as long as you are blessed with the stay in Madīna-tul-Munawwaraĥ.
4. If possible, spend most of your time in Masjid-un-Nabawī in the state of cleanness, offering Ṣalāĥ, reciting the Quran and Ṣalāt-'Alan-Nabī and making Żikr. Worldly conversation should be avoided in any Masjid, especially in this Holy Masjid.

Mihrab of Masjid-un-Nabawi صَلَّى اللهُ تَعَالٰی عَلَیْهِ وَاٰلِهٖ وَسَلَّم
Orchard of Jannah

Mihrab of Masjid-un-Nabawi صَلَّى اللهُ تَعَالٰی عَلَیْهِ وَاٰلِهٖ وَسَلَّم
Orchard of Jannah

An ancient memorable image of the Holy Ka'bah

5. How wonderful it would be for you to be blessed with keeping a fast in Madīna-tul-Munawwarah, especially on a hot summer day as intercession is promised to the one doing so!

6. Every good deed performed here is equivalent to fifty thousand good deeds. Therefore, make strenuous efforts to perform worship. Do reduce your intake. As long as possible, give charity especially to the deserving locals.

7. Recite the entire Quran at least once here and once in the Ḥaṭīm of the Holy Ka'bah.

8. As it is an act of worship to look at the Holy Ka'bah and the Holy Quran, it is also an act of worship to look at the blessed mausoleum. Therefore, reap its blessings reverently in abundance and present Ṣalāt and Salām.

9. After the daily five Ṣalāhs or every morning and evening, present yourself in front of the Golden Grilles in the direction of the blessed face of the Holy Prophet صَلَّى اللهُ تَعَالٰى عَلَيْهِ وَاٰلِهٖ وَسَلَّم and present Salām.

10. Whether you are in the city or in suburbs, whenever you see the Green Dome, turn towards it immediately and recite Ṣalāt and Salām with hands folded respectfully. Do not proceed without doing it as this is contrary to manners.

11. As long as possible, try to offer Ṣalāh in the very first Masjid made in the era of the Beloved Prophet صَلَّى اللهُ تَعَالٰى عَلَيْهِ وَاٰلِهٖ وَسَلَّم. Its length and width were 50 yards each. The very first Masjid was extended later on. To offer Ṣalāh in the extended area of the Masjid is also like offering Ṣalāh in Masjid-un-Nabawī.

12. Do not do Ṭawāf [i.e. move around] the blessed mausoleum. Neither prostrate yourself nor bow down like Rukū'. The reverence for the Holy Prophet صَلَّى اللهُ تَعَالٰى عَلَيْهِ وَاٰلِهٖ وَسَلَّم lies in obeying him. *(Derived from Bahār-e-Sharī'at, vol. 1, pp. 1227-1228)*

Recite near Golden Grille

If anyone recites the Quranic verse one time

إِنَّ اللّٰهَ وَمَلٰٓئِكَتَهٗ يُصَلُّوْنَ عَلَى النَّبِيِّ ؕ
يٰٓاَيُّهَا الَّذِيْنَ اٰمَنُوْا صَلُّوْا عَلَيْهِ وَسَلِّمُوْا تَسْلِيْمًا ﴿۵۶﴾

standing in front of the sacred grave of the Beloved and Blessed Prophet صَلَّى اللهُ تَعَالٰى عَلَيْهِ وَاٰلِهٖ وَسَلَّم and then recites صَلَّى اللّٰهُ عَلَيْكَ وَسَلَّمَ يَا رَسُوْلَ اللّٰهِ 70 times, an angel replies saying, 'O so and so person! May Allah عَزَّوَجَلَّ send Salām upon you!' The angel then makes Du'ā for that person, 'O Allah عَزَّوَجَلَّ, fulfill his every need.'

(Al-Mawāĥib-ul-Ladunniyaĥ, vol. 3, pp. 412)

Don't turn your back towards Golden Grille for Du'ā

Whenever you get the privilege of being present in front of the Golden Grille, do not look here and there; looking inside the Grille is a great daring. With back towards the Qiblaĥ, stand almost two yards away from the Grille and say Salām whilst facing towards the sacred Muwājaĥaĥ. Make Du'ā also whilst facing the sacred Muwājaĥaĥ. There are certain people over there who insist that you face the Qiblaĥ to make Du'ā. Do not listen to them. Never turn your back towards the Noble Prophet صَلَّى اللهُ تَعَالٰى عَلَيْهِ وَاٰلِهٖ وَسَلَّم, who is the Ka'baĥ of the Ka'baĥ!

Reward of fifty thousand I'tikāf

Whenever you enter the blessed Masjid, do not forget to make the intention of I'tikāf. By doing this, you will get the reward of fifty thousand Nafl I'tikāf. In addition, it will also become permissible to eat, drink and do Ifṭār within the Masjid. The intention for I'tikāf is as follows:

نَوَيْتُ سُنَّتَ الْاِعْتِكَافِ

***Translation:** I make the intention of Sunnaĥ I'tikāf*[1].

Reward of five Hajj daily

One should particularly offer 40 Ṣalāĥ in Masjid-un-Nabawī. In fact, offer all your Farḍ Ṣalāĥ in this blessed Masjid. The Beloved and Blessed Prophet صَلَّى اللهُ تَعَالٰى عَلَيْهِ وَاٰلِهٖ وَسَلَّم has stated, 'Whosoever makes Wuḍū and leaves with the intention of offering Ṣalāĥ in my Masjid, this is equivalent to one Hajj for him.'

(Shu'ab-ul-Īmān, vol. 3, pp. 499, Ḥadīš 4191)

Say Salām orally

Say memorized Salām orally in the court of the Noble Prophet صَلَّى اللهُ تَعَالٰى عَلَيْهِ وَاٰلِهٖ وَسَلَّم as it seems rather strange to say Salām and make Du'ā there reading from a book. The Prophet of mankind, the Peace of our heart and mind, the most Generous and Kind صَلَّى اللهُ تَعَالٰى عَلَيْهِ وَاٰلِهٖ وَسَلَّم is resting in his sacred grave facing the Qiblaĥ with complete physical life, and is fully aware of even our heart-feelings. Therefore, it does not seem appropriate to say Salām reading from a book.

Look at it in this way. If you are present in the court of your Murshid (i.e. spiritual guide), will you say Salām to him reading from a book? Certainly not! In fact, you would say Salām with the words that come to your mind spontaneously. I hope that you may have understood my point. Remember that this is that honourable court where hearts are looked at, not eloquent expressions.

---

[1] In fact, when you enter the blessed Masjid from either Bāb-us-Salām or Bāb-ur-Raḥmaĥ, you will find a pillar in front of you with the inscription 'نَوَيْتُ سُنَّتَ الْاِعْتِكَاف' in gold letters. This is to remind the devotees of Rasūl.

Old woman blessed with grand vision

During my (the author's) visit to Madīnaĥ in 1405 A.H., the late Ḥājī Ismā'īl, a spiritual brother of mine, told me the following parable. Almost two or three years back, an 85-year-old woman came to perform Hajj. During her visit to Madīnaĥ, whilst she was present in front of the Golden Grille, she made Salām in the court of the Beloved and Blessed Prophet صَلَّى اللهُ تَعَالٰى عَلَيْهِ وَاٰلِهٖ وَسَلَّم in her broken words. Meanwhile, she caught sight of a lady reciting Ṣalāt and Salām in extremely eloquent words reading from a book.

Dejected, the old woman said, 'Yā Rasūlallāĥ صَلَّى اللهُ تَعَالٰى عَلَيْهِ وَاٰلِهٖ وَسَلَّم! I am not an educated person, and cannot make Salām in excellent and eloquent words. You are great and glorious. You will be accepting the Salām of only those who make Salām in your court in an excellent manner. How can I expect you to like the Salām of mine, an uneducated person.' She then left weeping.

When she went to sleep at night, her sleeping fortune awoke, blessing her with the vision of the Holy Prophet صَلَّى اللهُ تَعَالٰى عَلَيْهِ وَاٰلِهٖ وَسَلَّم in her dream. The blessed lips of the Beloved Prophet صَلَّى اللهُ تَعَالٰى عَلَيْهِ وَاٰلِهٖ وَسَلَّم began to move and the following words were uttered, 'Why are you becoming disappointed? I have accepted your Salām before everyone else's.'

صَلُّوْا عَلَى الْحَبِيْب صَلَّى اللهُ تَعَالٰى عَلٰى مُحَمَّد

Await expectantly!

It is an act of worship and reward to look at the Green Dome and the blessed Ḥujraĥ. Try to spend most of your time in Masjid-un-Nabawī reciting Ṣalāt and Salām eagerly and looking at the blessed Ḥujraĥ reverentially. Imagine as though our Beloved and Blessed Prophet صَلَّى اللهُ تَعَالٰى عَلَيْهِ وَاٰلِهٖ وَسَلَّم would soon come out of his blessed Ḥujraĥ.

Let your tears flow in the desire of being blessed with the vision of the Prophet of Raḥmaĥ, the Intercessor of Ummaĥ صَلَّى اللهُ تَعَالٰی عَلَيْهِ وَاٰلِهٖ وَسَلَّم.

A Memon Ḥājī blessed with seeing the Holy Prophet ﷺ

During my (the author's) visit to Madīnaĥ on the occasion of the Hajj of 1400 A.H., I met a young Ḥājī from Karachi who told me that he was once sitting by the Green Grille behind the blessed Ḥujraĥ towards the blessed back of the Beloved Prophet صَلَّى اللهُ تَعَالٰی عَلَيْهِ وَاٰلِهٖ وَسَلَّم when he saw in wakefulness that the Prophet of Raḥmaĥ, the Intercessor of Ummaĥ صَلَّى اللهُ تَعَالٰی عَلَيْهِ وَاٰلِهٖ وَسَلَّم had come out of the blessed Ḥujraĥ. The Noble Prophet صَلَّى اللهُ تَعَالٰی عَلَيْهِ وَاٰلِهٖ وَسَلَّم said to that young Ḥājī, 'Ask for whatever you desire!'

That young Ḥājī goes onto say that he was so enraptured and engrossed in the blessed vision that he dared not ask for anything. The Prophet of Raḥmaĥ صَلَّى اللهُ تَعَالٰی عَلَيْهِ وَاٰلِهٖ وَسَلَّم then returned to his blessed Ḥujraĥ, leaving the young Ḥājī overwhelmed.

Do not spit in sacred streets

Neither spit in the streets of Makkaĥ and Madīnaĥ nor blow your nose there. Aren't you aware that the Beloved and Blessed Prophet صَلَّى اللهُ تَعَالٰی عَلَيْهِ وَاٰلِهٖ وَسَلَّم passed these streets!

Jannat-ul-Baqī'

The sacred tombs and graves in Jannat-ul-Baqī' and Jannat-ul-Ma'lā have been destroyed. The graves of thousands of eminent companions, great Awliyā, and devotees and those of even countless family members of the Holy Prophet صَلَّى اللهُ تَعَالٰی عَلَيْهِ وَاٰلِهٖ وَسَلَّم have been obliterated.

Therefore, if you enter the graveyard, there is a possibility that you might actually be walking on the grave of any companion or devotee of Rasūl, whereas walking on the grave of even an ordinary Muslim is Ḥarām in Sharī'aĥ. It is stated in *Rad-dul-Muḥtār* that if a certain path was built after demolishing the graves underneath it, it is Ḥarām to walk on that path. *(Rad-dul-Muḥtār, vol. 1, pp. 612)* In fact, if there is even a doubt about a path being new, then it is impermissible and sin to walk on it. *(Durr-e-Mukhtār, vol. 3, pp. 183)* Therefore, it is a Madanī request that you make Salām standing outside the boundary of Jannat-ul-Baqī', not its main entrance. The proper method is to make Salām with your back towards the Qiblaĥ and your face towards the faces of the buried ones.

Salām to those buried in Jannat-ul-Baqī'

اَلسَّلَامُ عَلَيْكُمْ دَارَ قَوْمٍ مُّؤْمِنِيْنَ فَاِنَّـآ اِنْ شَآءَ اللّٰهُ بِكُمْ لَاحِقُوْنَ ط اَللّٰهُمَّ اغْفِرْ لِاَهْلِ الْبَقِيْعِ الْغَرْقَدِ ط اَللّٰهُمَّ اغْفِرْ لَنَا وَلَهُمْ ط

Salām be upon you, O the believers living here. اِنْ شَآءَ اللّٰه عَزَّوَجَلَّ, *we are about to meet you. O Allah* عَزَّوَجَلَّ, *forgive those buried in Baqī'. O Allah* عَزَّوَجَلَّ, *forgive us and them.*

Broken heart

Alas! There was a time when this sacred place used to be 'served' by the Aĥl-us-Sunnaĥ. The Imāms of the blessed Masājid were also true devotees, from the Aĥl-us-Sunnaĥ. During the sermon of Jumu'aĥ, indicating with his hands towards the Prophet's sacred grave in Masjid-un-Nabawī, when the Imām recited اَلصَّلٰوةُ وَالسَّلَامُ عَلٰى هٰذَا النَّبِيِّ (i.e. Ṣalāt and Salām be upon this Nabī صَلَّى اللهُ تَعَالٰى عَلَيْهِ وَاٰلِهٖ وَسَلَّم), thousands

Jannat-ul-Baqi

An ancient memorable image of Jannat-ul-Baqi

Bab-ul-Baqi

Bab-ul-Baqi

of devotees of Rasūl would become overcome with emotion and start weeping.

Farewell visit

When the heart breaking moment of departure from Madīnaĥ arrives, proceed towards the sacred Muwājaĥaĥ weeping. If you cannot weep, wear a weeping look on the face. Recite Ṣalāt and Salām whilst weeping. Then express your feelings in an imploring manner like this:

Al-Wada' Yā Rasūlallāĥ ﷺ

اَلْوَدَاعُ يَا رَسُوْلَ اللّٰهِ ط اَلْوَدَاعُ يَا رَسُوْلَ اللّٰهِ ط اَلْوَدَاعُ يَا رَسُوْلَ اللّٰهِ ط
اَلْفِرَاقُ يَا رَسُوْلَ اللّٰهِ ط اَلْفِرَاقُ يَا رَسُوْلَ اللّٰهِ ط اَلْفِرَاقُ يَا رَسُوْلَ اللّٰهِ ط
اَلْفِرَاقُ يَا حَبِيْبَ اللّٰهِ ط اَلْفِرَاقُ يَا نَبِيَّ اللّٰهِ ط اَلْاَمَانُ يَا حَبِيْبَ اللّٰهِ ط
لَا جَعَلَهُ اللّٰهُ تَعَالٰى اٰخِرَ الْعَهْدِ مِنْكَ وَلَا مِنْ زِيَارَتِكَ وَلَا مِنَ الْوُقُوْفِ
بَيْنَ يَدَيْكَ اِلَّا مِنْ خَيْرٍ وَّعَافِيَةٍ وَّصِحَّةٍ وَّسَلَامَةٍ اِنْ عِشْتُ اِنْ شَآءَ
اللّٰهُ تَعَالٰى جِئْتُكَ وَ اِنْ مِّتُّ فَاَوْدَعْتُ عِنْدَكَ شَهَادَتِيْ وَاَمَانَتِيْ وَعَهْدِيْ
وَمِيْثَاقِيْ مِنْ يَّوْمِنَا هٰذَا اِلٰى يَوْمِ الْقِيٰمَةِ وَهِيَ شَهَادَةُ اَنْ لَّآ اِلٰهَ اِلَّا اللّٰهُ
وَحْدَهٗ لَا شَرِيْكَ لَهٗ وَاَشْهَدُ اَنَّ مُحَمَّدًا عَبْدُهٗ وَرَسُوْلُهٗ ط ﴿ سُبْحٰنَ رَبِّكَ
رَبِّ الْعِزَّةِ عَمَّا يَصِفُوْنَ ﴿۱۸۰﴾ وَسَلٰمٌ عَلَى الْمُرْسَلِيْنَ ﴿۱۸۱﴾ وَالْحَمْدُ لِلّٰهِ رَبِّ
الْعٰلَمِيْنَ ﴿۱۸۲﴾ ﴾ اٰمِيْنَ، اٰمِيْنَ، اٰمِيْنَ، يَا رَبَّ الْعٰلَمِيْنَ بِحَقِّ طٰهٰ وَ يٰسٓ

Al-Wadā' Tājdār-e-Madīnaĥ

Āĥ! Ab waqt-e-rukhṣat ĥay āyā
Al-Wadā' Tājdār-e-Madīnaĥ
Ṣadma-e-ĥijr kaysay saĥūn gā
Al-Wadā' Tājdār-e-Madīnaĥ
Bay-qarārī baṙĥī jā raĥī ĥay
Ĥijr kī ab gĥaṙī ā raĥī ĥay
Dil ĥuwā jātā ĥay pāraĥ pāraĥ
Al-Wadā' Tājdār-e-Madīnaĥ

Kis ṭaraḥ shauq say mayn chalā tĥā
Dil kā ghunchaĥ khushī say kĥilā tĥā
Āĥ! Ab cĥūttā ĥay Madīnaĥ
Al-Wadā' Tājdār-e-Madīnaĥ

Kūay Jānā kī rangīn fazāon!
Ay mu'aṭṭar mu'ambar ĥawāon
Lo Salām ākhirī ab ĥamārā
Al-Wadā' Tājdār-e-Madīnaĥ

Kāsh! Qismat mayrā sātĥ daytī
Mawt bĥī yāwarī mayrī kartī
Jān qadmaun pay qurbān kartā
Al-Wadā' Tājdār-e-Madīnaĥ

Sauz-e-ulfat say jaltā raĥūn mayn
'Ishq mayn tayray gĥultā raĥūn mayn
Mujĥ ko dīwānaĥ samjĥay zamānaĥ
Al-Wadā' Tājdār-e-Madīnaĥ

Mayn jaĥān bĥī raĥūn mayray Āqā
Ĥo nazar mayn Madīnay kā jalwaĥ
Iltijā mayrī maqbūl farmā
Al-Wadā' Tājdār-e-Madīnaĥ

Kucĥ na ḥusn-e-'amal kar sakā ĥūn
Nażr chand ashk mayn kar raĥā ĥūn
Bas yeĥī ĥay mayrā kul asāsaĥ
Al-Wadā' Tājdār-e-Madīnaĥ

Ānkĥ say ab ĥuwā kĥūn jārī
Rūḥ per bĥī ĥay ab ranj tārī
Jald 'Aṭṭār ko pĥir bulānā
Al-Wadā' Tājdār-e-Madīnaĥ

Like before, present Salām in the blessed courts of Shaykhayn Karīmayn رضی اللہ تعالیٰ عنہما. Make Du'ā tearfully and plead for repeated visits to Madīnaĥ. Ask for an easy death with Īmān in Madīnaĥ and burial in Jannat-ul-Baqī'.

Then return with tears in eyes, repeatedly turning around to look at the Prophet's sacred mausoleum with wistfulness. Leave like the child who is being separated from his loving mother, crying and looking back at her all the time expecting her to call him back and embrace him. How fortunate would be the one who, at such a moment, is blessed with the embrace by the Beloved and Blessed Prophet صَلَّى اللّٰهُ تَعَالٰى عَلَيْهِ وَاٰلِهٖ وَسَلَّم and with death at his blessed feet!

صَلُّوْا عَلَى الْحَبِيْب صَلَّى اللّٰهُ تَعَالٰى عَلٰى مُحَمَّد
تُوْبُوْا اِلَى الله اَسْتَغْفِرُ الله
صَلُّوْا عَلَى الْحَبِيْب صَلَّى اللّٰهُ تَعَالٰى عَلٰى مُحَمَّد

Ziyārāt (holy sites) in Makka-tul-Mukarramaĥ

Birthplace of Holy Prophet ﷺ

'Allāmaĥ Quṭbuddīn عَلَيْهِ رَحْمَةُ اللّٰهِ الْمُبِيْن has said: The Du'ā made at the birthplace of the Holy Prophet صَلَّى اللّٰهُ تَعَالٰى عَلَيْهِ وَاٰلِهٖ وَسَلَّم is accepted. An easy way to get there is to exit via any of the adjacent doors of the mount Marwaĥ. In front of the doors is a big space for Ṣalāĥ-offering people. This sacred house is situated on the other side of the space and will appear from distance, اِنْ شَآءَ اللّٰه عَزَّوَجَلَّ. The mother of Sultan Ĥārūn Rashīd عَلَيْهِ رَحْمَةُ اللّٰهِ الْمَجِيْد had a Masjid constructed on this spot but this extremely sacred house has now been converted into a Madrasaĥ and library. A board with the writing مَكْتَبَةُ مَكَّةَ الْمُكَرَّمَة 'Maktabaĥ Makka-tal-Mukarramaĥ' is on display here.

Jabal Abū Qubays

This is the first mountain of the world. It lies outside Masjid-ul-Ḥarām near Ṣafā and Marwaĥ. The Du'ā made at this mountain is accepted. The people of Makkaĥ when affected by droughts used to come here and make Du'ā. It is stated in a Ḥadīš that Ḥajar-ul-Aswad descended onto it from Paradise. *(Attarghīb Wattarĥīb, vol. 2, pp. 125, Ḥadīš 30)*

This mountain is also referred to as 'Al-Amīn' as Ḥajar-ul-Aswad remained intact over it during the storm of Sayyidunā Nūḥ. On the occasion of the construction of the Holy Ka'baĥ, this mountain called out to Sayyidunā Ibrāĥīm عَلٰی نَبِیِّنَا وَ عَلَیْہِ الصَّلٰوۃُ وَالسَّلَام and told him that Ḥajar-ul-Aswad was present over it. *(Balad-ul-Amīn, pp. 204)*

It is also reported that this is the spot where Ḥajar-ul-Aswad descended from Paradise and where the Beloved and Blessed Prophet صَلَّی اللہُ تَعَالٰی عَلَیْہِ وَاٰلِہٖ وَسَلَّم split the moon. As Makka-tul-Mukarramaĥ is surrounded by mountains, people used to climb this mountain for sighting the moon. As remembrance, a Masjid named Masjid Ḥilāl was built here which used to be called Masjid Bilāl by some people. وَاللہُ وَرَسُوْلُہٗ اَعْلَم

A royal palace has been constructed over the mountain, because of which it is no longer possible to behold this holy Masjid. During the Hajj of 1409 AH a bomb exploded near the palace, martyring many Ḥujjāj. As a result, it is now a high security area. In view of the security of the palace, the Wuḍū area that existed in the tunnel of the mountain has also been demolished. It is reported that Sayyidunā Ādam عَلٰی نَبِیِّنَا وَ عَلَیْہِ الصَّلٰوۃُ وَالسَّلَام is buried in the cave Kanz situated over the very same mountain Abū Qubays. According to another authentic narration he عَلَیْہِ السَّلَام is buried in Masjid Khayf in Minā. وَاللہُ وَرَسُوْلُہٗ اَعْلَم

House of Khadīja-tul-Kubrā رَضِیَ اللہُ عَنْہَا

As long as the Noble Prophet صَلَّی اللہُ تَعَالٰی عَلَیْہِ وَاٰلِہٖ وَسَلَّم lived in Makkaĥ, he صَلَّی اللہُ تَعَالٰی عَلَیْہِ وَاٰلِہٖ وَسَلَّم stayed in this blessed house. Except for Sayyidunā Ibrāĥīm رَضِیَ اللہُ تَعَالٰی عَنْہُ all other blessed offspring of the Holy Prophet صَلَّی اللہُ تَعَالٰی عَلَیْہِ وَاٰلِہٖ وَسَلَّم including Sayyidatunā Fāṭimaĥ رَضِیَ اللہُ تَعَالٰی عَنْہَا were born in this sacred house. Many a time, Sayyidunā Jibrāīl عَلَیْہِ السَّلَام presented himself in the court of the Holy Prophet صَلَّی اللہُ تَعَالٰی عَلَیْہِ وَاٰلِہٖ وَسَلَّم in the same house. The Beloved Prophet صَلَّی اللہُ تَعَالٰی عَلَیْہِ وَاٰلِہٖ وَسَلَّم also received many Quranic revelations in this house. After Masjid-ul-Ḥarām, there is no place in Makkaĥ superior to this house but regretfully it has now been obliterated completely, and a walkway has been made here. Exiting via the adjacent door of the mount Marwaĥ, you can only behold the aura of this house looking towards left with desperate eyes.

Cave of Jabal Šaur

This cave is situated on the right side of Makkaĥ towards the suburb of Masfalaĥ approximately 4 kilometres away. This is the sacred cave which is mentioned in the Holy Quran. This is that blessed cave where the Holy Prophet صَلَّى اللّٰهُ تَعَالٰى عَلَيْهِ وَاٰلِهٖ وَسَلَّم and his beloved companion, Sayyidunā Abū Bakr Ṣiddīq رَضِىَ اللّٰهُ تَعَالٰى عَنْهُ spent three nights during migration (Ĥijraĥ). When the enemies reached the mouth of the cave in search of them, Sayyidunā Abū Bakr Ṣiddīq رَضِىَ اللّٰهُ تَعَالٰى عَنْهُ became dejected and said: Yā Rasūlallāĥ! Our enemies have approached us. If they look down, they will see us. Comforting and encouraging him, the Holy Prophet صَلَّى اللّٰهُ تَعَالٰى عَلَيْهِ وَاٰلِهٖ وَسَلَّم said:

Grieve not, no doubt Allah (عَزَّوَجَلَّ) is with us. لَا تَحْزَنْ اِنَّ اللّٰهَ مَعَنَا ۚ

[Kanz-ul-Īmān (Translation of Quran)] (Part 10, Sūraĥ At-Taubaĥ, verse 40)

This is the mountain where Qābīl martyred Sayyidunā Ĥābīl.

Cave of Ḥirā

This is the place where the Holy Prophet صَلَّى اللّٰهُ تَعَالٰى عَلَيْهِ وَاٰلِهٖ وَسَلَّم used to do worship and meditation prior to declaring his Prophethood. This cave faces the direction of the Qiblaĥ. This is where the Beloved and Blessed Prophet صَلَّى اللّٰهُ تَعَالٰى عَلَيْهِ وَاٰلِهٖ وَسَلَّم received the first revelation (i.e. first five verses of Sūraĥ Al-'Alaq). The cave is situated in Jabal Ḥirā on the eastern side of Masjid-ul-Ḥarām about 3 kilometres away. This sacred cave is also called 'Jabal Nūr'. The cave of Ḥirā is superior to the cave of Šaur as the Holy Prophet صَلَّى اللّٰهُ تَعَالٰى عَلَيْهِ وَاٰلِهٖ وَسَلَّم spent only 3 nights in the latter while he صَلَّى اللّٰهُ تَعَالٰى عَلَيْهِ وَاٰلِهٖ وَسَلَّم lived for a longer period of time in the former.

Dār-ul-Arqam

Dār-ul-Arqam was situated in the vicinity of the mount Ṣafā. When the situation in early Islam became very desperate, our Beloved and Blessed Prophet صَلَّى اللّٰهُ تَعَالٰى عَلَيْهِ وَاٰلِهٖ وَسَلَّم sought refuge in this blessed house. Several eminent people embraced Islam in this house such as Sayyidunā Ḥamzaĥ, Sayyidunā 'Umar رَضِىَ اللّٰهُ تَعَالٰى عَنْهُمَا etc.

It is in this house that the verse يٰۤاَيُّهَا النَّبِيُّ حَسْبُكَ اللّٰهُ وَمَنِ اتَّبَعَكَ مِنَ الْمُؤْمِنِيْنَ ﴿۶۴﴾ was revealed. On this spot, the mother of caliph Ĥārūn Rashīd عَلَيْهِ رَحْمَةُ اللّٰهِ الْمَجِيْد had a Masjid constructed which was renovated by many succeeding caliphs during their reign. No sign of this house exists now and it has been included in Masjid-ul-Ḥarām.

Masfalaĥ

This is indeed a very historic locality. Sayyidunā Ibrāĥīm عَلَيْهِ السَّلَام used to live here. Eminent Ṣaḥābaĥ like Sayyidunā Abū Bakr, Sayyidunā 'Umar and Sayyidunā Ḥamzaĥ رَضِىَ اللّٰهُ تَعَالٰى عَنْهُم also lived here. This area lies in the direction of Mustajār (wall of the Holy Ka'baĥ).

Jannat-ul-Ma'lā

After Jannat-ul-Baqī', Jannat-ul-Ma'lā is the world's holiest graveyard. Sayyidatunā Khadīja-tul-Kubrā, Sayyidunā 'Abdullāĥ Ibn 'Umar and many companions رَضِىَ اللّٰهُ تَعَالٰى عَلَيْهِمْ اَجْمَعِيْن, saints, Awliyā and pious people are resting here.

The sacred graves have been obliterated in the name of making roads there. It is better to stand outside the graveyard and make Salām from far.

اَلسَّلَامُ عَلَيۡكُمۡ يَا اَهۡلَ الدِّيَارِ مِنَ الۡمُؤۡمِنِيۡنَ وَ الۡمُسۡلِمِيۡنَ وَ اِنَّآ اِنۡ شَآءَ اللّٰهُ بِكُمۡ لَاحِقُوۡنَ ط نَسۡئَلُ اللّٰهَ لَنَا وَ لَكُمُ الۡعَافِيَةَ ط

Salām be upon you, O the believers from amongst Mu`mins and Muslims living here! We are about to meet you, اِنۡ شَآءَاللہ عَزَّوَجَلَّ. We ask Allah عَزَّوَجَلَّ for your well being and ours.

Make Du'ā for yourself, your parents, family, friends and the entire Ummaĥ, and make Īṣāl-e-Šawāb for those buried in Jannat-ul-Ma'lā. Du'ā is accepted here.

Masjid Jinn

This Masjid is situated near Jannat-ul-Ma'lā. Listening to the recitation of the Holy Quran from the Beloved and Blessed Rasūl صَلَّی اللهُ تَعَالٰی عَلَيۡهِ وَاٰلِهٖ وَسَلَّم during Ṣalāt-ul-Fajr, a group of jinn embraced Islam in this Masjid.

Masjid-ur-Rāyaĥ

This Masjid is situated in the vicinity of Masjid Jinn on the right-hand side. The word رَايَه (Rāyaĥ) in Arabic refers to a flag. This is the historic spot where the Noble Rasūl صَلَّی اللهُ تَعَالٰی عَلَيۡهِ وَاٰلِهٖ وَسَلَّم planted a flag on the occasion of the conquest of Makkaĥ.

Masjid Khayf

This Masjid is located in Minā. The Beloved and Blessed Prophet صَلَّی اللهُ تَعَالٰی عَلَيۡهِ وَاٰلِهٖ وَسَلَّم offered Ṣalāĥ here on the occasion of Ḥijja-tul-Wadā'. He صَلَّی اللهُ تَعَالٰی عَلَيۡهِ وَاٰلِهٖ وَسَلَّم has said: 'صَلّٰى فِيۡ مَسۡجِدِ الۡخَيۡفِ سَبۡعُوۡنَ نَبِيًّا' That is, seventy Prophets عَلَيۡهِمُ السَّلَام offered Ṣalāĥ in Masjid Khayf. *(Al-Mu'jam-ul-Awsaṭ, vol. 4, pp. 117, Ḥadīš 5407)* He صَلَّی اللهُ تَعَالٰی عَلَيۡهِ وَاٰلِهٖ وَسَلَّم has further stated that the graves of seventy Prophets عَلَيْهِمُ السَّلَام are present in Masjid Khayf. *(Al-Mu'jam-ul-Kabīr, vol. 12, pp. 316, Ḥadīš 13525)*

This Masjid has now greatly been extended. The visitors should behold this Masjid with reverence and present Salām in the courts of the Prophets عَلَيْهِمُ السَّلَام in following words:

اَلسَّلَامُ عَلَيْكُمْ يَا اَنْۢبِيَاءَ اللّٰهِ وَرَحْمَةُ اللّٰهِ وَبَرَكَاتُهٗ ط

Then make Īṣāl-e-Šawāb and Du'ā.

Masjid Ji'irrānaĥ

This Masjid is located about 26 kilometres from Makkaĥ on the road to Ṭāif. You should put on Iḥrām for 'Umraĥ here as the Beloved and Blessed Prophet صَلَّى اللّٰهُ تَعَالٰى عَلَيْهِ وَاٰلِهٖ وَسَلَّم also put on Iḥrām for 'Umraĥ here on his return after the conquest of Ṭāif. Yūsuf Bin Māĥak عَلَيْهِ رَحْمَةُ اللّٰهِ الْخَالِق has said, 'Three hundred Prophets عَلَيْهِمُ السَّلَام put on Iḥrām for 'Umraĥ at Ji'irrānaĥ. The Beloved and Blessed Prophet صَلَّى اللّٰهُ تَعَالٰى عَلَيْهِ وَاٰلِهٖ وَسَلَّم drove his blessed stake into the ground, causing very sweet and cold spring water to gush out!

(Balad-ul-Amīn, pp. 221; Akhbār Makkaĥ, Juz 5, pp. 62-69)

It is said that there is a well here. Sayyidunā Ibn 'Abbās رَضِىَ اللّٰهُ تَعَالٰى عَنْهُمَا has said: On his return from Ṭāif, the Holy Prophet صَلَّى اللّٰهُ تَعَالٰى عَلَيْهِ وَاٰلِهٖ وَسَلَّم stayed here and distributed the wealth of Ghanīmaĥ here. He صَلَّى اللّٰهُ تَعَالٰى عَلَيْهِ وَاٰلِهٖ وَسَلَّم put on the Iḥrām of 'Umraĥ here on 28 Shawwāl-ul-Mukarram. *(Balad-ul-Amīn, pp. 220-221)* This area is named after a Qurayshī woman, Ji'irrānaĥ. *(Balad-ul-Amīn, pp. 137)* [The Urdu-speaking] people refer it to as 'Baŕā 'Umraĥ', i.e. the place of big 'Umraĥ.

This is indeed a very special place. Sayyidunā 'Abdul Ḥaq Muḥaddiš Ďihlvī عَلَيْهِ رَحْمَةُ اللّٰهِ الْقَوِى has stated in '*Akhbār-ul-Akhyār*' that his Murshid Sayyidunā 'Abdul Waĥĥāb Muttaqī عَلَيْهِ رَحْمَةُ اللّٰهِ الْقَوِى has strongly advised him to put on the Iḥrām of 'Umraĥ at Ji'irrānaĥ, if possible. His Murshid has further stated that Ji'irrānaĥ is such a sacred place that once he spent a night there, and was blessed with the vision of the Holy Prophet صَلَّى اللهُ تَعَالٰى عَلَيْهِ وَاٰلِهٖ وَسَلَّم a hundred times in his dream within a part of that single night اَلْحَمْدُ لِلّٰهِ عَلٰى اِحْسَانِهٖ. It was a routine of Sayyidunā 'Abdul Waĥĥāb Muttaqī عَلَيْهِ رَحْمَةُ اللّٰهِ الْقَوِى that he used to walk all the way to Ji'irrānaĥ in the state of fast in order to put on the Iḥrām of 'Umraĥ. *(Mulakhkhaṣ az: Akhbār-ul-Akhyār, pp. 278)*

Tomb of Sayyidatunā Maymūnaĥ رَضِىَ اللهُ عَنْهَا

It is situated on Madīnaĥ road near the area called Nawāriyaĥ. By the time of the writing of this account, a way to get to this blessed grave is that you go by the public transport bus # 2A or 13 which normally passes Masjid 'Āishaĥ on Madīnaĥ road. The last stop of this bus is Nawāriyaĥ which is about 17 kilometres from Makkaĥ. Get off here and walk towards Makkaĥ.

After you have walked for about 10 to 15 minutes on the same side of the road, you will find a checkpoint ahead of which lies 'Mawqif Ḥujjāj' [i.e. a place for Ḥujjāj to stay]. A little distance ahead of it is an enclosed area where the blessed tomb of Sayyidatunā Maymūnaĥ رَضِىَ اللهُ تَعَالٰى عَنْهَا is situated. This sacred tomb is located in the middle of the road. According to many people, when a bulldozer was brought here to demolish the sacred tomb, the bulldozer turned upside down many times. Eventually it was enclosed by walls. How great the Karāmat of our mother Sayyidatunā Maymūnaĥ رَضِىَ اللهُ تَعَالٰى عَنْهَا is!

11 places in Masjid-ul-Ḥarām where Holy Prophet صَلَّى اللهُ عَلَيْهِ وَسَلَّم offered Ṣalāĥ

1. Inside Baytullāĥ, i.e. inside the Ka'baĥ
2. Behind Maqām-u-Ibrāĥīm

3. At the corner of Maṭāf opposite Ḥajar-ul-Aswad

4. In between Ḥaṭīm and the door of the Ka'baĥ near Rukn 'Irāqī

5. Maqām Ḥufraĥ which is located between the door of the Ka'baĥ and Ḥaṭīm at the base of the wall of Ka'baĥ. It is also called 'Maqām-e-Imāmat-e-Jibrāīl.'

   This is the place where the Prophet of Raḥmaĥ, the Intercessor of Ummaĥ صَلَّى اللهُ تَعَالٰى عَلَيْهِ وَاٰلِهٖ وَسَلَّم blessed Jibrāīl Amīn to lead Ṣalāĥ five times. This is the spot where Sayyidunā Ibrāĥīm عَلَيْهِ السَّلَام prepared the soil for the construction of the Ka'baĥ.

6. In the direction of the sacred door of the Holy Ka'baĥ (to offer Ṣalāĥ facing the direction of the door of the Ka'baĥ is superior to all other directions[1]).

7. Towards the direction of Mīzāb-ur-Raḥmaĥ. This is said to be the direction towards which the Holy Prophet صَلَّى اللهُ تَعَالٰى عَلَيْهِ وَاٰلِهٖ وَسَلَّم is facing in his blessed grave.

8. The entire area of Ḥaṭīm, especially below Mīzāb-ur-Raḥmaĥ

9. In between Rukn Aswad and Rukn Yamānī

10. Near Rukn Shāmī. He صَلَّى اللهُ تَعَالٰى عَلَيْهِ وَاٰلِهٖ وَسَلَّم would offer Ṣalāĥ here in such a manner that his blessed back was towards Bāb-ul-'Umraĥ, whether he was inside or outside Ḥaṭīm.

11. The spot where Sayyidunā Ādam عَلٰى نَبِيِّنَا وَعَلَيْهِ الصَّلٰوةُ وَالسَّلَام used to offer his Ṣalāĥ, which is either on the left or the right of Rukn Yamānī. It is also said that the place where Sayyidunā Ādam عَلٰى نَبِيِّنَا وَعَلَيْهِ الصَّلٰوةُ وَالسَّلَام offered Ṣalāĥ is Mustajār. *(Kitāb-ul-Hajj, pp. 274)*

---

[1] It is said that Pakistan and India are situated in the direction of the blessed door of Ka'baĥ. اَلْحَمْدُ لِلّٰهِ عَلٰى اِحْسَانِهٖ ؕ وَاللهُ تَعَالٰى اَعْلَمُ وَرَسُوْلُهٗ اَعْلَم

Ziyārāt [holy sites] in Madīna-tul-Munawwaraĥ

Orchard of Jannaĥ

The space between the blessed Ḥujraĥ (which is now included in the blessed mausoleum) of the Noble Prophet صَلَّى اللهُ تَعَالٰى عَلَيْهِ وَاٰلِهٖ وَسَلَّم and his Mimbar (pulpit) with its length 22 meters and width 15 meters is 'رَوْضَةُ الْجَنَّةِ' i.e. an orchard of Paradise. The Holy Prophet صَلَّى اللهُ تَعَالٰى عَلَيْهِ وَاٰلِهٖ وَسَلَّم has stated, 'مَا بَيْنَ بَيْتِيْ وَمِنْبَرِىْ رَوْضَةٌ مِّنْ رِّيَاضِ الْجَنَّةِ' i.e. the space between my house and the Mimbar is an orchard from amongst the orchards of Paradise.' *(Bukhārī, vol. 1, pp. 402, Ḥadīš 1195)* Colloquially, it is called 'رِيَاضُ الْجَنَّةِ' but the correct words are 'رَوْضَةُ الْجَنَّةِ'.

Masjid Qubā

About 3 kilometres from Madīnaĥ lies an ancient village called 'Qubā' where this Masjid is situated in south-western direction. The excellence of this Masjid has been described even in the Quran and authentic Aḥādīš. Devotees of Rasūl can reach from Masjid-un-Nabawī to Masjid Qubā by walking with a medium pace within almost 40 minutes. It is stated in *Ṣaḥīḥ Bukhārī* that the Beloved Prophet صَلَّى اللهُ تَعَالٰى عَلَيْهِ وَاٰلِهٖ وَسَلَّم used to travel to this Masjid every Saturday either by walking or by riding. *(Bukhārī, vol. 1, pp. 402, Ḥadīš 1193)*

Reward of 'Umraĥ

Here are two sayings of the Noble Prophet صَلَّى اللهُ تَعَالٰى عَلَيْهِ وَاٰلِهٖ وَسَلَّم:

1. To offer Ṣalāĥ in Masjid Qubā is equivalent to 'Umraĥ.

   (Tirmižī, vol. 1, pp. 348, Ḥadīš 324)

2. The person who makes Wuḍū at his home and then offers Ṣalāĥ in Masjid Qubā will be given the reward of 'Umraĥ. *(Ibn Mājaĥ, vol. 2, pp. 175, Ḥadīš 1412)*

Grave of Sayyidunā Ḥamzaĥ رَضِیَ اللّٰہُ عَنۡہُ

Sayyidunā Ḥamzaĥ رَضِیَ اللّٰہُ تَعَالٰی عَنۡہُ was martyred during the battle of Uḥud in 3 A.H. His blessed grave is also situated in the vicinity of this holy mountain. Besides the graves of many other eminent martyrs of the battle of Uḥud, the graves of Sayyidunā Muṣ'ab Bin 'Umayr and Sayyidunā 'Abdullāĥ Bin Jaḥsh رَضِیَ اللّٰہُ تَعَالٰی عَنۡہُمَا are also situated here. Furthermore, most of the 70 companions martyred during the battle of Uḥud also rest inside the enclosed area.

Excellence of making Salām to martyrs of Uḥud

Shaykh 'Abdul Ḥaq Muḥaddiš Diĥlvī عَلَیۡہِ رَحۡمَۃُ اللّٰہِ الۡقَوِی has stated in his book *Jażb-ul-Qulūb*, 'Whosoever passes by the graves of the martyrs of Uḥud and makes Salām to them, the martyrs, in reply, keep making Salām to him till the Day of Judgement. Many people have heard Salām from these martyrs with their own ears, especially Salām from Sayyidunā Ḥamzaĥ رَضِیَ اللّٰہُ تَعَالٰی عَنۡہُ has been heard many times.'

(Jażb-ul-Qulūb, pp. 177)

Salām in court of Sayyidunā Ḥamzaĥ رَضِیَ اللّٰہُ عَنۡہُ

اَلسَّلَامُ عَلَيْكَ يَا سَيِّدَنَا حَمْزَةُ ط اَلسَّلَامُ عَلَيْكَ يَا عَمَّ رَسُوْلِ اللّٰهِ ط
اَلسَّلَامُ عَلَيْكَ يَا عَمَّ نَبِيِّ اللّٰهِ ط اَلسَّلَامُ عَلَيْكَ يَا عَمَّ حَبِيْبِ
اللّٰهِ ط اَلسَّلَامُ عَلَيْكَ يَا عَمَّ الْمُصْطَفٰى ط اَلسَّلَامُ عَلَيْكَ يَا سَيِّدَ
الشُّهَدَآءِ وَيَا اَسَدَ اللّٰهِ وَاَسَدَ رَسُوْلِهٖ ط اَلسَّلَامُ عَلَيْكَ يَا سَيِّدَنَا
عَبْدَ اللّٰهِ بْنَ جَحْشٍ ط اَلسَّلَامُ عَلَيْكَ يَا مُصْعَبَ بْنَ عُمَيْرٍ ط
اَلسَّلَامُ عَلَيْكُمْ يَا شُهَدَآءَ اُحُدٍ كَآفَّةً عَامَّةً وَّرَحْمَةُ اللّٰهِ وَبَرَكَاتُهٗ ط

The Sacred Graves of Sayyiduna Hamzah رضی اللہ تعالیٰ عنہ

Sayyiduna Mus'ab bin Umair رضی اللہ تعالیٰ عنہ

Sayyiduna Abdullah bin Jahsh رضی اللہ تعالیٰ عنہ

The Sacred Graves of Sayyiduna Hamzah رضی اللہ تعالیٰ عنہ

Sayyiduna Mus'ab bin Umair رضی اللہ تعالیٰ عنہ

Sayyiduna Abdullah bin Jahsh رضی اللہ تعالیٰ عنہ

Ghers Well

Roma Well

Salām be upon you, O Sayyidunā Ḥamzaĥ رَضِیَ اللهُ تَعَالٰی عَنْهُ! Salām be upon you, O the uncle of Allah's Prophet! Salām be upon you, O the uncle of Allah's Nabī! Salām be upon you, O the uncle of Allah's beloved. Salām be upon you, O the uncle of the chosen one. Salām be upon you, O the leader of the martyrs and the lion of Allah عَزَّوَجَلَّ and His Prophet صَلَّی اللهُ تَعَالٰی عَلَیْهِ وَاٰلِهٖ وَسَلَّم! Salām be upon you also, O 'Abdullāĥ Bin Jaḥsh رَضِیَ اللهُ تَعَالٰی عَنْهُ. Salām be upon you, O Muṣ'ab Bin 'Umayr رَضِیَ اللهُ تَعَالٰی عَنْهُ. Salām, mercy and blessings of Allah عَزَّوَجَلَّ be upon all of you, O the martyrs of Uḥud.

✽✽✽

Collective Salām to martyrs of Uḥud

اَلسَّلَامُ عَلَیۡکُمۡ یَا شُهَدَآءُ یَا سُعَدَآءُ یَا نُجَبَآءُ یَا نُقَبَآءُ یَآ اَهۡلَ الصِّدۡقِ وَالۡوَفَآءِ ط اَلسَّلَامُ عَلَیۡکُمۡ یَا مُجَاهِدِیۡنَ فِیۡ سَبِیۡلِ اللّٰهِ حَقَّ جِهَادِهٖ ط ﴿سَلٰمٌ عَلَیۡکُمۡ بِمَا صَبَرۡتُمۡ فَنِعۡمَ عُقۡبَی الدَّارِ ﴿۲۴﴾﴾ اَلسَّلَامُ عَلَیۡکُمۡ یَا شُهَدَآءَ اُحُدٍ کَآفَّةً عَآمَّةً وَّرَحۡمَةُ اللّٰهِ وَبَرَکَاتُهٗ ط

Salām be upon you all, O martyrs, O pious ones, O virtuous ones, O leaders, O the truthful and the trustworthy! Salām be upon you all, O the ones who fought in the path of Allah عَزَّوَجَلَّ and fulfilled the right of Jihad! 'Peace be upon you for your patience, what an excellent last abode then you got.' Salām be upon you all, O martyrs of Uḥud! Salām, mercy and blessings of Allah عَزَّوَجَلَّ be upon you all!

✽✽✽

How to visit these holy sites?

My dear visitors of Makkaĥ and Madīnaĥ! For the acquisition of blessings I have mentioned only a few holy sites. For further information about holy sites and faith-refreshing parables, interested devotees of Rasūl should study the book '*Āshiqān-e-Rasūl kī Ḥikāyatayn ma' Makkay Madīnay kī Ziyāratayn*' published by Maktaba-tul-Madīnaĥ, the publishing department of Dawat-e-Islami. Your Īmān will be refreshed. However, not everyone is able enough to get to these holy sites just by reading about them from this book.

There are two ways to visit these sites. Firstly, you can get to these sites via vehicles available outside Masjid-un-Nabawī where every morning the drivers consistently shout 'Ziyāraĥ Ziyāraĥ.' The vehicle will take you to the five Masājid, Masjid Qubā and the resting place of Sayyidunā Ḥamzaĥ رَضِیَ اللّٰہُ تَعَالٰی عَنْہُ.

Secondly, if you wish to visit further sites of Makkaĥ and Madīnaĥ, you will have to hire a person who is familiar with these sites.

صَلُّوْا عَلَی الْحَبِیْب   صَلَّی اللّٰہُ تَعَالٰی عَلٰی مُحَمَّد

◆◆◆

اَلْحَمْدُ لِلّٰهِ رَبِّ الْعٰلَمِيْنَ وَ الصَّلٰوةُ وَالسَّلَامُ عَلٰى سَيِّدِ الْمُرْسَلِيْنَ
اَمَّا بَعْدُ فَاَعُوْذُ بِاللّٰهِ مِنَ الشَّيْطٰنِ الرَّجِيْمِ ط بِسْمِ اللّٰهِ الرَّحْمٰنِ الرَّحِيْمِ ط

Offences and their Expiations

Keep in mind some essential terms etc. prior to studying rulings described in the form of questions & answers.

Definition of *Dam** etc.

1. ***Dam:*** A *Dam* (dʌm) implies one goat (male or female, sheep, ram or the seventh part of a cow or camel).

2. **Badanaĥ:** A Badanaĥ implies a camel or a cow (including a bull and a buffalo etc.). All these animals must be of the qualities required for the ritual sacrifice (performed on Eid-ul-Aḍḥā).

3. **Ṣadaqaĥ:** A Ṣadaqaĥ implies the amount of one Ṣadaqaĥ Fiṭr[1].

Leniency in *Dam* etc.

If the offence occurs due to sickness or severe heat or cold or wound or blisters/boils or the extreme discomfort caused by lice; this is called an 'unintentional offence.' If such an unintentional offence occurs that makes *Dam* Wājib, there is the option in this case either

* In this book, the word '*Dam*' has been used in the sense of an expiation with its pronunciation as 'dʌm.' It must not be pronounced as 'dæm.' Note that this word has been italicized in the whole book with its '*D*' capitalized. [Translator's Note]

[1] The amount of one Ṣadaqaĥ Fiṭr is 1.920 kilograms of wheat or its flour or the money equivalent to the value of this much wheat or 3.840 kilograms of barley or dates or the money equivalent to it.

to pay *Dam* or donate Ṣadaqaĥ to six Masākīn instead of *Dam*. If six Ṣadaqāt are donated to the same Miskīn[1], it will be considered as one Ṣadaqaĥ. Therefore, it is necessary to give six Ṣadaqāt to six different Masākīn.

The second option is that six Masākīn can be provided with two full meals (such that they are full) instead of paying *Dam*. The third option is that if he does not want to donate Ṣadaqaĥ etc., he can observe three fasts; thus his *Dam* will get paid. If such an unintentional offence occurs that makes Ṣadaqaĥ Wājib, then there is the choice either to pay Ṣadaqaĥ or keep one fast instead.

(Mulakhkhaṣ az: Baĥār-e-Sharī'at, vol. 1, pp. 1162)

Important rulings regarding *Dam*, Ṣadaqaĥ and fasts

In case of observing expiatory fast, it is a condition that its intention must be made within the night, i.e. before Ṣubḥ-e-Ṣādiq. The intention may be made in these words: '*I am going to observe fast for such and such expiation.*' Iḥrām is not a condition for these fasts. Similarly, it is also not a condition to observe such fasts consecutively.

The act of donating Ṣadaqaĥ and that of observing the fast may be performed in one's own country as well. However, it is preferable to donate Ṣadaqaĥ and food to the Masākīn of Ḥaram. It is a condition that the animal for *Dam* and Badanaĥ be slaughtered within Ḥaram.

Rulings for sacrifice of Hajj and meat of animal of *Dam*

It is a condition for the sacrifice performed in gratitude to Hajj that it be performed within the limits of Ḥaram. The meat of this animal can be eaten by the sacrifice-performing person as well as the rich and the poor, but that of the one slaughtered to pay *Dam* or Badanaĥ

[1] A Miskīn is the one who does not possess anything and who has to beg others for food or clothes for covering the body. Begging is Ḥalāl (allowed) for him.

etc. can only be eaten by the deserving people. The expiation-paying person and the Ghanī people cannot eat it.

(Mulakhkhaṣ az: Bahār-e-Sharī'at, vol. 1, pp. 1162-1163)

Whether it is the sacrifice of *Dam* or gratitude, there is no harm in taking the meat out of Ḥaram after the slaughter but it is essential that the animal be slaughtered within the limits of Ḥaram.

Fear Allah عَزَّوَجَلَّ

I have observed that people deliberately commit the 'offence' but do not pay the expiation. This act of theirs leads them to committing two sins: (i) committing the offence deliberately and (ii) not paying the expiation.

Therefore, they must pay the expiation, and repentance will also be Wājib for them. However, if an offence occurs unknowingly or under coercion or by mistake, just expiation is enough in this case, repentance is not Wājib. Further, it must also be remembered that whether the offence occurs deliberately or by mistake, knowingly or unknowingly, willingly or under coercion, whilst one is asleep or awake, unconscious or conscious and whether one commits the offence himself or causes someone else to do it, expiation must be paid. If the expiation is not paid, it will be a sin.

When it comes to paying for the offence, some people even say: '*Allah* عَزَّوَجَلَّ *will forgive us*', and then they do not pay *Dam* etc. Such people should remember the fact that paying *Dam* etc. has been declared Wājib by Sharī'aĥ, and evading *Dam* etc. deliberately is non-compliance with Sharī'aĥ, which is itself a severe sin. Some wealth-loving unwise Ḥujjāj even ask such a question as: It is just a sin, *Dam* is not Wājib (مَعَاذَاللّٰه). Alas! All they are concerned about is to save a few coins only ignoring the fact that they have deserved a severe torment due to the sin. To trivialize a sin leads to serious consequences and even Kufr in some cases. May Allah عَزَّوَجَلَّ bless us all with a Madanī mindset!

آمِیْن بِجَاہِ النَّبِیِّ الْاَمِیْن صَلَّی اللّٰہُ تَعَالٰی عَلَیْہِ وَاٰلِہٖ وَسَلَّم

Double expiation for Qārin

A Qārin has to pay two expiations in all the cases in which there is the commandment of one expiation (i.e. a *Dam* or a Ṣadaqaĥ). *(Ĥidāyaĥ, vol. 1, pp. 171)* If a minor commits an offence, there is no expiation.

Details of double expiation for Qārin

Many books contain the ruling that two *Dams* or Ṣadaqāt become due for a Qārin in such cases where one *Dam* or Ṣadaqaĥ becomes Wājib for a Mufrid or Mutamatte'. Although this ruling is correct, it applies only in certain conditions. In other words, it is not so that two *Dams* would be declared due for a Qārin in each and every case where one *Dam* will become due for a Mufrid or Mutamatte'. Therefore, the full details of this ruling are being given below so that there is no misconception.

Here is a summary of what 'Allāmaĥ Shāmī قُدِّسَ سِرُّہُ السَّامِی has stated in this context: If a Mufrid commits any of such acts declared Ḥarām because of being in the state of Iḥrām, he is required to pay one *Dam*, whereas if a Qārin or the one considered Qārin in terms of rulings commits such an act, he is required to pay two *Dams*. The same ruling will apply as regards Ṣadaqaĥ, i.e. a Qārin will have to pay two Ṣadaqāt because he has put on the Iḥrām of both Hajj and 'Umraĥ.

However, if a Qārin misses any of the Wājib acts of Hajj – for example, if he has missed Sa'ī or Ramī or has performed the Ṭawāf of Hajj or 'Umraĥ in the state of uncleanness or without Wuḍū or has cut the grass of Ḥaram – double expiation will not be imposed on him in these cases because these acts are forbidden not because of Iḥrām but rather these are forbidden in Ḥaram and are Wājib in Hajj and 'Umraĥ.

'Allāmaĥ 'Alī Qārī عَلَيۡهِ رَحۡمَةُ اللّٰهِ الۡبَارِى has stated full details of this ruling: Under the rules, if a Mufrid commits any of such acts forbidden due to Iḥrām he is required to pay one *Dam* or Ṣadaqaĥ. If a Qārin or the one considered Qārin in terms of rulings commits such an act he has to pay two *Dams* or Ṣadaqāt because of putting on the Iḥrām of both Hajj and 'Umraĥ but there are certain conditions in which even a Qārin is required to pay only one *Dam* or Ṣadaqaĥ etc. (The reason for it is that those certain acts are not forbidden due to Iḥrām.)

1. If a person intending to perform Hajj and 'Umraĥ passes Mīqāt without Iḥrām and puts on Iḥrām of Hajj Qirān at the place where he has reached instead of coming back, he is required to pay only *Dam* because he has committed a forbidden act before he had put on the Iḥrām of Hajj Qirān.

2. If a Qārin or the one considered Qārin in terms of rulings has cut a tree of Ḥaram, he is required to pay only one penalty because cutting trees of Ḥaram is not forbidden because of Iḥrām.

3. If a person who has made a Shar'ī vow to go to perform Hajj or 'Umraĥ on foot departed on some conveyance to perform Hajj Qirān, for example, during the days of Hajj he is required to pay one *Dam* (because of travelling by the vehicle).

4. If someone performed Ṭawāf-uz-Ziyāraĥ in the state of uncleanness or without Wuḍū, only one penalty will be paid because the acts forbidden in Ṭawāf-uz-Ziyāraĥ are confined

to Hajj only. Likewise, if a person performing only 'Umraĥ performed the Ṭawāf of 'Umraĥ in the abovementioned state, he is to pay only one penalty (*Dam* or Ṣadaqaĥ).

5. If a Qārin or the one considered Qārin in terms of rulings returned from 'Arafāt before the Imām without any valid reason, and the sun has not yet set, he is required to pay one *Dam* because this is one of the Wājib acts of Hajj and has nothing to do with the Iḥrām of 'Umraĥ.

6. If a Qārin or the one considered Qārin in terms of rulings did not perform the ritual stay in Muzdalifaĥ without any valid reason, he is required to pay one *Dam*.

7. If he gets Ḥalq done without slaughtering the animal, he is required to pay one *Dam*.

8. If he gets Ḥalq done after the days of ritual sacrifice have passed, he is required to pay one *Dam*.

9. If he slaughtered the animal of ritual sacrifice after the days of ritual sacrifice have passed, he is required to pay one *Dam*.

10. If he did not perform Ramī at all or missed so much part of it which makes it obligatory to pay *Dam* or Ṣadaqaĥ, he is required to pay one *Dam* or Ṣadaqaĥ.

11. If he missed the Sa'ī of either 'Umraĥ or Hajj, he is required to pay one *Dam*.

12. If he missed Ṭawāf-e-Ṣadr (i.e. farewell Ṭawāf), he is required to pay one *Dam* because this is related to the Āfāqī Ḥājī and has nothing to do with the 'Umraĥ-performing person.

Note: The rule of two penalties described above applies to every such person who has 'gathered' two Iḥrāms irrespective of whether he has done so as a Sunnaĥ or not. For example, if a Mutamatte' has brought Ḥadī[1] or has not brought Ḥadī but has put on the Iḥrām of Hajj before being out of the Iḥrām of 'Umraĥ, he has gathered two Iḥrāms, which is a Sunnaĥ in this case. Two Iḥrāms can also be gathered without a Sunnaĥ. For instance, if the residents of Makkaĥ or those considered residents of Makkaĥ have put on the Iḥrām of Hajj Qirān, they have gathered two Iḥrāms.

Similarly, every such person who has gathered Iḥrāms of two Hajj or two 'Umraĥ with one intention or two intentions or has done so with one intention in the beginning but has added another intention later on, he has also gathered two Iḥrāms. In the same manner, if a person who has put on Iḥrām with the intention of performing hundred Hajj or hundred 'Umraĥ commits any offence before he has performed them, he is required to pay hundred penalties in this case. *(Al-Mutaqassiṭ lil-Qārī, pp. 406-410 Mulakhkhaṣan)*

Questions and answers about Ṭawāf-uz-Ziyāraĥ

Question 1: If a woman who was performing Ṭawāf-uz-Ziyāraĥ experienced menses during the Ṭawāf, what should she do?

Answer: She must discontinue the Ṭawāf instantly and get out of Masjid-ul-Ḥarām. If she continued the Ṭawāf or stayed within the Masjid, she would be sinner.

Question 2: What is the ruling if she experienced menses after she has performed four rounds of Ṭawāf? Also state the ruling if this happens before four rounds.

---

[1] Ḥadī is the animal brought to Ḥaram for ritual sacrifice.

Answer: If a woman experiences menses whilst performing Ṭawāf, she must discontinue the Ṭawāf immediately irrespective of whether she had performed four rounds or less than four. It is not permissible to perform Ṭawāf or stay in the Masjid in the state of menses. She must also get out of Masjid-ul-Ḥarām immediately. If possible, she should perform Tayammum before she exits the Masjid as it is safer to do so.

If she has experienced menses after she had performed four or more than four rounds, she must complete the same previously discontinued Ṭawāf after she has attained cleanness. If she experienced menses after three or less three rounds, she can still resume her previously discontinued Ṭawāf. If a woman who was aware of her routine of menses has experienced menses after performing three rounds of Ṭawāf, and she had so much time before experiencing menses that she could have performed four rounds but did not do, she is required to pay *Dam* in this case because of delaying four rounds. She would also be a sinner.

It is stated in *Baĥār-e-Sharī'at*, 'If she had so much time that she could perform Ṭawāf but did not do and has experienced menses or post-natal bleeding, she is a sinner. *(Baĥār-e-Sharī'at, vol. 1, pp. 1145)* However, if she has performed four rounds, she is not required to pay any penalty because of delaying three rounds because it is Wājib to perform most part of Ṭawāf-uz-Ziyāraĥ within its stipulated time, not whole of it.

It is stated in *Baĥār-e-Sharī'at*, 'It is one of the Wājib acts of Hajj to perform most part of Ṭawāf Ifāḍaĥ during the days of ritual sacrifice. The Ṭawāf performed on returning from 'Arafāt is called Ṭawāf Ifāḍaĥ and its other name is Ṭawāf-uz-Ziyāraĥ. If a person has performed most part within the stipulated time, he/she can perform the remaining part, i.e. three rounds even after the days of ritual sacrifice have passed. *(ibid, pp. 1049)*

If the woman experienced menses after she had performed four rounds and then she continued to perform the remaining three rounds (in the state of uncleanness) whether or not due to some compulsion, *Dam* will be due. The same ruling would apply if she left for her country after performing four rounds, missing three rounds without any reason. If she repeats the Ṭawāf performed in the state of menses, *Dam* will become void, though she repeats it after the days of ritual sacrifice have passed. If she has performed three rounds in the state of cleanness and the rest four in uncleanness, she is required to pay Badanaĥ. Furthermore, it is also Wājib to repeat this Ṭawāf.

It is stated in *Baĥār-e-Sharī'at*: If the whole of or most part, i.e. four rounds of a Farḍ Ṭawāf is performed in the state of uncleanness or menses or post-natal bleeding, Badanaĥ is due. Repetition is Wājib after the attainment of cleanness in this case. If it is done without Wuḍū, *Dam* is due. *(ibid, pp. 1175)* In case of repeating it after the attainment of cleanness, Badanaĥ will become void as stated above.

Ṭawāf-uz-Ziyāraĥ of menses-experiencing woman whose flight is booked

Question 3: What should a woman do if she is experiencing menses and has not yet performed Ṭawāf-uz-Ziyāraĥ while her seat for return flight has already been booked?

Answer: If possible, she should get the reservation of her seat cancelled and perform Ṭawāf-uz-Ziyāraĥ after attaining purity. If the cancellation of reservation causes difficulty for her or her travelling companions, she can perform Ṭawāf-uz-Ziyāraĥ in the same state because of compulsion, but Badanaĥ will be due to her. Further, it is also necessary for her to repent as entering the Masjid and performing the Ṭawāf in the state of uncleanness are both sin. If she succeeds in repeating Ṭawāf-uz-Ziyāraĥ after attaining purity from menses by the sunset of 12th Żul-Ḥijjaĥ, expiation will become void (i.e. Badanaĥ will no longer remain due to her). If she manages to repeat Ṭawāf-uz-Ziyāraĥ after purity after 12th Żul-Ḥijjaĥ, the expiation of Badanaĥ will become void but that of *Dam* will still be due to her.

Question 4: Some women take tablets to prevent menses during the usual days of their menstrual periods. Can a woman whose menses has ceased during the days of her usual menstrual periods as a result of taking anti-menses tablets perform Ṭawāf-uz-Ziyāraĥ?

Answer: She can do. (She should consult a lady doctor because sometimes the use of these tablets is harmful. If it is likely that immediate harm will be caused by these tablets, then they should not be used. However, the Ṭawāf performed when the menses have ceased is valid.)

Question 5: If someone performed Ṭawāf-uz-Ziyāraĥ in unclean clothes[1] or without Wuḍū, what would be the expiation?

Answer: If someone performed Ṭawāf-uz-Ziyāraĥ without Wuḍū, *Dam* will become Wājib. It is Mustaḥab to repeat it in the state of Wuḍū and *Dam* will also no longer remain Wājib in this case. Even if he repeated it after 12th Żul-Ḥijjaĥ, *Dam* will become void [not Wājib]. To perform any type of Ṭawāf in unclean clothes is Makrūĥ Tanzīĥī. If someone did so, there would be no expiation.

---

[1] Here 'unclean clothes' refer to the clothes with which any uncleanliness like urine etc. has come into contact to such an extent that offering Ṣalāĥ in those clothes is not allowed by Sharī'aĥ. [Translator's Note]

Very important point about intention of Ṭawāf

Question 6: A person reached Masjid-ul-Ḥarām on 10th Żul-Ḥijjaĥ to perform Ṭawāf-uz-Ziyāraĥ but made the intention of Nafl Ṭawāf by mistake; what should such a person do?

Answer: His Ṭawāf-uz-Ziyāraĥ has been performed. Keep in mind that though making an intention for Ṭawāf is Farḍ as Ṭawāf is not valid without it; making intention for a particular Ṭawāf is not a condition. Every Ṭawāf offered with mere intention of Ṭawāf is valid. Even during the specific time when a particular Ṭawāf is offered, if someone offered Ṭawāf with the intention of some other type of Ṭawāf, the offered Ṭawāf will be considered the particular Ṭawāf, not the intended one.

For example, someone wearing Iḥrām for 'Umraĥ came to Masjid-ul-Ḥarām from out of Mīqāt but performed Ṭawāf without the intention of Ṭawāf of 'Umraĥ or made the intention of just Ṭawāf or made the intention of Nafl Ṭawāf, his Ṭawāf will be considered the Ṭawāf for 'Umraĥ in all cases. Similarly, the very first Ṭawāf performed by a Qārin will be considered his Ṭawāf of 'Umraĥ and his second Ṭawāf will be Ṭawāf-ul-Qudūm. *(Al-Maslak-ul-Mutaqassiṭ lil-Qārī, pp. 145)*

Question 7: What is the expiation for the one who went to his country without performing Ṭawāf-uz-Ziyāraĥ?

Answer: Mere expiation will not be sufficient as his Hajj will not be valid in this case. There is no substitute for this. It is mandatory for such a person to return to Makkaĥ and perform Ṭawāf-uz-Ziyāraĥ. Unless he offers Ṭawāf-uz-Ziyāraĥ, his conjugal relations with his wife will not be permissible even if many years pass. If a married woman has committed this mistake, her conjugal relations with her husband will not be permissible unless she has offered Ṭawāf-uz-

Ziyāraĥ. If an unmarried man or woman has made this mistake, their conjugal relations with their spouses after they get married will not also be permissible unless they have offered Ṭawāf-uz-Ziyāraĥ.

Questions and answers about Ṭawāf-ur-Rukhṣat

Question 1: Can the person who has performed Ṭawāf-ur-Rukhṣat go to Masjid-ul-Ḥarām to offer Ṣalāĥ, if his departure is delayed? Is he required to perform Ṭawāf-ur-Rukhṣat again at the time of departure?

Answer: He can do so. Further, he can also perform as many 'Umraĥ and Ṭawāf as possible. It is not Wājib to repeat Ṭawāf-ur-Rukhṣat but it is Mustaḥab to do so. Ṣadr-ush-Sharī'aĥ رحمة الله تعالى عليه has stated: If a person has intended to depart and has performed Ṭawāf-ur-Rukhṣat but he had to stay due to some reason and has not intended to stay, the previously performed Ṭawāf is enough in this case but it is still Mustaḥab to perform Ṭawāf again so that the last act he performs is Ṭawāf.

(Baĥār-e-Sharī'at, vol. 1, pp. 1151; 'Ālamgīrī, vol. 1, pp. 234)

Important ruling of Ṭawāf-ur-Rukhṣat

Question 2: Having performed Hajj before leaving for his country, if a person has the intention of staying at the house of his relative in Jeddah for two days and then he has the intention of visiting Madīnaĥ, when should he perform Ṭawāf-ur-Rukhṣat?

Answer: He should perform Ṭawāf-ur-Rukhṣat before going to Jeddah. Any Nafl Ṭawāf offered after Ṭawāf-uz-Ziyāraĥ is considered Ṭawāf-ur-Rukhṣat as the time of Ṭawāf-ur-Rukhṣat for an Āfāqī Ḥājī starts right after Ṭawāf-uz-Ziyāraĥ. It has already been described that every type of Ṭawāf offered with the mere intention of Ṭawāf is valid. In short, if any Nafl Ṭawāf is offered after Ṭawāf-uz-Ziyāraĥ before departure, that Nafl Ṭawāf will be considered Ṭawāf-ur-Rukhṣat.

Question 3: If the menses of an Āfāqī woman starts at the time of departure, how should she deal with the matter of Ṭawāf-ur-Rukhṣat? Should she stay or leave after paying *Dam*?

Answer: Ṭawāf-ur-Rukhṣat is no longer Wājib for her. She can leave. There is no need to pay *Dam*.

(Derived from: Bahār-e-Sharī'at, vol. 1, pp. 1151)

Question 4: Is Ṭawāf-ur-Rukhṣat Wājib even for those living in Makkaĥ or Jeddah?

Answer: No. Ṭawāf-ur-Rukhṣat is Wājib at the time of departure only for Āfāqī Ḥujjāj, i.e. those coming from out of Mīqāt for performing Hajj.

Question 5: Is Ṭawāf-ur-Rukhṣat Wājib at the time of departure for those who have come to perform Hajj from Madīnaĥ?

Answer: It is Wājib for them to perform Ṭawāf-ur-Rukhṣat because they are Āfāqī Ḥājī. Madīnaĥ is situated out of Mīqāt.

Question 6: Is Ṭawāf-ur-Rukhṣat Wājib for the performer of 'Umraĥ?

Answer: No. It is Wājib for only Āfāqī Ḥājī at the time of departure.

Miscellaneous questions and answers about Ṭawāf

Question 1: If the chest or back of the one doing Ṭawāf turns towards the Ka'baĥ for a short duration unintentionally or due to crowd pressure, what should he do?

Answer: He should repeat the distance for which his chest or back faced the Ka'baĥ during Ṭawāf. It is preferable to repeat that round.

Raising hands when uttering Takbīr of Ṭawāf

Question 2: What is the Sunnaĥ of raising hands during the Takbīr of Ṭawāf in front of Ḥajar-ul-Aswad? Should a person raise his hands up to his ears or shoulders?

Answer: There are different verdicts of Islamic scholars in this regard. It is stated in *Fatāwā of Hajj and 'Umraĥ*: Men have to raise their hands up to their ears as they do to initiate Ṣalāĥ. As for women, they are to raise their hands up to their shoulders as they do in the beginning of Ṣalāĥ. *(Fatāwā Hajj-o-'Umraĥ, part 1, pp. 127)*

Question 3: How is it to perform Ṭawāf with hands folded as in Ṣalāĥ?

Answer: It is not Mustaḥab to do so. To avoid it is better.

What if one forgets the rounds during Ṭawāf?

Question 4: If someone forgets the number of rounds or is in doubt about the number of rounds during Ṭawāf, what is the solution to this problem?

Answer: If the Ṭawāf is Farḍ such as Ṭawāf-uz-Ziyāraĥ or Wājib such as Ṭawāf-ur-Rukhṣat, he has to perform Ṭawāf again from the beginning. If an honest person informs about the number of the rounds, it is better to believe what he has said. If two honest men inform, it is strongly advisable to believe them. If the Ṭawāf is neither Farḍ nor Wājib but, for example, if it is Ṭawāf-ul-Qudūm (that is Sunnaĥ for the Qārin and the Mufrid) or if it is any Nafl Ṭawāf, he should act according to his probable assumption on such an occasion. *(Rad-dul-Muḥtār, vol. 3, pp. 582)*

What if the Wuḍū invalidates during Ṭawāf?

Question 5: If someone's Wuḍū becomes invalid during the third round of Ṭawāf and he goes to make Wuḍū, how should he resume his Ṭawāf on return?

Answer: He may restart his Ṭawāf from the beginning. He is also allowed to resume from where he discontinued. This ruling is applicable only when Wuḍū becomes invalid during any of the first three rounds. If Wuḍū becomes invalid after one has performed four or more than four rounds one cannot restart Ṭawāf from the first round. Instead, he will have to resume from where he discontinued. It is also not necessary to resume from the direction of Ḥajar-ul-Aswad. *(Durr-e-Mukhtār, Rad-dul-Muḥtār, vol. 3, pp. 582)*

Important ruling of Ṭawāf for Ma'żūr Shar'ī

Question 6: If someone is Ma'żūr Shar'ī due to the problem of passing urine drops after urination, how long his Wuḍū for Ṭawāf will remain valid?

Answer: His Wuḍū will remain valid for as long as the time of that Ṣalāĥ is valid. Ṣadr-ush-Sharī'aĥ رَحْمَةُ اللّٰهِ تَعَالٰى عَلَيْه has stated: If the time of Ṣalāĥ ends after the Ma'żūr Shar'ī has performed four rounds of Ṭawāf, he is required to make Wuḍū and perform Ṭawāf as the Wuḍū of a Ma'żūr Shar'ī person becomes invalid after the time of Ṣalāĥ ends. It is Ḥarām to perform Ṭawāf without Wuḍū. Therefore, he must make Wuḍū and perform the remaining rounds of Ṭawāf. If the time of Ṣalāĥ ends before he has performed four rounds, he is still required to make Wuḍū and perform the remaining rounds. It is preferable in the latter case to perform the Ṭawāf from beginning. *(Bahār-e-Sharī'at, vol. 1, pp. 1101; Al-Maslak-ul-Mutaqassiṭ, pp. 167)*

Remember that only the discharge of urine drops after urination does not render a person Ma'żūr Shar'ī. It has great details. To know details about this issue, please study the book '*Laws of Ṣalāĥ*' (from page 24 to 26) published by Maktaba-tul-Madīnaĥ, the publishing department of Dawat-e-Islami.

Ruling for Nafl Ṭawāf performed by woman experiencing menses

Question 7: If a woman has performed Nafl Ṭawāf when experiencing menses, what is the ruling for her?

Answer: She has become a sinner, and it is Wājib for her to pay a *Dam*. 'Allāmaĥ Shāmī قُدِّسَ سِرُّهُ السَّامِى has stated: If a woman has performed a Nafl Ṭawāf in the state of menses or uncleanness [when Ghusl is Farḍ for her], she is required to pay a *Dam*. If she performed it without Wuḍū, she is to pay a Ṣadaqaĥ. *(Rad-dul-Muḥtār, vol. 3, pp. 661)*

If a person who had performed the Ṭawāf in the state of uncleanness or without Wuḍū repeats the Ṭawāf after he has attained cleanness or made Wuḍū, expiation will become void. However, if someone has deliberately done so, he will have to repent of it as it is a sin to perform the Ṭawāf during menses or without Wuḍū.

Question 8: If someone started eighth round considering it the seventh one but he recalled during the eighth round that it is eighth, what should he do now?

Answer: He should end his Ṭawāf during the same (eighth) round. However, if someone started eighth round deliberately, it will amount to the commencement of a new Ṭawāf and, therefore, all the seven rounds of the new Ṭawāf will have to be completed. *(ibid, pp. 581)*

Question 9: If one round of the Ṭawāf for 'Umraĥ is missed, what will be the expiation?

Answer: Ṭawāf for 'Umraĥ is Farḍ. If even one round of Ṭawāf for 'Umraĥ is missed, *Dam* will be Wājib. If Ṭawāf is not performed at all or most (i.e. four or more than four) rounds are missed, there will be no expiation but it is mandatory to perform the Ṭawāf or the remaining four rounds as the case may be. *(Lubāb-ul-Manāsik, pp. 353)*

Question 10: What is the penalty for the Qārin or the Mufrid who has missed Ṭawāf-ul-Qudūm?

Answer: Though there is no expiation, doing so is the abandonment of Sunnat-ul-Muakkadaĥ, which is disliked.

(Lubāb-ul-Manāsik & Al-Maslak-ul-Mutaqassiṭ, pp. 352)

Ruling of performing Ṭawāf on the first or second floor of Masjid-ul-Ḥarām

Question 11: How is it to perform Ṭawāf on the roof of Masjid-ul-Ḥarām?

Answer: The Farḍ Ṭawāf of the Holy Ka'baĥ performed on the roof of Masjid-ul-Ḥarām is valid provided there is no wall in between [the Ṭawāf-performing person and the Holy Ka'baĥ]. However, if there is enough space in the Maṭāf of the ground floor, it is Makrūĥ in this case to perform Ṭawāf on the roof because climbing or walking over the roof of the Masjid unnecessarily is Makrūĥ.

Furthermore, the person performing Ṭawāf on the roof of Masjid-ul-Ḥarām remains away from the Holy Ka'baĥ instead of remaining closer to it besides facing needless hardships and tiredness. It is preferable to remain close to the Holy Ka'baĥ during Ṭawāf and it is forbidden to inflict needless hardship on oneself. However, if there is no space on the ground floor or one cannot delay performing Ṭawāf due to some Shar'ī reason, the Ṭawāf performed on the roof is permissible without it being Makrūĥ, i.e. there is no harm in it in this case. وَاللّٰهُ تَعَالٰى اَعْلَم *(Māĥnāmaĥ Ashrafiyaĥ, June 2005, 11th Fiqĥī Seminar, pp. 14)*

How is it to recite Munājāt aloud during Ṭawāf

Question 12: How is it to make Du'ā or recite Munājāt or Na'at etc. loudly during Ṭawāf?

Answer: To recite Munājāt etc. so loudly that the voice causes inconvenience to other Ṭawāf-performing or Ṣalāĥ-offering people is Makrūĥ Taḥrīmī, impermissible and a sin. However, there is no harm in reciting it in a low voice provided no one is inconvenienced by it. There is a matter of concern for those whose mobile ringtones cause great inconvenience to worshippers during Ṭawāf. They should repent. Remember that these rulings apply not only to Masjid-ul-Ḥarām but also to all other Masājid and places. Musical ringtone is impermissible even if one is not in Masjid.

Questions and answers about Iḍṭibā' and Raml

Question 1: If someone forgot to perform Raml during the first round of the Ṭawāf performed before Sa'ī, what should he do?

Answer: Performing Raml is Sunnaĥ during the first three rounds only. It is Makrūĥ to perform it during every round. Therefore, if someone forgets to perform Raml during the first round, he should perform it during the second and third rounds. If Raml is missed during the first two rounds, it should be done during the third round. If it is not performed during the first three rounds, it can no longer be performed during the rest four rounds.

(Durr-e-Mukhtār, Rad-dul-Muḥtār, vol. 3, pp. 583)

Question 2: If Iḍṭibā' and Raml are not performed during the Ṭawāf in which these are to be performed, what will be the expiation?

Answer: Though there is no expiation for missing Iḍṭibā' and Raml, it is deprivation from a great Sunnaĥ.

Question 3: How is it to perform Raml during all the seven rounds?

Answer: It is Makrūĥ Tanzīĥī. However, there is no expiation for it. *(Rad-dul-Muḥtār, vol. 3, pp. 584)*

Questions and answers about Sa'ī

Question 1: If a Ḥājī returned to his country without performing Sa'ī at all, what should he do now?

Answer: Sa'ī is Wājib for Hajj. Therefore, *Dam* would be Wājib for the one who did not perform Sa'ī at all or missed four or more than four rounds of Sa'ī. If he missed less than four rounds, he has to give a Ṣadaqaĥ for each missed round. *(Baĥār-e-Sharī'at, vol. 1, pp. 1177)*

Question 2: If a person who has missed the Sa'ī of Hajj and returned to his country without paying *Dam* is granted the privilege of performing Hajj again after two years by the grace of Allah عَزَّوَجَلَّ, can he now perform the Sa'ī he missed two years back?

Answer: He can perform the missed Sa'ī, and *Dam* will also become void in this case but one should not return to his country without performing Sa'ī thinking that he would perform it later on because anyone can meet his death anytime. Even if he has remained alive, there is no guarantee that he would visit these holy places again.

Question 3: After performing four rounds of Sa'ī for Hajj, if someone took off Iḥrām (i.e. he got Ḥalq done, giving up the observance of the restrictions of Iḥrām) what should he do now?

Answer: He must give three Ṣadaqāt. However, if he performs the remaining three rounds even after Ḥalq etc., expiation will become void. Remember! The period of Hajj or Iḥrām is not a precondition for Sa'ī. If a person who has not performed Sa'ī performs it any time in his lifetime, his Wājib will be fulfilled (and he will no longer be required to pay the expiation).

Question 4: If someone performed Sa'ī before Ṭawāf, what should he do now?

Answer: Ṣadr-ush-Sharī'aĥ رَحْمَةُ اللهِ تَعَالٰی عَلَیْه has stated: It is a condition to perform Sa'ī after the whole of or most part of Ṭawāf has been performed. Therefore, if performed before Ṭawāf or after three rounds of it, Sa'ī will not be valid. It is also a condition that Iḥrām starts before Sa'ī whether it is the Iḥrām of Hajj or that of 'Umraĥ.

In short, Sa'ī cannot be performed before Iḥrām. If someone performs the Sa'ī of Hajj before the ritual stay in 'Arafaĥ, it is a condition to perform Sa'ī in the state of Iḥrām. If he performs Sa'ī after the ritual stay in 'Arafaĥ, it is a Sunnaĥ in this case to perform Sa'ī after he has taken off Iḥrām. As for the Sa'ī of 'Umraĥ, it is Wājib to perform it in Iḥrām. That is, if he gets his head shaved after Ṭawāf and then performs Sa'ī, the Sa'ī will be valid but *Dam* will be Wājib because of missing a Wājib act. *(Baĥār-e-Sharī'at, vol. 1, pp. 1109)*

Questions and answers about kissing and caressing

Question 1: How is it to touch wife in the state of Iḥrām?

Answer: Touching wife without lust is permissible but holding her hands or touching her body with lust is Ḥarām. If someone lustfully kisses his wife or caresses her body, *Dam* will be Wājib for him. Whether these actions are done to a woman or an Amrad [a beardless beautiful boy] there is the same ruling. *(Durr-e-Mukhtār, Rad-dul-Muḥtār, vol. 3, pp. 667)* If the wife who is in the state of Iḥrām also feels lust during these actions of her husband, she will also have to pay *Dam*. *(Baĥār-e-Sharī'at, vol. 1, pp. 1173)*

Question 2: If someone has lustful thoughts or looks at someone else's private part and ejaculates, what will be the expiation?

Answer: There will be no expiation in this case. *('Ālamgīrī, vol. 1, pp. 244)* As for taking a glance at a non-Maḥram woman or an Amrad or having lustful thoughts about them, this is a Ḥarām act leading to

Hell even when one is not in the state of Iḥrām. If these filthy thoughts come into someone's mind, he should reject them instead of enjoying them. These rulings are the same for women.

Question 3: Is there any expiation, if nocturnal emission takes place in the state of Iḥrām.

Answer: There is no expiation. *('Ālamgīrī, vol. 1, pp. 244)*

Question 4: Allah عَزَّوَجَلَّ forbid, if a Muḥrim commits masturbation, what will be the expiation?

Answer: If ejaculation takes place as a result of masturbation, *Dam* will be Wājib, otherwise, it is Makrūĥ. *(ibid)* This is a shameful, impermissible and Ḥarām act leading to Hell irrespective of whether or not one is in the state of Iḥrām.

A'lā Ḥaḍrat رَحْمَةُ اللهِ تَعَالٰى عَلَيْه has said: On the Day of Judgement, those who masturbate will be resurrected with their palms pregnant, and thus will be disgraced in front of a great multitude of people. *(Mulakhkhaṣ az: Fatāwā Razawiyyaĥ, vol. 22, pp. 244)*

An important question

Question 5: If someone feels lust while shaking hands with Amrad[1] what is the penalty?

Answer: *Dam* will be Wājib. There is no specification for Amrad & non-Amrad in this matter. If both felt lust, and the other is also a Muḥrim, he must also pay *Dam*.

---

[1] If one feels lust due to seeing or touching a boy or man, it is mandatory to stay away from such a person irrespective of whether or not one is in the state of Iḥrām. If lust intensifies as a result of shaking hands with him or touching or talking to him, then all these acts are not permissible. For detailed information about it, study the booklet '*Abuses of the People of Lūṭ*' published by Maktaba-tul-Madīnah, the publishing department of Dawat-e-Islami.

Walking hand in hand with wife

Question 6: If the husband and the wife when performing Ṭawāf or Sa'ī hand in hand with each other feel lust, what will be the ruling?

Answer: *Dam* will become Wājib for the one who feels lust. If both of them have felt lust, both will have to pay a *Dam* each. If men holding each others' hands in the state of Iḥrām feel lust, there is the same ruling.

Questions and answers about intercourse

Question 1: Can Hajj become even invalid due to intercourse?

Answer: Yes. If a Muḥrim indulges in intercourse prior to the ritual stay in 'Arafāt, his Hajj will become invalid. He will have to pay *Dam* and perform Hajj again as Qaḍā the very next year besides performing the remaining rites of that invalid Hajj as usual. *('Ālamgīrī, vol. 1, pp. 244)*

If the woman is also a Muḥrimaĥ, there is the same expiation for her. If there is a risk of indulging in this act once again, it is advisable to stay away from each other avoiding even seeing each other from the commencement of the Iḥrām of Qaḍā to its end.

(Baĥār-e-Sharī'at, vol. 1, pp. 1173)

Question 2: If a person who is unaware of rulings indulges in intercourse in ignorance, then?

Answer: Whether someone indulges in intercourse forgetfully or intentionally, willingly or under coercion, Hajj will become invalid in all the cases and *Dam* will have to be paid. If he has intercourse again at another time, another *Dam* will be Wājib. However, *Dam* will not be Wājib if he abandons the intention of Hajj prior to his indulgence in intercourse.

Question 3: Does the 'Iḥrām' of a Ḥājī become invalid owing to intercourse?

Answer: No. Iḥrām still exists as usual (i.e. the restrictions of Iḥrām are still to be observed). The acts that were impermissible for the Muḥrim before are impermissible even after having intercourse. All other rulings still apply. *(Baĥār-e-Sharī'at, vol. 1, pp. 1175)*

Question 4: If someone's Hajj becomes invalid and he puts on a new Iḥrām instantly for the Hajj of the very same year, then?

Answer: He will neither be exempted from expiation nor will his Hajj of this year be valid as it had already become invalid. In any way, he would not be able to skip the Qaḍā of Hajj the following year. *(ibid)*

Question 5: Can a Mutamatte' who has removed his Iḥrām having performed 'Umraĥ have intercourse with his wife, whereas many days are still left in the commencement of Hajj-rites?

Answer: He may do so as long as he has not put on Iḥrām for Hajj.

Question 6: If someone has intercourse with his wife having put on the Iḥrām for 'Umraĥ before performing Ṭawāf etc., what is the expiation in this case?

Answer: If he has intercourse with his wife before performing four rounds of Ṭawāf, his 'Umraĥ will become invalid in this case. He has to redo the 'Umraĥ and pay *Dam*. If he does so after performing four or more than four rounds of Ṭawāf, his 'Umraĥ will be valid. However, he will still have to pay *Dam*. *(Durr-e-Mukhtār, vol. 3, pp. 676)*

Question 7: Is there any penalty for the Mu'tamir (i.e. the person performing 'Umraĥ) who has intercourse having performed Ṭawāf and Sa'ī but before getting Ḥalq done?

Answer: Yes. He has to pay *Dam*. His conjugal relations with his wife will be permissible only after getting Ḥalq or Qaṣr done.

Questions and answers about cutting nails

Question 1: If a person who is unaware of this ruling cuts the nails of his both hands and feet in ignorance, is there any leniency for him?

Answer: On such an occasion, ignorance is not an excuse. Whether someone commits an offence forgetfully or deliberately, willingly or under coercion, he will have to pay expiation in all cases. Ṣadr-ush-Sharī'aĥ رَحْمَةُ اللهِ تَعَالٰی عَلَيْه has stated: If he has trimmed all five nails of one hand and one foot or all twenty nails of both hands and both feet in one sitting, he will be required to give one *Dam*. If he has trimmed less than five nails of a hand or foot, he is required to pay a Ṣadaqaĥ for each trimmed nail. Even if he has trimmed four nails of each hand and each foot, he has to pay sixteen Ṣadaqāt. However, if the amount of sixteen Ṣadaqāt is equivalent to that of a *Dam*, he can pay a little less than the amount of *Dam* or he is allowed to pay *Dam*. If he has trimmed all five nails of one hand or those of one foot in one sitting and all five nails of the other in another sitting, two *Dam* will be Wājib for him. Likewise, if he has trimmed the nails of both hands and both feet in four different sittings, four *Dam* will be Wājib for him. *(Baĥār-e-Sharī'at, vol. 1, pp. 1172; 'Ālamgīrī, vol. 1, pp. 344)*

Question 2: If a person trims nails with his teeth, what is the penalty?

Answer: Whether one cuts nails with his teeth or a razor or a knife or nail-clipper, the ruling is the same. *(Baĥār-e-Sharī'at, vol. 1, pp. 1172)*

Question 3: Can a Muḥrim cut the nails of someone else?

Answer: No, he cannot. The ruling is the same as for shaving someone else's hair. *(Al-Maslak-ul-Mutaqassiṭ lil-Qārī, pp. 332)*

Questions and answers about removal of hair

Question 1: Allah عَزَّوَجَلَّ forbid! If a Muḥrim shaves his beard, what is the penalty?

Answer: Shaving or trimming the beard less than a fist-length is a Ḥarām act leading to Hell. It is even more strictly Ḥarām in the state of Iḥrām in which not even the hair of head can be cut.

Ṣadr-ush-Sharī'aĥ رَحْمَةُاللهِ تَعَالٰى عَلَيْه has stated: If the Muḥrim has removed hair from one fourth part of his head or beard more than it, he is required to pay a *Dam*. If the hair is removed from less than one fourth part of the head, Ṣadaqaĥ is due. If the Muḥrim has less hair in his beard, and has removed all hair that is equivalent to the one fourth part of a full beard, *Dam* is due, otherwise Ṣadaqaĥ. If the Muḥrim has removed a little amount of hair from different places of his head, and the total amount of removed hair is equivalent to the one fourth part of the head, *Dam* will be Wājib, otherwise Ṣadaqaĥ. *(Bahār-e-Sharī'at, vol. 1, pp. 1170; Rad-dul-Muḥtār, vol. 3, pp. 659)*

Question 2: Can a woman crop her hair?

Answer: No. If she crops the hair of a quarter of her head or that of her whole head equal to a finger digit in length, she will have to pay *Dam*. In case of cropping the hair by less than a finger digit in length, she will have to pay Ṣadaqaĥ. *(Lubāb-ul-Manāsik, pp. 327)*

Question 3: If a Muḥrim has removed pubic hair or that of the neck or the armpit, what is the ruling?

Answer: If he has removed hair from the whole of the neck or from the whole of one armpit, he is required to pay a *Dam*. If he has removed hair from half of or even more than half of but less than the whole of any of these parts, he is to pay a Ṣadaqaĥ. The same ruling applies to pubic hair. Even if he has removed hair from both armpits, he is to pay only *Dam*. *(Baĥār-e-Sharī'at, vol. 1, pp. 1170; Durr-e-Mukhtār, Rad-dul-Muḥtār, vol. 3, pp. 659)*

Question 4: If a person gets shaved the hair of his head, beard and armpits etc. in one sitting, how many expiations will he have to pay?

Answer: Only one *Dam* will be Wājib even if all the hair of the whole body from head to toe is removed in one sitting. However, if the hair of different body-parts is removed in different sittings, *Dam* will be Wājib according to the number of sittings.

(Durr-e-Mukhtār, Rad-dul-Muḥtār, vol. 3, pp. 659-661)

Question 5: If hair falls during Wuḍū, is there any expiation for it?

Answer: Of course. If Muḥrim's 2 or 3 strands of hairs fall during Wuḍū or due to scratching the body or combing hair, he is to donate a handful of grain or a piece of bread or a date as charity for each fallen hair. If more than three hairs fall, he will have to pay Ṣadaqaĥ. *(Baĥār-e-Sharī'at, vol. 1, pp. 1171)*

Question 6: If some of the hairs of a Muḥrim are burnt by the fire of the stove while cooking food, then?

Answer: He will have to pay Ṣadaqaĥ. *(ibid)*

Question 7: If a Muḥrim gets his moustache shaved, what is the expiation?

Answer: Whether he gets his whole moustache shaved or gets it trimmed, he will have to pay Ṣadaqaĥ. *(ibid)*

Question 8: If someone gets the hair of his chest shaved, what should he do?

Answer: Except the hair of head, beard, neck, armpit and that of under-navel, if one gets the hair of any other part of his body shaved, he will have to pay Ṣadaqaĥ only. *(ibid)*

Question 9: Is there any leniency for the person whose hair falls involuntarily out of the disease of hair-falling?

Answer: There will be no expiation even if, without him touching the hair, all of his hair falls involuntarily or due to illness. *(ibid)*

Question 10: What will be the expiation, if a Muḥrim shaves another Muḥrim's head?

Answer: If the time for the removal of Iḥrām has arrived, both of them may shave each others' hair. If the time for the removal of Iḥrām has not yet arrived, there will be different rulings with regard to expiation. If a Muḥrim shaves another Muḥrim's head, expiation will be due not only for the one whose head was shaved but the one who shaved the head will also have to pay Ṣadaqaĥ. If a Muḥrim shaves the head of a non-Muḥrim (the one who is not in the state of Iḥrām) or trims his moustache or nails, (the Muḥrim) should give some charity to the Masākīn. *(Bahār-e-Sharī'at, vol. 1, pp. 1142, 1171)*

Question 11: Can a non-Muḥrim shave the head of a Muḥrim or not?

Answer: He cannot do so before its proper time. If he does so, expiation will become due not only for the Muḥrim, but the non-Muḥrim will also have to pay Ṣadaqaĥ. *(ibid, pp. 1171)*

Question 12: What is the ruling if a Muḥrim has removed his hair with depilatory [i.e. hair-removing] powder or cream?

Answer: It is stated in *Bahār-e-Sharī'at*: The ruling is the same whether hair is shaved, cut, trimmed or removed using anything. *(ibid)*

Questions and answers about use of perfume

Question 1: In the state of Iḥrām, if a person took the bottle of perfume in his hand, causing some fragrance to come into contact with his hand, is there any expiation for it?

Answer: Seeing this, if people comment that a lot of fragrance has come into contact with hand, *Dam* will be Wājib even if it is in contact with a small part. If very little amount of fragrance comes into contact with the body, Ṣadaqaĥ will become due.

(Baĥār-e-Sharī'at, vol. 1, pp. 1163)

Question 2: If a Muḥrim applies fragrant oil into his head, what should he do?

Answer: If fragrance comes into contact with the whole of a big part of the body such as thigh, face, shin or head, *Dam* will be Wājib irrespective of whether it happens out of applying fragrant oil or scent. *(ibid)*

Question 3: If fragrance comes into contact with bedding or Iḥrām or someone else applies it to them, what should be done?

Answer: The amount of fragrance should be observed. If the amount of fragrance is much, *Dam* will be due; if the amount is less, Ṣadaqaĥ will be due.

Question 4: If fragrance is applied to the carpet, bedding, pillow or shawl, etc. of lodging, what should Muḥrim do?

Answer: The Muḥrim should avoid using them. If he did not take care, resulting in the fragrance coming into contact with any of his body parts, there will be two different rulings depending upon the amount of fragrance. If the amount of fragrance that has come into contact is much, *Dam* will be Wājib; if it is less, Ṣadaqaĥ will be

Wājib. If no fragrance has come into contact with any of the body parts of Muḥrim, no expiation will be due. However, it is still better to avoid such things. The Muḥrim should talk to the landlord to provide any other lodging or alternatively he can spread an odourless shawl over the floor or bedding. Similarly, he can change the covering of the pillow or wrap it in some odourless sheet.

Question 5: After Muḥrim has made the intention of Iḥrām, is it necessary for him to remove the fragrance applied to the body before the intention of Iḥrām?

Answer: No. Ṣadr-ush-Sharī'aĥ رَحْمَةُ اللهِ تَعَالٰى عَلَيْه has stated: If the fragrance applied to the body before the intention of Iḥrām spreads, coming into contact with other parts of the body after the intention of Iḥrām, no expiation is due. *(Baĥār-e-Sharī'at, vol. 1, pp. 1163)*

Question 6: If the Muḥrim is wearing a bag or belt with a bottle of fragrance in its pocket before he has made the intention of Iḥrām, is it necessary for him to take the bottle out after he has made the intention of Iḥrām? If the fragrance from the bottle of fragrance comes into contact with the hand, will expiation be due in this case?

Answer: It is not necessary to take the bottle out of the bag or the belt after he has made the intention of Iḥrām. If this fragrance comes into contact with the hand etc. after the intention of Iḥrām, expiation will be due as it is not the fragrance applied to the body or clothes before the intention of Iḥrām.

Question 7: Before making the intention of Iḥrām, if someone is wearing a perfumed bag around his neck with a perfumed handkerchief and a perfumed rosary of Ṭawāf in the bag, can he use these things after the intention of Iḥrām?

Answer: To smell the fragrance of these things deliberately is Makrūĥ. However, it is allowed to use them provided the fragrance applied to them would not come into contact with the Iḥrām or the body but it is obviously very difficult to protect the body or the Iḥrām from fragrance when using rosary or handkerchief. Therefore, it is safer to avoid using these things.

Question 8: Before making the intention of Iḥrām, if someone puts fragrance-applied two or three extra shawls onto his lap or wears them and, after making the intention of Iḥrām, removes the extra ones; can he use those shawls in the state of that Iḥrām?

Answer: If the liquid form of the fragrance still exists, those shawls cannot be used. However, if no liquid form exists, only fragrance emanates from them, one can use them in this case but it is still Makrūĥ Tanzīĥī. Ṣadr-ush-Sharī'aĥ رَحْمَةُ اللهِ تَعَالٰى عَلَيْه has stated: If someone has applied fragrance to shawls etc. before the intention of Iḥrām and has used them in the state of Iḥrām, it is Makrūĥ to do so but no expiation will be due. *(ibid, pp. 1165)*

Question 9: If one or both the shawls of Iḥrām become unclean out of nocturnal emission or any other reason, two other shawls are available, but fragrance had been applied to them before, can Muḥrim use them?

Answer: If the liquid form of the fragrance or its coating still exists, Muḥrim cannot wear those shawls. If he wears them expiation will be due. However, if no coating of fragrance exists, Muḥrim can use them even if fragrance is emanating from them. However, it is still Makrūĥ Tanzīĥī to use such shawls without a Shar'ī reason. Islamic jurists have stated: It is impermissible in the state of Iḥrām to wear a piece of cloth that has a coating of fragrance on it.

('Ālamgīrī, vol. 1, pp. 222)

It is stated in *Baĥār-e-Sharī'at*: If he applied fragrance [to those shawls] before he put on Iḥrām and has put on those shawls in the state of Iḥrām, it is Makrūĥ to do so but no expiation is due.

(Baĥār-e-Sharī'at, vol. 1, pp. 1165)

Question 10: If fragrance comes into contact with a Muḥrim whilst he was kissing Ḥajar-ul-Aswad or touching Rukn Yamānī or clinging to Multazam, what should he do?

Answer: If a significant amount of fragrance has come into contact, *Dam* will have to be paid. If small amount of fragrance has come into contact Ṣadaqaĥ will have to be given. *(Baĥār-e-Sharī'at, vol. 1, pp. 1164)* (Muḥrim should make someone else judge whether much amount or small amount of fragrance has come into contact with him. As there is the expiation of *Dam* in case of much amount of fragrance coming into contact, Muḥrim's Nafs may well declare much amount as small amount.)

Question 11: Can a Muḥrim deliberately smell a fragrant flower or not?

Answer: No. It is Makrūĥ Tanzīĥī for the Muḥrim to deliberately smell fragrance or any fragrant thing. However, there is no expiation. *(ibid, pp. 1163)*

Question 12: How is it to eat uncooked cardamom or silver-coated seeds of cardamom?

Answer: No. It is Ḥarām. If the Muḥrim eats pure fragrance such as musk, saffron, cardamom, clove or cinnamon in so much amount that it comes into contact with most part of the mouth, *Dam* will be Wājib. If the fragrance comes into contact with lesser part of the mouth, Ṣadaqaĥ will be Wājib. *(ibid, pp. 1164)*

Question 13: Can a Muḥrim eat fragrant food, aniseed, betel nuts, creamy biscuits, toffees, etc.?

Answer: There is no harm in eating the fragrance cooked in food even if fragrance is still emanating from it. Similarly, if fragrance is not added at the time of cooking but after the cooking, and the fragrance has vanished, eating that meal is also permissible. If uncooked fragrance is mixed into food or medicine, and the amount of fragrance exceeds that of odourless food or medicine etc., the ruling for pure fragrance will apply in this case, and expiation will be due. If such fragrance comes into contact with most part of the mouth, *Dam* will be Wājib. If it comes into contact with lesser part of the mouth, Ṣadaqaĥ will be Wājib. If the amount of grain etc. exceeds that of pure fragrance, there will be no expiation. If pure fragrance emanates from such food, it is Makrūĥ Tanzīĥī to eat it.

Question 14: How is it to have soft drinks, fragrance-added beverages, fruit-juices, etc.?

Answer: If sandalwood fragrance is added to the beverage, it is allowed to drink it because sandalwood fragrance is cooked before being added to the beverage. If an essence is also added to the beverage to make it fragrant, it is usually added to the cooked beverage after it has been cooled. The essence is obviously added to the beverage in small amount. The ruling on this type of essence-added beverage is that if a Muḥrim has drunk it three times or more, *Dam* will be due otherwise Ṣadaqaĥ.

It is stated in *Baĥār-e-Sharī'at*: If a Muḥrim has drunk a fragrance-added beverage, *Dam* will be due provided fragrance is dominant. If the fragrance is in small amount but the Muḥrim has drunk such a beverage three times or more, *Dam* will be due, otherwise Ṣadaqaĥ.

(Baĥār-e-Sharī'at, vol. 1, pp. 1165)

Question 15: Can a Muḥrim apply coconut oil to his head etc.?

Answer: There is no harm in it. Even so, the rulings of pure fragrance will apply in case of applying sesame and olive oil. They cannot be applied to the body even if they are odourless. However, expiation will not be Wājib in case of eating them, sniffing them, applying them on wound or dropping them into the ear. *(ibid, pp. 1166)*

Question 16: How is it to apply fragrant kohl into eyes in the state of Iḥrām?

Answer: It is Ḥarām. 'Allāmaĥ Maulānā Muftī Muhammad Amjad 'Alī A'ẓamī عَلَيْهِ رَحْمَةُ اللهِ الْقَوِى has stated: In case of using needle once or twice while applying kohl, Ṣadaqaĥ will be Wājib. In case of using needle thrice or more while applying kohl, *Dam* will become Wājib. There is no harm in using the kohl that has no fragrance in it provided it is necessary. To use even such odourless kohl unnecessarily is Makrūĥ and undesirable. *(Bahār-e-Sharī'at, vol. 1, pp. 1164)*

Question 17: Is removing fragrance necessary for the one who has paid the expiation for using it?

Answer: As the use of fragrance is an offence in the state of Iḥrām, removing fragrance from the body or cloth is Wājib. If fragrance is not removed after paying expiation, *Dam* will be Wājib again. *(Bahār-e-Sharī'at, vol. 1, pp. 1166)*

Use of fragrant soap in the state of Iḥrām

Question 18: Fragrant soaps, shampoo and powder are usually available in the hotels of Makkaĥ and Madīnaĥ and Muḥrims freely wash their hands etc. with these things. Similarly, fragrant soaps are provided to Muḥrims at the airport and in the aeroplane. Furthermore, fragrant powder is provided to Muḥrims in the hotels of Makkaĥ and Madīnaĥ to wash clothes and pots. What is the Shar'ī ruling on using such things?

Answer: If those in the state of Iḥrām use these things, no expiation will be due. (However, it is Makrūĥ to use them with the intention of using fragrance.)[1] *(Derived from: Iḥrām and Fragrant Soap)*

Muḥrim and rose-garlands

Question 19: Can a pilgrim wear a rose-made garland at the airport after he has made the intention of Iḥrām?

Answer: He cannot wear a rose-made garland after making the intention of Iḥrām because rose is a pure fragrance-smelling flower and can cause the body or clothes to have its fragrance. If a larger portion of the cloth is having rose-fragrance and Muḥrim had that cloth on for 12 hours, *Dam* will be due; otherwise Ṣadaqaĥ. If a little fragrance has come into contact with as much portion of the cloth as a hand-span or less than it, and the Muḥrim had it on for 12 hours, Ṣadaqaĥ is due. If he had it on for less than 12 hours, it is Wājib to give a handful of wheat to a Shar'ī Faqīr.

If the fragrance is in small quantity but has come into contact with more than a hand-span portion of the cloth, the ruling of fragrance coming into contact with a larger portion will apply in this case, i.e. if Muḥrim has worn this cloth for 12 hours, *Dam* is due, and if he had it on for less than 12 hours, Ṣadaqaĥ is due. If clothes have had

[1] For the guidance of Ummaĥ, Dawat-e-Islami's Majlis Taḥqīqāt Shar'iyyaĥ has issued this Fatwā with mutual agreement, and has obtained endorsement from three erudite scholars of Aĥl-us-Sunnaĥ: (1) Muftī A'ẓam Pakistan 'Allāmaĥ 'Abdul Qayyūm Ĥazarvī (2) Sharaf-e-Millat 'Allāmaĥ Muhammad 'Abdul Ḥakīm Sharaf Qādirī (3) Fayz-e-Millat 'Allāmaĥ Fayz Aḥmad Owaysī (رحمهم الله تعالى). Maktaba-tul-Madīnaĥ has issued a booklet entitled, '*Iḥrām and Fragrant Soap*'. Those seeking further details should study this booklet or download it from Dawat-e-Islami's website: www.dawateislami.net

no fragrance in them despite Muḥrim wearing the garland, no expiation will be due. *(Iḥrām and Fragrant Soap, pp. 35-36)*

Question 20: If a Muḥrim has shaken hands with someone, resulting in the latter's hand fragrance coming into contact with that of Muḥrim, what is the ruling?

Answer: If pure fragrance has come into contact with Muḥrim's hand, expiation will be due. If pure fragrance has not come into contact and it has only caused the hand to have fragrance, no expiation will be due because Muḥrim has not benefitted from pure fragrance. However, it is still advisable to remove this fragrance by washing the hand. *(Iḥrām and Fragrant Soap, pp. 35)*

Question 21: Can a Muḥrim wash his head or beard with a fragrant shampoo?

Answer: Here is the translation of some excerpts from pages 25 to 28 of the booklet, '*Iḥrām and Fragrant Soap*': If the cause of the use of fragrance being forbidden is taken into consideration, it seems rationally justified to prohibit applying fragrant shampoo to the head or the beard. And expiation should also be declared due, as is the ruling on washing the head and the beard with Khiṭmī (a fragrant herb). The use of this fragrant herb softens hair, killing lice and is therefore impermissible for Muḥrim. It is stated in *Durr-e-Mukhtār*: To wash the head or the beard with Khiṭmī is Ḥarām as it is a type of fragrance or kills lice. *(Durr-e-Mukhtār, vol. 3, pp. 570)*

Since Imām Abū Yūsuf and Imām Muhammad رَحِمَهُمَا اللّٰهُ تَعَالٰی have not declared it fragrance, its use will be considered to be a partial offence and will result in Ṣadaqaĥ being Wājib. To wash the head with fragrant shampoo also seems to be a partial offence as the fragrance added to shampoo is heated, negating the ruling of fragrance.

However, two other causes, i.e. softening hair and killing lice are still found. Therefore, Ṣadaqaĥ should be Wājib.

It is also noteworthy to know whether the same ruling applies if a beardless and bald Muḥrim has used the shampoo. Apparently, the verdict of expiation should not be made in this case as the causes of prohibition, i.e. softening hair and killing lice are not found. And if the causes do not exist, the ruling will not also apply. However, if dirt is removed, the use of shampoo will be Makrūĥ even for such a beardless and bald person. As for using it for washing hands, the ruling for soap will apply in this case as shampoo is also a type of soap in liquid form that is pasteurized [i.e. heated with a special process].

Question 22: In Masjid-ul-Ḥarām and Masjid-un-Nabawī, a type of scented solution is used to clean the floor which comes into contact with the feet of millions of Muḥrims. What is the ruling?

Answer: No expiation will be due because it is not fragrance. Even if it were pure fragrance, no expiation would still be Wājib because this solution is mixed into water before being used for cleaning the floor. Obviously, the amount of water is much more than that of the solution. The ruling is that no expiation will be due if liquid fragrance is mixed into any other liquid that is in greater amount.

As for the general ruling regarding beverages described in the books of Islamic jurisprudence, it refers to the act of mixing solid fragrance into some liquid. 'Allāmaĥ Ḥusayn Bin Muhammad 'Abdul Ghanī Makkī عَلَيْهِ رَحْمَةُ اللّٰهِ الْقَوِى has stated on page 316 of the book '*Irshād-us-Sārī*': If rose-water is mixed into sugar-added water (i.e. a type of beverage) and the amount of rose-water is less than that of sugar-added water, as usually is, no expiation will be due in this case. Favouring the very same viewpoint, 'Allāmaĥ 'Alī Qārī عَلَيْهِ رَحْمَةُ اللّٰهِ الْبَارِى

has narrated a similar ruling in the book '*Ṭarābulusī*' and it has its basis in the book '*Muḥīṭ*'. *(ibid, pp. 28-29)*

Question 23: If Muḥrim has used toothpaste, what is the expiation?

Answer: If fragrance added to toothpaste is heated, as it is usually done, expiation will not be due in this case as stated in the foregoing details. *(ibid, pp. 33)* However, if Muḥrim used toothpaste with the intention of removing smell from the mouth or having fragrance, then it is Makrūĥ. A'lā Ḥaḍrat رحمۃ اللہ تعالٰی علیہ has stated: If fragrance is cooked after being added to the ingredients of tobacco, then it is permissible to eat it even if fragrance is emanating from it. However, it is Makrūĥ to use it with the intention of having fragrance.

(Fatāwā Razawiyyaĥ, vol. 10, pp. 716)

Questions and answers about wearing stitched clothes etc.

Question 1: If a Muḥrim put on stitched clothing forgetfully and removed them after ten minutes as soon as he recalled, will there be any expiation etc. for him?

Answer: Yes. Ṣadaqaĥ will be Wājib even if he wears stitched clothes just for a moment, whether deliberately or forgetfully. If a Muḥrim has worn stitched dress for the duration of a day or night[1] or more, *Dam* will be Wājib even if he does so for many consecutive days. *(Fatāwā Razawiyyaĥ referenced, vol. 10, pp. 757)*

Question 2: If a Muḥrim covers his head with a cap or a turban or shawl of Iḥrām, or if a male Muḥrim forgets to take off stitched

[1] The duration of a day or that of a night means, for example, from sunrise to sunset or vice versa; or from noon to midnight or vice versa. *(Footnote: Anwār-ul-Bashāraĥ ma' Fatāwā Razawiyyaĥ, vol. 10, pp. 757)*

clothes or cap before he makes the intention of Iḥrām, or if the face of Muḥrim is covered by someone else's shawl in crowd, what is the penalty for it?

Answer: Whether an offence is committed deliberately or by mistake or due to someone else' carelessness, expiations must be paid in any case. As it is a sin to commit an offence deliberately, repentance will also be Wājib. Now note the details of expiation. If a male Muḥrim covers the whole of or one quarter of his head for the consecutive period of a day or night or more, *Dam* will be Wājib.

Likewise, if a male or a female Muḥrim covers the whole of or one quarter of his/her face for the consecutive period of a day or night or more, *Dam* will be Wājib. In case of covering less than one quarter of head/face for the period of a day or night or in case of covering the whole of face or head for less than the period of a day or night, Ṣadaqaĥ will be due. In case of covering less than one quarter for less than the period of a day or night, there is no expiation but it is a sin. *(ibid, pp. 758)*

Question 3: Can a Muḥrim wipe his nose with a piece of cloth due to flu?

Answer: He cannot wipe his nose with a piece of cloth. He can blow his nose into a piece of cloth or towel keeping it distant from the nose. Ṣadr-ush-Sharī'aĥ, Badr-uṭ-Ṭarīqaĥ 'Allāmaĥ Maulānā Muftī Muhammad Amjad 'Alī A'ẓamī عَلَيْهِ رَحْمَةُ اللهِ الْقَوِى has stated: There is no harm in covering the ear and the back of the neck. Similarly, Muḥrim can place his empty hand onto his nose. However, if Muḥrim has placed his hand with a piece of cloth in it over his nose, though expiation will not be due, it is Makrūĥ and a sin to do so.

(Baĥār-e-Sharī'at, vol. 1, pp. 1169)

Questions and answers about using tissue paper in the state of Iḥrām

Question 1: Can a Muḥrim use tissue paper to wipe sweat from his face or nose due to flu or water after making Wuḍū?

Answer: A Muḥrim cannot do so.

Question 2: How is it to wear a mask made of cloth or tissue paper?

Answer: It is impermissible and a sin to do so. If conditions are met, expiation will also be due.

Question 3: If Muḥrim has worn a scented mask, what will be the ruling?

Answer: If a Muḥrim has worn a scented mask that contains fragrance in liquid form, resulting in the liquid fragrance coming into contact with the body, the ruling of fragrance will apply in this case. That is, if the fragrance is in small amount and has not come into contact with an entire part of the body, Ṣadaqaĥ will be due. If fragrance is in large amount or has come into contact with an entire part of the body, *Dam* will be due. If pure fragrance does not exist but rather fragrance is only emanating from the tissue paper, no expiation is required even if the Muḥrim has wiped the face etc. with it or his face or hand is having fragrance due to touching the tissue paper. This is because pure fragrance is not found in the tissue paper, and the main purpose of using tissue paper is not to benefit from fragrance. *(Iḥrām and Fragrant Soap, pp. 31)*

If a Muḥrim has entered a room where incense or frankincense is burnt to spread fragrance, causing his clothes to have fragrance in them, expiation is not required because he has not benefitted from pure fragrance. *('Ālamgīrī, vol. 1, pp. 241)*

Question 4: Can a Muḥrim use stitched shawl at the time of sleeping for covering his body?

Answer: He can do so. Rather, there is no harm in using even more than one shawl provided the face is uncovered, even if both feet are fully covered.

Question 5: When travelling by air or by bus, if a Muḥrim goes to sleep with his face resting on a pillow or on the backrest of the seat in front of him, what is the ruling in this case?

Answer: Although no expiation is required for sleeping with the face resting on a pillow, it is Makrūĥ Taḥrīmī to do so. As for sleeping with the face resting on the backrest of the seat in front of Muḥrim, it is permissible to do so because a seat is normally hard like a door, unlike a pillow that is soft.

Question 6: Can a Muḥrim sleep with his face resting on his knees? There is no expiation for sleeping with the face resting on a pillow but it is Makrūĥ. Why?

Answer: If the face is resting only on the knees, i.e. only on the hard part of the knees, this is permissible because the ruling applies depending upon the hard thing wrapped or covered or put into the cloth, not the cloth itself, just as Islamic scholars have stated the ruling of a sack or a bundle of something (except that of clothes). However, this is very unlikely that the face of Muḥrim rests only on the knees when sleeping. What is likely is that some part of the face will be resting on the hard part of the knee and some part of it will be in contact with the cloth only. Therefore, this should be avoided, otherwise this can result in expiation being due. As for a pillow, it is soft like a piece of cloth (and therefore it is prohibited for Muḥrim to sleep with his face resting on it), but a pillow is not considered cloth in all cases (therefore, expiation is not due).

Question 7: Is it allowed for a Muḥrim to sleep in a sleeping bag to protect against cold, covering his entire body except the face and the head?

Answer: Yes. It is allowed for a Muḥrim to do so because this is not referred to as wearing clothes.

Question 8: If a Muḥrim has the problem of passing drops after urination, what should he do?

Answer: It is advisable for him to tie an unstitched Taĥband (i.e. a piece of cloth used to cover the lower part of the body). To tie a Taĥband in the state of Iḥrām is absolutely permissible provided it is unstitched. *(Mulakhkhaṣ az: Fatāwā Razawiyyaĥ, vol. 10, pp. 664)*

Question 9: Is there any expiation for wearing stitched clothes due to the compulsion of illness etc.?

Answer: Yes. If a Muḥrim wears clothes from head to toe due to sickness, it will be considered one unintentional offence[1]. If he has worn clothes for the period of a day or night or more than it, *Dam* will be Wājib. In case of wearing clothes for less than this period, Ṣadaqaĥ will be Wājib.

If there is the need of wearing just one cloth due to illness but he wears two clothes; for example, if there is the need of wearing just shirt but he wears stitched vest as well, though there will be just one expiation in this case, he will be considered a sinner.

If he wears the extra clothes on any other part of the body, for example, there is the need of wearing just trousers but he wears shirt as well, there will be one unintentional offence and one intentional offence. *(Baĥār-e-Sharī'at, vol. 1, pp. 1168; 'Ālamgīrī, vol. 1, pp. 242)*

---

[1] See the ruling about unintentional offence on page 181.

Question 10: If a Muḥrim wears full dress unnecessarily, how many expiations will he have to pay?

Answer: If he wears his full dress unnecessarily at the same time, it will be considered only one offence. If he wears one cloth necessarily and the other unnecessarily, there will be two offences in this case. *(Baĥār-e-Sharī'at, vol. 1, pp. 1168)*

Question 11: If a Muḥrim hides his face in his hands or someone places his hand onto the Muḥrim's head, is there any harm in it?

Answer: To place one's own hand or that of someone else onto the head or the nose in the state of Iḥrām is permissible. 'Allāmaĥ 'Alī Qārī عَلَيْهِ رَحْمَةُ اللّٰهِ الْبَارِى has stated: To place one's own hand or that of someone else onto the head or the nose in the state of Iḥrām is unanimously permissible as this is not referred to as covering or hiding the head or the nose. *(Lubāb-ul-Manāsik wal-Maslak-ul-Mutaqassiṭ, pp. 123)*

Question 12: Can a Muḥrim stroke his face after he has made Du'ā?

Answer: He can do so because it is allowed to place the hand onto the face. The bearded Islamic brother should take care not to remove any hair when stroking his face after Du'ā or Wuḍū.

Question 13: If a Muḥrim puts stitched clothes onto his shoulder, is there any expiation?

Answer: There is no expiation. Ṣadr-ush-Sharī'aĥ رَحْمَةُ اللّٰهِ تَعَالٰى عَلَيْه has stated: What is prohibited is to wear stitched clothes as they are usually worn. On the contrary, if a Muḥrim has used a shirt as Taĥband or has wrapped a pyjama around his waist without putting his feet into the parts of the pyjama, there is no harm in it. Similarly, if he has spread a robe over his shoulders without putting his hands into sleeves, no expiation is due but it is Makrūĥ to do so. If he has put stitched clothes over his shoulders, there is no harm in it. *(Bahār-e-Sharī'at, vol. 1, pp. 1169)*

Question and answer about ritual stay in 'Arafāt

Question: Can the ritual stay in 'Arafāt be carried out at the night of 10th Żul-Ḥijjaĥ?

Answer: Yes. The stipulated time for the ritual stay in 'Arafāt is from the commencement of the timing of Ẓuĥr of 9th Żul-Ḥijjaĥ to the commencement of the timing of Fajr of 10th Żul-Ḥijjaĥ. *('Ālamgīrī, vol. 1, pp. 229)*

Question and answer about ritual stay in Muzdalifaĥ

Question: If a person has no worry, when should he leave for Minā from Muzdalifaĥ?

Answer: He should leave when only as much time is left in the sunset as two Rak'āt Ṣalāĥ can be offered (with a Sunnaĥ-conforming manner of recitation of Quran and other Ażkār etc.) To stay till sunset is contrary to a Sunnat-ul-Muakkadaĥ and it is disliked to do so but no *Dam* etc. is Wājib. However, if a person left for Minā but was stuck in the crowd and the sun set whilst he was still in Muzdalifaĥ, he will not be considered to have missed the Sunnaĥ. (This answer is extracted from *Fatāwā Hajj and 'Umraĥ* part 2 from page 83 to 87).

Question and answer about Ramī

Question: If, any day, someone threw stones more than half of the total number, for example, he was to throw twenty one stones at the three satans on 11th Żul-Ḥijjaĥ but he threw eleven stones, what is the expiation?

Answer: He will have to pay one Ṣadaqaĥ for each missed stone. Ṣadr-ush-Sharī'aĥ رَحْمَةُ اللهِ تَعَالٰی عَلَيْه has stated: If a person missed Ramī of all days or missed whole of or most part of the Ramī of a day - for example, if he threw three stones on 10th Żul-Ḥijjaĥ or threw 10 stones on 11th Żul-Ḥijjaĥ etc. or if he performed the whole of or most part of a day's Ramī on the other day - *Dam* is to be paid in all these cases.

If he missed less than half of the Ramī of a day - for example, if he threw four stones and did not throw the rest three on 10th Żul-Ḥijjaĥ or if he threw eleven stones and did not throw the rest ten on other days or threw stones the other day - he is to pay one Ṣadaqaĥ for every stone not thrown. If the total amount of Ṣadaqaĥ is equivalent to a *Dam*, he should pay a little less than the amount of *Dam*.

(Bahār-e-Sharī'at, vol. 1, pp. 1178)

Questions and answers about ritual sacrifice

Question 1: Can the Mutamatte' who has performed the Ramī of 10th Żul-Ḥijjaĥ perform ritual sacrifice and Ḥalq in Jeddah?

Answer: He cannot do so as Jeddah is out of the limits of Ḥaram. Therefore, if these two rites (i.e. sacrifice and Ḥalq) are done in Jeddah, two *Dam* will be Wājib.

Question 2: If a Mutamatte' and a Qārin performed sacrifice before Ramī or got Ḥalq done before sacrifice, what would be the expiation?

Answer: *Dam* will have to be paid in both the cases.

Question 3: If a Mufrid (the one performing Hajj Ifrād) gets his Ḥalq done before performing sacrifice, is there any expiation?

Answer: No. Performing sacrifice is not Wājib for a Mufrid, it is Mustaḥab for him. *(ibid, pp. 1140)* If he wishes to perform sacrifice, it is better for him to do Ḥalq first, then perform sacrifice.

Questions and answers about Ḥalq and Taqṣīr

Question 1: If a Ḥājī gets his head shaved after 12th Żul-Ḥijjaĥ out of Ḥaram, what will be the expiation for him?

Answer: He will have to pay two *Dams*; one for getting Ḥalq done out of Ḥaram and the other for getting it done after 12th Żul-Ḥijjaĥ. *(Rad-dul-Muḥtār, vol. 3, pp. 666)*

Question 2: Can the Ḥalq for 'Umraĥ be done out of Ḥaram?

Answer: No. If it is done out of Ḥaram, *Dam* will become Wājib. However, there is no restriction of time for it.

(Durr-e-Mukhtār, Rad-dul-Muḥtār, vol. 3, pp. 666)

Question 3: Is it Wājib even for those working in Jeddah etc. to have Ḥalq or Taqṣīr done every time they perform 'Umraĥ?

Answer: Yes. Otherwise the restrictions of Iḥrām will not come to an end.

Question 4: If a woman has short hair (as in fashion these days) and she is also enthusiastic about performing 'Umraĥ but fears the loss of all hair due to repeated Qaṣr, what should she do? If the length of the hair of a woman is shorter than that of a finger digit, Qaṣr for 'Umraĥ is not possible for her. What is the ruling for her in case of performing 'Umraĥ?

Answer: As long as a woman has hair on her head, it will remain Wājib for her to do Qaṣr every time she performs 'Umraĥ. The Beloved and Blessed Prophet صَلَّى اللهُ تَعَالٰى عَلَيْهِ وَاٰلِهٖ وَسَلَّم has stated: It is (Wājib) for women to do Qaṣr, not Ḥalq. *(Abū Dāwūd, vol. 2, pp. 295, Ḥadīš 1984)*

If the length of the hair of a woman is shorter than that of a finger digit, she is exempted from doing Qaṣr because it is not possible for her. To have Ḥalq done is already forbidden for her. What she is advised to do in such a situation is to get out of the restrictions of Iḥrām near the end of the days of ritual sacrifice (i.e. after the sunset of 12th Żul-Ḥijja-til-Ḥarām) provided she is going to perform the 'Umraĥ that is related to Hajj. Even if she does not wait till the above-mentioned time, no expiation will be due.

Miscellaneous questions and answers

Question 1: If a Muḥrim sustained head or facial injury, and he is compelled to bandage it, will he be sinner?

Answer: Under the condition of being compelled to take such an act he will not be sinner, however, he will have to pay expiation for the unintentional offence.

Therefore, if a Muḥrim used such a large bandage that covered one quarter or more than one quarter of his head or face for the period of a day or night or more, *Dam* will become Wājib. If less than one quarter of the face or the head was covered, Ṣadaqaĥ will be Wājib. (See the details of unintentional offence on page 181). Except for the head and the face, there is no harm in having bandage on any other part of the body. Further, a woman can have bandage even on her head in compulsion.

Question 2: While waiting to perform Hajj, can a Mutamatte' and a Qārin perform 'Umraĥ in this period?

Answer: Since the Qārin is still in the state of Iḥrām he cannot do so. As for the Mutamatte', there is a difference of opinion amongst Islamic scholars in this matter. It is better for a Mutamatte' to perform as many Nafl Ṭawāf as possible. Even if he performs 'Umraĥ, according to some scholars, there is no harm in it. However, after performing the rites of Hajj, everyone, i.e. the Mutamatte', the Qārin and the Mufrid can perform 'Umraĥ.

Question 3: Those living in Arab outside Mīqāt such as Dammam and Riyadh etc. are not allowed by government but they deceivingly pass Mīqāt without Iḥrām and put on it after they have passed it and then perform Hajj. What is the ruling for such people?

Answer: It is impermissible to present oneself to be disgraced by violating the law. In case of passing Mīqāt without Iḥrām, it would be Wājib to return to Mīqāt and put on Iḥrām. If someone passed Mīqāt without Iḥrām and performed Hajj or 'Umraĥ, he will be required to pay *Dam* besides being a sinner. If he has returned to Mīqāt the same year before the commencement of the rites of Hajj or 'Umraĥ and has put on any type of Iḥrām, *Dam* will become void, otherwise not.

Question 4: If someone has had Ḥalq done before performing the Sa'ī of Hajj or 'Umraĥ, and many days have passed since he did so, what is the ruling?

Answer: It is a Sunnaĥ for a Hajj-performing person to have Ḥalq done before Sa'ī. That is, doing Sa'ī before Ḥalq is contrary to Sunnaĥ. Therefore, if someone gets Ḥalq done before he has performed Sa'ī, there is no harm in it. Even if many days have passed since he did so, no expiation will be due because there is no time limit for Sa'ī. However, if he has returned to his 'country' without performing Sa'ī, *Dam* will be due in this case because of missing a Wājib. If he comes back and performs Sa'ī, *Dam* will no longer remain Wājib. However, it is still better for him to give *Dam* as it is in the interest of the destitute.

This ruling will apply only when Ḥalq is performed within its stipulated time, i.e. the days of ritual sacrifice after the Ramī of 10th Żul-Ḥijja-til-Ḥarām. If someone gets Ḥalq done before he has performed Ramī or after the days of ritual sacrifice have passed, *Dam* will be Wājib for him. If an 'Umraĥ-performing person gets Ḥalq done before Sa'ī, *Dam* will be due for him. If he has performed complete Ṭawāf or most (i.e. four) rounds of it, he will get out of the restrictions of Iḥrām otherwise not. Even if many days have passed, the commandment of Sa'ī will not become void as it is Wājib and will have to be performed.

Question 5: If a person who has made the intention of Hajj Ifrād took off Iḥrām after he has performed 'Umraĥ, what should he do and what is the expiation?

Answer: To take off the Iḥrām of Hajj after performing 'Umraĥ is not permissible and the person doing so will not also get out of the restrictions of Iḥrām but rather he will remain Muḥrim as usual. It is mandatory for him to take off Iḥrām after he has performed the rites of Hajj. To make the intention of taking off Iḥrām without performing the rites of Hajj is not sufficient. Since the restrictions of Iḥrām still exist, expiation will also be due in case of committing forbidden acts. However, only one expiation will be due even if he has committed all the acts forbidden in Iḥrām. For example, if he has put on stitched clothes, applied fragrance, had his head shaved etc., he is required to pay only *Dam* for all these acts. It is now mandatory for him to take off the stitched clothes and put on unstitched Iḥrām again, to repent and to perform the rites of Hajj with the intention of the Iḥrām of the same previous Hajj.

Question 6: If a person who wants to perform the ritual sacrifice of Eid-ul-Aḍḥā puts on Iḥrām after the appearance of the moon of Żul-Ḥijjaĥ, should he trim nails and remove unnecessary hair etc.

or not because it is Mustaḥab for him not to trim nails etc. in those days? What is preferable for him?

Answer: If a Ḥājī is in the need of cutting his nails and hair etc. it is preferable and Mustaḥab for him to do so. Remember! If so many days have passed since he last trimmed his nails that 40 days will pass in case of putting on Iḥrām without cutting nails and hair, it is necessary to trim nails because it is a sin to leave the nails untrimmed for more than 40 days.

Question 7: Is it allowed to start performing 'Umraĥ on 13th Żul-Ḥijja-til-Ḥarām?

Answer: No. It is Makrūĥ Taḥrīmī (impermissible and a sin) to put on the Iḥrām of 'Umraĥ during the days of Tashrīq, i.e. from 9th to 13th Żul-Ḥijja-til-Ḥarām. If someone puts on Iḥrām of 'Umraĥ during these days, *Dam* would be due. ***(Durr-e-Mukhtār, vol. 3, pp. 547)***

How is it to put on Iḥrām after the sunset of 13th Żul-Ḥijja-til-Ḥarām

Question 8: Is it not allowed even for locals who have not performed Hajj that year to perform 'Umraĥ during those five days i.e. 9th to 13th Żul-Ḥijja-til-Ḥarām?

Answer: It is Makrūĥ Taḥrīmī even for them to put on the Iḥrām of 'Umraĥ and perform 'Umraĥ during those days. This ruling is the same for Āfāqī, Ḥillī and Mīqātī. What is actually forbidden during these days is to put on the Iḥrām of 'Umraĥ. One can perform 'Umraĥ any day throughout the year but it is Makrūĥ Taḥrīmī to put on the Iḥrām of 'Umraĥ during these five days. If a person who has put on Iḥrām before 9th Żul-Ḥijja-til-Ḥarām performs 'Umraĥ with the same Iḥrām during these five days, there is no harm in it.

However, it is still better to perform 'Umraĥ after these five days have passed. *(Lubāb-ul-Manāsik, pp. 466)*

Question 9: If a Ḥillī or Ḥaramī performs 'Umraĥ as well as Hajj during the months of Hajj, what is the ruling for him?

Answer: *Dam* will be Wājib for him because he is only allowed to perform Hajj Ifrād that contains no 'Umraĥ. However, he can perform 'Umraĥ only.

Question 10: How is it for a Muḥrim to wash hands before and after the meal? If he did not wash hands before the meal, germs will go into the stomach, and if he did not wash them after the meal, the hands will remain smelly with stains on them. What should he do?

Answer: He can wash hands before and after the meal without using soap. If there is any other type of stain or dirt on the hands, he can wipe them with a piece of cloth taking care not to remove any hair.

Question 11: How is it for a Muḥrim to dry his hands and face with a handkerchief after making Wuḍū?

Answer: He cannot touch cloth to face (a male Muḥrim cannot touch it even to his head); the rest of the body can be dried with such precaution that neither dirt be removed nor any strand of hair is broken.

Question 12: Is a Muḥrimaĥ allowed to wear a veil-attached cap or a projected veil in such a way that it does not touch her face?

Answer: She can do so, but if the veil touches the whole of her face even for a short while as a result of wind or her own hand's touching the veil mistakenly, expiation will become due.

Question 13: Should a Muḥrim apply soap onto his head while getting Ḥalq done?

Answer: He should not use soap as this will remove dirt, and removal of dirt from the body is Makrūĥ in the state of Iḥrām.

Question 14: Can a woman experiencing her menstrual periods make the intention of Iḥrām?

Answer: She can make the intention, but she cannot offer Nafl Ṣalāĥ of Iḥrām. Further, she will have to perform Ṭawāf after attaining purity.

Question 15: How is it to wear stitched slippers in the state of Iḥrām?

Answer: If the instep (i.e. the upper raised portion of the foot) remains uncovered, there is no harm in wearing such slippers.

Question 16: How is it to use safety pins or buttons or tie knots in the Iḥrām?

Answer: To do so is contrary to Sunnaĥ and a disliked act but no *Dam* etc. is Wājib.

Question 17: Usually, the Ḥujjāj pay a *Dam* as a caution. How is it to do so? In case of learning later on that a *Dam* was actually Wājib, will that cautiously paid *Dam* be sufficient or not?

Answer: If the *Dam* was paid after it being Wājib, it will suffice; if it was paid before, and *Dam* had become Wājib afterwards during an 'Umraĥ etc. that previous *Dam* will not be sufficient.

Question 18: Can a Muḥrim take dirt out of his nose or ear?

Answer: It is a Sunnaĥ to clean the inside of the nose in Wuḍū. Therefore, remove the dried mucus if it has accumulated in the nose. Similarly, if rheum of eyes has dried on eye-lashes etc. it is also Farḍ to remove it in Wuḍū and Ghusl. But take care not to break any hair. As for removing dirt from the ear, no Islamic scholar has explicitly allowed to remove it. Therefore, the ruling of removing bodily dirt will apply in this case, i.e. it is Makrūĥ Tanzīĥī to remove it but no hair should break.

Question 19: Can a person perform 'Umraĥ on behalf of his living parents?

Answer: He can do. The reward of every type of deed including Farḍ Ṣalāĥ, fast, Hajj, Zakāĥ or any supererogatory act may be donated to the living as well as the dead (Muslims).

Question 20: Kindly state expiations for killing louse in the state of Iḥrām.

Answer: If a Muḥrim kills one of his own lice on his body or clothes or throws it away, he has to donate a piece of bread. If he kills or throws away two or three lice, he has to donate a handful of grain. In case of more than three lice, he will have to pay a Ṣadaqaĥ.

If a Muḥrim washes his head or cloth or puts it in the sunshine for killing lice, there is the same expiation for it as for killing lice. If someone else kills Muḥrim's louse at the command of the Muḥrim, the Muḥrim will have to pay expiation even if the one killing the louse is not in the state of Iḥrām. There is no expiation for killing the louse that has fallen onto the ground etc. or the one that is on another person's body or clothes even if the other person is also in the state of Iḥrām.

HAJJ AKBAR

Question: How is it to call the Hajj performed on Friday as Hajj Akbar?

Answer: There is no harm in it. Allah عَزَّوَجَلَّ has said in verse number 3 of Surah At-Taubah part 10:

وَ اَذَانٌ مِّنَ اللّٰهِ وَرَسُوْلِهٖۤ اِلَى النَّاسِ يَوْمَ الْحَجِّ الْاَكْبَرِ

And there is proclamation from Allah and His Prophet to all people on the day of Great Pilgrimage.

[Kanz-ul-Īmān (Translation of Quran)] (Part 10, Sūrah At-Taubah, verse 3)

Commenting on the foregoing verse, 'Allāmah Maulānā Sayyid Muhammad Na'īmuddīn Murādābādī عَلَيْهِ رَحْمَةُ اللّٰهِ الْهَادِى has stated: Hajj was declared to be Hajj Akbar because 'Umrah used to be called Hajj Aṣghar in those days. According to another exegesis, that Hajj was referred to Hajj Akbar because the Holy Prophet صَلَّى اللّٰهُ تَعَالٰى عَلَيْهِ وَاٰلِهٖ وَسَلَّم performed Hajj that year. As that Hajj took place on a Friday, the Muslims call the Hajj taking place on Friday Hajj Akbar as it reminds them of Hajj Wadā'. *(Tafsīr Khazāin-ul-'Irfān, pp. 354)*

The Beloved and Blessed Prophet صَلَّى اللّٰهُ تَعَالٰى عَلَيْهِ وَاٰلِهٖ وَسَلَّم has stated: The best day of 'Arafah from among the days is the one that falls on a Friday and the Hajj of this day is preferable to seventy such Hajj that do not take place on Friday. *(Fatḥ-ul-Bārī, vol. 9, pp. 231, Taḥt Al-Ḥadīš 4606)*

Guidance for those working in Arab

Question 1: If the inhabitants of Makka-tul-Mukarramah or those working over there go to 'Ṭāif', is it necessary for them to put on the Iḥrām for Hajj or 'Umrah on return?

Answer: Keep this principle in mind that if the people of Makka-tul-Mukarramaĥ go out of the limits of Ḥaram for a piece of work but remain within Mīqāt (such as Jeddah), they do not need to put on Iḥrām on return. However, if they go out of Mīqāt (such as Madīna-tul-Munawwaraĥ, Ṭāif, Riyadh etc.), it is not permissible for them to return without Iḥrām. No matter a driver goes out of Mīqāt and returns many times a day, Hajj or 'Umraĥ will become Wājib for him each time. If he comes to Makka-tul-Mukarramaĥ without Iḥrām, *Dam* will become Wājib for him. However, if he put on Iḥrām outside Mīqāt the very same year, *Dam* will become void.

Ḥīlaĥ for not putting on Iḥrām

Question 2: If a person who works in Jeddah comes to Jeddah for work from his country, for example, from Pakistan, is Iḥrām necessary for him?

Answer: If he has the intention of going to Jeddah, there is no need of Iḥrām; rather, he can go to even Makka-tul-Mukarramaĥ from Jeddah without Iḥrām. Therefore, the person wishing to enter Ḥaram without Iḥrām can do so with the help of a Ḥīlaĥ provided that he makes firm intention to go first to such place as Jeddah without the intention of going to Makka-tul-Mukarramaĥ with the intention of Hajj and 'Umraĥ.

For example, he went to Jeddah for business or trade, and after completing his business transactions he made intention to visit Makka-tul-Mukarramaĥ from there. If he had already made the intention of going to Makkaĥ, he cannot go without Iḥrām in this case. This Ḥīlaĥ is not permissible for the one performing Hajj Badal on behalf of someone else.

How is it to ask for financial help for Hajj or 'Umraĥ?

Question: Some poor devotees, overwhelmed by the feeling of devotion, ask people for financial help for 'Umraĥ or Hajj-pilgrimage; is it permissible to do so?

Answer: It is Ḥarām. Ṣadr-ul-Afāḍil Maulānā Na'īmuddīn Murādābādī عَلَیْہِ رَحْمَۃُ اللّٰہِ الْہَادِی has narrated, 'Some Yemeni would leave for Makka-tul-Mukarramaĥ for performing Hajj without provisions calling themselves Mutawakkil[1], but after reaching Makka-tul-Mukarramaĥ, they would start begging people for financial help. Sometimes they would even snatch things from people committing dishonesty.

The following verse was revealed about such people and it was commanded to go on the pilgrimage with provisions so that others would not be burdened. It was prohibited to beg for financial help. One must take provisions with him and the best provision is piety.' *(Khazāin-ul-'Irfān, pp. 67 – Maktaba-tul-Madīnaĥ)* Allah عَزَّوَجَلَّ says in part 2, Sūraĥ Al-Baqaraĥ, verse 197:

وَ تَزَوَّ دُوْا فَاِنَّ خَیْرَ الزَّادِ التَّقْوٰی

And take provisions with you (for the journey); so the best provision is piety.

[Kanz-ul-Īmān (Translation of Quran)] (Part 2, Sūraĥ Al-Baqaraĥ, verse 197)

The Holy Prophet صَلَّی اللّٰہُ تَعَالٰی عَلَیْہِ وَاٰلِہٖ وَسَلَّم has stated, 'One who asks people for (money etc.), whereas he is not facing destitution, nor does he have so many family members that he cannot provide for, will come on the Day of Judgement with no flesh on his face.'

(Shu'ab-ul-Īmān, vol. 3, pp. 274, Ḥadīš 3526)

---

[1] Mutawakkil means the one who trusts Allah عَزَّوَجَلَّ.

Dear devotees of Madīnaĥ! Have patience! The prohibition on begging for money etc. is emphasized so much that some Islamic jurists have stated that a Muḥrim should apply fragrance to his body after bath before putting on Iḥrām provided he has his own fragrance. If he does not have fragrance, he should not ask someone for it because this is also a type of begging. *(Rad-dul-Muḥtār, vol. 3, pp. 559)*

صَلُّوْا عَلَى الْحَبِيْب صَلَّى اللّٰهُ تَعَالٰى عَلٰى مُحَمَّد

How is it to overstay for Hajj on 'Umraĥ-Visa?

Question 1: Some people go to Ḥaramayn Ṭayyibayn (Makkaĥ and Madīnaĥ) from their country during Ramadan on 'Umraĥ-visa, but they overstay there or return to their country having performed Hajj despite the expiry of their visa. Is it permissible by Sharī'aĥ?

Answer: It is the law in most counties that a foreigner is not allowed to stay without a visa. The very same law is in force in Makkaĥ and Madīnaĥ. If the one overstaying there despite the expiry of his visa is apprehended by the police, he will be imprisoned even if he is in the state of Iḥrām. He would neither be allowed to perform 'Umraĥ nor Hajj; instead, he will be deported to his country after being punished legally.

Remember! If there is a chance that the violation of a law will lead to disgrace, bribery and lying, etc. it is not permissible to violate such a law. A'lā Ḥaḍrat, Imām-e-Aĥl-e-Sunnat, Maulānā Shāĥ Imām Aḥmad Razā Khān عَلَيْهِ رَحْمَةُ الرَّحْمٰن has stated, 'Some of the permissible acts are considered to be crimes by law and, if committed, invite disgrace and discomfort for a person. To invite such a trouble for oneself is impermissible. *(Fatāwā Razawiyyaĥ, vol. 17, pp. 370)*

Therefore, illegal overstay in any country of the world even in Makkaĥ for 'Hajj' is not permissible. To say that a person is able to stay for 'Hajj' by illegal means by the grace of Allah عَزَّوَجَلَّ and His Prophet صَلَّى اللّٰهُ تَعَالٰى عَلَيْهِ وَاٰلِهٖ وَسَلَّم is a very challenging remark in the matter of Sharī'aĥ.

Ruling for the Ṣalāĥ of illegal stayer

Question 2: One who stays in Makkaĥ or any other city of Saudi Arabia without visa to perform Hajj should offer complete Ṣalāĥ or Qaṣr?

Answer: Those who have travelled to Makkaĥ on 'Umraĥ visas with the intention of staying there illegally for Hajj or those intending to reside illegally in any country of the world after the expiration of their visas will be considered 'residents' for as long as they live in that city or village in which they were already residing at the time of expiration of their visas. No matter they live there for decades they will remain 'residents'.

However, if they travelled from that city or village with an intention to cover a distance of 92 km or more, they would become 'traveller' as soon as they would go out of the inhabited areas [of the city or the village], invalidating their intention of stay. For example, someone went to Makka-tul-Mukarramaĥ from Pakistan on 'Umraĥ visa and, at the time of expiry of his visa, he was in Makkaĥ-tul-Mukarramaĥ as a 'resident' then the rulings of a 'resident' will apply to him. If, for instance, he goes to Madīna-tul-Munawwaraĥ, he will become a 'traveller' no matter he stays there for years. He will remain a 'traveller' even if he returns to Makka-tul-Mukarramaĥ and he will have to offer Qaṣr [shortened] Ṣalāĥ. However, if his visa is renewed, he can make a new intention to stay.

To cause discomfort to pigeons and locusts in Ḥaram

Question 1: How is it to frighten the pigeons and locusts of Ḥaram into flying without any reason?

Answer: A'lā Ḥaḍrat رَحْمَةُ اللهِ تَعَالٰى عَلَيْه has stated: It is forbidden to frighten the pigeons of Ḥaram into flying. *(Malfūẓāt-e-A'lā Ḥaḍrat, pp. 208)*

Question 2: How is it to cause discomfort to the pigeons and locusts in Ḥaram?

Answer: It is Ḥarām to do so. Ṣadr-ush-Sharī'aĥ رَحْمَةُ اللهِ تَعَالٰى عَلَيْه has stated, 'To hurt an animal of Ḥaram or to cause pain to it in any way is Ḥarām for all. This ruling will apply regardless of whether the person committing these mistakes is in the state of Iḥrām or not.' *(Bahār-e-Sharī'at, vol. 1, pp. 1186)*

Question 3: Can Muḥrims slaughter pigeons and eat them?

Answer: It is stated on page 1180 of the 1st volume of *Bahār-e-Sharī'at*: If a Muḥrim has slaughtered a wild animal, it will not be Ḥalāl and will remain carrion[1]. If he has also eaten its meat after paying expiation, he will be required to pay the expiation again for eating it. If he had paid no expiation before eating, only one expiation will be sufficient in this case.

Question 4: Is it allowed to catch and eat the locust of Ḥaram?

Answer: It is Ḥarām to do so. (Basically, a locust is Ḥalāl and can be eaten even if dead like fish. It is not necessary to slaughter it.)

Question 5: Outside Masjid-ul-Ḥarām, countless locusts are trampled under foot and are lying dead or injured. What is the ruling if someone has eaten them?

---

[1] Murdār, not considered lawfully slaughtered

Answer: If someone has eaten these locusts, no expiation is due. To eat that animal is Ḥarām which is hunted in Ḥaram and is rendered Ḥalāl by being slaughtered lawfully (as per Sharī'aĥ) like a deer etc. The cause of such a hunted animal being Ḥarām is that the animal hunted in Ḥaram is considered carrion (Murdār) which is Ḥarām to be eaten. The reason why it is Ḥalāl to eat locust is that there is no condition for slaughtering it as per Shar'ī method. It will remain Ḥalāl no matter it is slaughtered in any way. Even if trampled under foot or strangled, it will remain Ḥalāl. However, it is not allowed to hunt locusts deliberately within the limits of Ḥaram.

Question 6: What is the expiation for slaughtering the wild terrestrial animal of Ḥaram (i.e. the one found on land)?

Answer: The expiation for it is to pay its price as Ṣadaqaĥ[1].

Question 7: How is it to slaughter and eat chicken in Ḥaram?

Answer: This is Ḥalāl. There is no harm in slaughtering and eating the meat of domesticated animals such as the chicken, the goat, the cow, the buffalo and the camel, etc. What is prohibited is to hunt terrestrial wild animals.

Question 8: There are usually swarms of locusts outside Masjid-ul-Ḥarām. If any locust is trampled under foot or crushed under the tyre of the vehicle, killing it or wounding it, what will be the ruling?

Answer: Expiation must be paid. It is stated on page 1184 of the first volume of the book '*Baĥār-e-Sharī'at*': A locust is also a terrestrial (land) animal. If someone kills it, he must give a date as expiation

[1] For detailed rulings on expiation, please study from pages 1179 to 1191 of Maktaba-tul-Madīnaĥ's published book '*Baĥār-e-Sharī'at* (volume 1)'. You will be amazed to have learnt rulings.

for it. It is stated on page 1181: To kill the animal deliberately is not a condition for expiation to be due. Even if the animal is killed by mistake, expiation is due.

Question 9: There are swarms of locusts in Masjid-ul-Ḥarām. Servants wipe the floor down, brutally killing or injuring locusts. Is there any alternative way to clean the floor? Similarly, it is said that some people catch pigeons and release them into some far-flung area or eat them. What is the ruling?

Answer: If locusts are in so large number that they cause inconvenience, there is no harm in killing them in this case. But if someone kills them for any other reason, he will have to pay the penalty whether he kills them deliberately or by mistake. If someone catches and kills a pigeon in Ḥaram, he must pay its penalty. Similarly, if someone has caught a pigeon of Ḥaram and released it outside Ḥaram, its penalty will remain due unless he is aware that the pigeon has safely returned to Ḥaram. In both cases, its penalty is to pay the price of the pigeon. The price will be set by two such people who are aware of such dealings in Ḥaram. If two people are not available, only one such person can set the price that must be paid.

Question 10: How is it to eat the fish of Ḥaram?

Answer: Fish is not a terrestrial animal and can be eaten. It can also be hunted, if necessary.

Question 11: What is the expiation if someone has killed the rat of Ḥaram?

Answer: There is no expiation. It is permissible to kill the rat. It is stated on page 1183 of the first volume of *Bahār-e-Sharī'at*: If any of the following animals attack a person, he can kill them. No expiation will be due. The animals include the crow, the kite, the wolf, the scorpion, the snake, the rat, the bandicoot, the mole, a violent dog (that tends to bite), the flea, the wasp, the mosquito, the tick[1], the tortoise, the crab, the moth, an ant that bites, the fly, the lizard and all insects of earth including badger, fox and jackal. Similarly, one can kill the animals that tend to attack humans like the lion, the tiger and the leopard. Likewise, there is no expiation for killing any of aquatic animals [i.e. the one found in water].

Cutting trees of Ḥaram

Question: Please give some advice on cutting the trees etc. of Ḥaram?

Answer: Stated here are some rulings extracted from page 1189 and 1190 of the 1st volume of *Bahār-e-Sharī'at*, the 1250-page publication of Maktaba-tul-Madīnah, the publishing department of Dawat-e-Islami: There can be four categories of trees in Ḥaram.

1. The tree is planted by someone and is of the type usually planted by people.
2. The tree is planted by someone but is not of the type planted by people.
3. The tree is not planted by someone but is of the type planted by people.
4. The tree is not planted by someone, nor is it of the type planted by people.

[1] A very small animal like an insect that lives under the skin of other animals and sucks their blood.

There is no expiation for cutting the trees that come into the first three categories. However, if there is an owner of the tree, he will claim compensation. As for cutting the tree coming into the fourth category, penalty must be paid, and if there is an owner of the tree, he will receive compensation as well. Penalty will be paid provided the tree is fresh before being cut, not damaged or uprooted. In order to pay the penalty, the one who has cut the tree is required to buy grains for as much money as is the price of the tree, and distribute it among the Masākīn (considered destitute by Sharī'aĥ). He must give one Ṣadaqaĥ to each Miskīn. If the quantity of grains bought for as much money as the price of the tree, is less than even one Ṣadaqaĥ, he must give it to only one Miskīn. It is not necessary to give these Ṣadaqāt to the Masākīn of Ḥaram. He can give the price of the tree as Ṣadaqaĥ or can also buy an animal of the same value and slaughter it in Ḥaram. To keep fast to pay this expiation is not sufficient.

Ruling: The tree that has dried can be uprooted and can be benefitted from. **Ruling:** If someone has plucked leaves off the tree, causing no damage to the tree, no expiation is required. Similarly, there is no harm in cutting a growing tree provided the owner has given permission. The one who has cut the tree is to pay its price to the owner. **Ruling:** If some people have jointly cut the tree, only one penalty will be jointly paid by all of them whether all are Muḥrim or non-Muḥrim or some are Muḥrim and some are non-Muḥrim.

Ruling: It is not permissible to make a Miswāk by cutting a twig off the Pilu (salvadora persica) tree or any other tree of Ḥaram. **Ruling:** If some trees are broken or damaged because of a person walking, camping or riding his animal, there is no expiation. **Ruling:** Due to the need, the Fatwā is that it is permissible to graze animals on the grass of Haram. As for cutting or uprooting it, there is the same ruling on it as on cutting the tree except for dry grass as well as the grass called Iżkhar because it is permissible to obtain any type of benefit from them. There is no harm in breaking and uprooting the white grass naturally growing after raining.

Question and answer about passing Mīqāt without Iḥrām

Question: If an Āfāqī did not put on Iḥrām at Mīqāt, instead he put on Iḥrām at Masjid 'Āishaĥ and performed 'Umraĥ; what is the ruling?

Answer: If an Āfāqī has departed for Makka-tul-Mukarramaĥ and entered Mīqāt without Iḥrām, *Dam* will be Wājib for him. To put on Iḥrām at Masjid 'Āishaĥ will not be sufficient in this case. What he is required to do is to pay a *Dam* or alternatively go out of Mīqāt and come back after having put on Iḥrām of 'Umraĥ, etc. from there. If he takes the second option, *Dam* will become void.

◆◆◆

اَلۡحَمۡدُ لِلّٰهِ رَبِّ الۡعٰلَمِیۡنَ وَ الصَّلٰوةُ وَالسَّلَامُ عَلٰی سَیِّدِ الۡمُرۡسَلِیۡنَ

اَمَّا بَعۡدُ فَاَعُوۡذُ بِاللّٰهِ مِنَ الشَّیۡطٰنِ الرَّجِیۡمِ ؕ بِسۡمِ اللّٰهِ الرَّحۡمٰنِ الرَّحِیۡمِ ؕ

Hajj of Children

(Questions and Answers)

Excellence of Ṣalāt-'Alan-Nabī ﷺ

The Holy Prophet صَلَّى اللهُ تَعَالٰى عَلَيْهِ وَاٰلِهٖ وَسَلَّم has stated, 'To make the Żikr of Allah عَزَّوَجَلَّ in abundance and to recite the Ṣalāt upon me alleviate destitution.' *(Al-Qaul-ul-Badī', pp. 273)*

صَلُّوۡا عَلَی الۡحَبِیۡب   صَلَّی اللّٰهُ تَعَالٰی عَلٰی مُحَمَّد

Question 1: Can the children also perform Hajj?

Answer: Yes. Sayyidunā 'Abdullāĥ Ibn 'Abbās رَضِیَ اللهُ تَعَالٰی عَنْهُمَا has said, 'The Noble Prophet صَلَّى اللهُ تَعَالٰى عَلَيْهِ وَاٰلِهٖ وَسَلَّم came across a caravan at Rauḥā and asked them, 'Who are you? They replied, 'We are Muslims.' Then they said, 'Who are you?' The Holy Prophet صَلَّى اللهُ تَعَالٰى عَلَيْهِ وَاٰلِهٖ وَسَلَّم replied, 'I am the Prophet of Allah.' A woman among them lifted up a child and said, 'Will his Hajj be valid?' The Beloved and Blessed Prophet صَلَّى اللهُ تَعَالٰى عَلَيْهِ وَاٰلِهٖ وَسَلَّم replied, 'Yes, and you will also be granted a reward for this.' *(Muslim, pp. 697, Ḥadīš 1336)*

The renowned exegetist Muftī Aḥmad Yār Khān عَلَيْهِ رَحْمَةُ الْحَنَّان has stated, 'The child will have a reward as he will perform Hajj, and she will also have a reward as she will help him perform it.' He رَحْمَةُ اللهِ تَعَالٰى عَلَيْه

has further stated, 'We have learnt from this Ḥadīš that children are rewarded for the virtuous deeds they perform, and their parents are also rewarded. Therefore, make them offer Ṣalāt and fast regularly.' *(Mirāt, vol. 4, pp. 88)*

Question 2: If a child performs Hajj, will his Farḍ be fulfilled?

Answer: No. One of the prerequisites for Hajj being Farḍ is 'puberty'. A'lā Ḥaḍrat Imām Aḥmad Razā Khān عَلَيْهِ رَحْمَةُ الرَّحْمٰن has stated, 'Hajj is not Farḍ upon a child. If he performs Hajj, it will be a Nafl one and only he will be granted a reward. However, the father or the guardian etc. of the child will gain the reward of teaching him. If conditions exist after the child has reached puberty, Hajj will become Farḍ upon him. The Hajj he performed in childhood will not suffice.' *(Fatāwā Razawiyyaĥ referenced, vol. 10, pp. 775)*

Question 3: How many types of children are there with regard to the rites of Hajj?

Answer: There are two types of children in this regard:

1. A mature child is the one who can distinguish between cleanness and uncleanness, sweet and bitter and is aware that Islam is a means of salvation. *(Irshād-us-Sārī Ḥāshiyaĥ Manāsik, pp. 37)*

2. An immature child is the one who cannot distinguish between the aforementioned things and is unaware of them.

Question 4: Will a mature child have to perform the rites of Hajj himself?

Answer: Yes. A mature child should perform all acts of Hajj himself. If he even misses Ramī etc. then he will not be required to pay expiation. *(Bahār-e-Sharī'at, vol. 1, pp. 1075)*

Question 5: If a mature child is able to perform some of rites of Hajj himself but unable to perform some others, can he authorise anyone else to perform those rites on his behalf?

Answer: 'Allāmaĥ 'Alī Qārī عَلَيْهِ رَحْمَةُ اللّٰهِ الْبَارِى has said, 'It is incorrect to authorise anyone to perform such rites on behalf of the mature child that he can perform himself, whereas it is correct to authorise anyone to perform such acts on his behalf that he cannot perform himself. However, if a child cannot himself offer the two Rak'āt Nafl Ṣalāĥ after Ṭawāf, no other person can offer it on his behalf. *(Al-Maslak-ul-Mutaqassiṭ lil-Qārī, pp. 113)*

Method of immature child's Hajj

Question 6: How will an immature child perform the rites of Hajj?

Answer: The rites for which an intention is required will be performed by the guardian, whereas the child can perform the rites for which no intention is required. The Islamic jurists رَحِمَهُمُ اللّٰهُ تَعَالٰى have said, 'If an immature child puts on Iḥrām himself and performs the rites of Hajj, the Hajj will not be valid. His guardian should perform the rites of Hajj on his behalf. However, the guardian will not offer the two Rak'āt Nafl Ṣalāĥ of Ṭawāf on behalf of the child. If his father and brother both accompany him, the father should perform the rites (Arkān). *('Ālamgīrī, vol. 1, pp. 236; Bahār-e-Sharī'at, vol. 1, pp. 1075)*

'Allāmaĥ Maulānā Muftī Amjad 'Alī A'ẓamī عَلَيْهِ رَحْمَةُ اللّٰهِ الْقَوِى has stated, 'Immature children cannot perform the acts for which an intention is required such as Iḥrām or Ṭawāf, but rather anyone should perform these acts on behalf of them. As for the acts for which an intention is not required such as Wuqūf-e-'Arafaĥ these children can perform them. *(Bahār-e-Sharī'at, vol. 1, pp. 1046)*

Question 7: Is it necessary to make the children perform Ghusl before they put on Iḥrām?

Answer: Yes. Presented below is a summary of a jurisprudential clause stated on page 557 of volume 3 of *Fatāwā Shāmī*: Both mature and immature children should perform Ghusl. However, the difference is that it is Mustaḥab for a mature child to perform the Ghusl himself and it is Mustaḥab for a guardian to order the mature child to perform Ghusl. As for an immature child, it is Mustaḥab for the guardian to help him perform Ghusl or ask his mother etc. to help him perform Ghusl.

Question 8: Will an immature child be made to put on Iḥrām?

Answer: Yes. Removing the stitched clothes from the body of the immature child, the guardian or anyone else should make him put on a shawl and a Taĥband. Thereafter, the father or, if the father is not present, then brother, or if the brother is not also present, then any other close blood relative should make the intention of Iḥrām on behalf of the child and prevent him from those acts forbidden for Muḥrim.

'Allāmaĥ Maulānā Muftī Muhammad Amjad 'Alī A'ẓamī عَلَيْهِ رَحْمَةُ اللّٰهِ الْقَوِى has stated, 'The stitched clothes of a child should be removed before his guardian or anyone of his blood relatives puts on Iḥrām on his behalf. Make him wear a shawl and a Taĥband and prevent him from every act which is not permissible for a Muḥrim.

(Bahār-e-Sharī'at, vol. 1, pp. 1075)

A mature child will make the intention of Iḥrām himself and the guardian cannot put on Iḥrām on his behalf. It is stated in *Shāmī*: 'If a child is mature, he will have to put on Iḥrām himself. It is not permissible for the guardian to put on Iḥrām on behalf of this child.' *(Rad-dul-Muḥtār, vol. 3, 535)*

If a mature child can put on Iḥrām himself, he will have to do it himself. The guardian cannot put on Iḥrām on his behalf, nor will the mature child become a Muḥrim if the guardian puts on Iḥrām. However, if a mature child cannot put on Iḥrām himself, the guardian will put on Iḥrām on his behalf.

Question 9: Will a guardian have to offer the Nafl of Iḥrām on behalf of an immature child?

Answer: No. A guardian cannot offer the Nafl of Iḥrām on behalf of an immature child.

Method of intention and Labbayk on behalf of an immature child

Question 10: Please let us know about the method of Labbayk and the intention of Iḥrām on behalf of an immature child.

Answer: A guardian should make the intention of Iḥrām on behalf of an immature child and say: 'اَحْرَمْتُ عَنْ فُلَانٍ' i.e. *I put on Iḥrām on behalf of so-and-so* [Mention the child's name instead of saying so-and-so]. Similarly, invoke Talbiyaĥ on his behalf in the following way: 'لَبَّيْكَ عَنْ فُلَانٍ' [Mention his name instead of saying so-and-so and complete the Talbiyaĥ].

The intention in Arabic will only be valid when its meaning is known. One can also make the intention in his mother tongue or in Urdu. For example, if the child's name is Ĥilāl Razā, make the intention like this: '*I put on Iḥrām on behalf of Ĥilāl Razā*'. Keep it in mind that it is a condition to make the intention in the heart, while uttering it verbally is Mustaḥab. If one has not uttered his intention verbally, there is no problem. To recite the Talbiyaĥ is necessary. It should be recited to such an audible voice that the reciter can hear it if there is no difficulty in hearing. Then say the following:

لَبَّيْكَ عَنْ هِلال رضا اَللّٰهُمَّ لَبَّيْكَ ط لَبَّيْكَ لَا شَرِيْكَ لَكَ لَبَّيْكَ ط

اِنَّ الْحَمْدَ وَالنِّعْمَةَ لَكَ وَالْمُلْكَ ط لَا شَرِيْكَ لَكَ ط

Method of Istilām of Ḥajar-ul-Aswad and intention of Ṭawāf on behalf of an immature child

Question 11: Please let us know about the intention of Ṭawāf and the method of Istilām of Ḥajar-ul-Aswad on behalf of an immature child.

Answer: Although it is sufficient to make the intention in the heart, it is better to utter it verbally. For example '*I intend to perform the seven rounds of Ṭawāf on behalf of Ĥilāl Razā*'. Afterwards, the Istilām being performed, will be also on behalf of the child.

Question 12: Will the guardian make a child perform Ṭawāf by walking him or carrying him in the lap?

Answer: Whichever method is convenient for him, he can adopt.

Question 13: Can guardian make the intention of his own Ṭawāf while walking a child or carrying him in the lap?

Answer: He can do so. In fact, he should do it. By doing this, the Ṭawāf of both of them will get performed. Remember that Istilām will have to be performed twice in every round once on behalf of himself and once on behalf of the child.

Question 14: How will a child perform the Ṭawāf?

Answer: A mature child should perform the Ṭawāf himself and offer the Nawāfil of Ṭawāf, whereas the guardian of an immature child should make him perform the Ṭawāf. However, the guardian should not offer the two Rak'āt of Ṭawāf on behalf of this child. *(Baĥār-e-Sharī'at, vol. 1, pp. 1075)*

Question 15: How can a child be made to perform Ramī?

Answer: A mature child will perform Ramī himself. Those accompanying an immature child should perform Ramī on his behalf. It is better to place stones onto the hand of the child and help perform Ramī. *(Mansik Mutawassiṭ, pp. 247; Fatāwā Razawiyyaĥ, vol. 10, pp. 667; Baĥār-e-Sharī'at, vol. 1, pp. 1148)*

Question 16: If a child misses any of Hajj rites or commits such an act which makes expiation or *Dam* due, what is the ruling in this regard?

Answer: If a child misses some act or commits a prohibited act, it is not Wājib upon him to do Qaḍā or pay expiation. Similarly, if the guardian of an immature child puts on Iḥrām on his behalf and the child commits some prohibited act, the father is not required to do Qaḍā or pay expiation.

('Ālamgīrī, vol. 1, pp. 236; Baĥār-e-Sharī'at, vol. 1, pp. 1075)

Question 17: What will one have to do if a child invalidates the Hajj?

Answer: If a child invalidates the Hajj, no *Dam* is Wājib upon him. It is also not Wājib to do Qaḍā of Hajj even if a mature child has done so. *('Ālamgīrī, vol. 1, pp. 236; Rad-dul-Muḥtār, vol. 3, pp. 673)*

Question 18: What is the ruling of a ritual sacrifice of Hajj offered by a child?

Answer: Regardless of which a child is mature or immature; no ritual sacrifice (of Hajj Tamattu' or Hajj Qirān) is Wājib upon him. *(Al-Maslak-ul-Mutaqassiṭ lil-Qārī, pp. 263)* The ritual sacrifice of Hajj Ifrād is not Wājib even upon adults.

Question 19: If the guardian wants to perform a ritual sacrifice of Hajj on behalf of a child, can he do it or not?

Answer: He can do so. But he should do it with his own money. If he spends the money of a child, he will have to make up for it. It means that he will have to return that money to the child.

Method of a child's 'Umraĥ

Question 20: Can a child be taken to perform the 'Umraĥ? If so, what is the method?

Answer: Yes, a child can be taken to perform 'Umraĥ. The previously mentioned same rulings of mature and immature child will apply here. However, one should ponder over the rulings of taking a very little child to the Masjid. The ruling is that if it is highly probable that a child would defecate or urinate in the Masjid, it is Makrūĥ Taḥrīmī to take him into the Masjid, otherwise it is Makrūĥ Tanzīĥī.

Question 21: Should a child be made to perform Ḥalq or Qaṣr?

Answer: Yes. However, a little girl should be made to perform Qaṣr. If there is a baby girl or a very little one, there is no harm in performing her Qaṣr.

Child and Naflī Ṭawāf

Question 22: What is the ruling for a child as regards a Naflī Ṭawāf?

Answer: A mature child should make the intention himself and offer the post-Ṭawāf Nafl Ṣalāĥ, whereas the guardian should make the intention on behalf of an immature child. There is no need to offer the Nawāfil of Ṭawāf.

Question 23: If a minor reaches puberty after he has entered Mīqāt without (putting on) Iḥrām, will *Dam* become Wājib upon him?

Answer: No. It is cited on page 1192 (volume 1) of *Bahār-e-Sharī'at*: If a minor reaches puberty after he has passed Mīqāt and put on Iḥrām, no *Dam* is necessary. Similarly, if he reaches puberty at Ḥil i.e. outside the Ḥaram but within the limits of Mīqāt, the rulings of Ḥillī will be applied. It means that if he wants to go for Hajj or 'Umraĥ, he should put on Iḥrām at Ḥil, or if he does not want to go for Hajj or 'Umraĥ, the rulings of Ḥaramī will be applied. In short, he will put on Iḥrām for Hajj within the Ḥaram, as for 'Umraĥ he will put on Iḥrām outside the Ḥaram. If he doesn't want to perform either, there is no need to put on Iḥrām.

Question 24: Can a child be taken to Masjid-un-Nabawī or not?

Answer: The Beloved Prophet صَلَّى اللهُ تَعَالٰى عَلَيْهِ وَاٰلِهٖ وَسَلَّم has said, 'Save the Masājid from children and the insane and trading and quarrels and raising voice and inflicting punishment and unsheathing swords.' *(Ibn Mājaĥ, vol. 1, pp. 415, Ḥadīš, 750)*

If it is highly probable that a child or an insane person if taken into the Masjid would defecate or urinate in the Masjid then it is Ḥarām otherwise Makrūĥ. People who take the shoes into the Masjid should make sure that if the shoes are stained with uncleanness, it should be cleaned off insomuch that there remains neither uncleanness nor foul smell. However, if you have cleaned shoes in such a way that neither there is the risk of the Masjid being unclean nor is there any foul smell, then it is not impermissible. Remember that walking into the Masjid with shoes on is the disrespect of the Masjid even if the shoes are clean.

It is not allowed to take small children, the insane (or an unconscious person or the one captured by a jinn) into the Masjid even for spiritual remedies etc. A baby cannot be brought into the Masjid even if it is packed into a napkin etc. If you have ever committed the mistake of bringing such children into the Masjid, repent instantly and make a firm intention of not doing it again. However, it is permissible to bring the children into Finā-e-Masjid, say the Imām's room, provided one does not have to pass through the actual part of the Masjid. If these are the manners of entering into an ordinary Masjid then the manners of entering into the Masjid-ul-Ḥarām and Masjid-un-Nabawī are absolutely great. A devotee of Rasūl can realise it.

There is a great need to secure the Masjidayn Karīmayn from the children. Nowadays the children run, shouting and sometimes they even defecate or urinate inside the Masjidayn Karīmayn. Alas! Those who take them into there do not pay any attention. Without any doubt, the children are immature and innocent, but those who take them there are at fault. If a mature child is taken into the Masjid, pay a close attention to him lest he should start playing around and interrupting those worshipping Allah عَزَّوَجَلَّ.

Child and paying visit to the Rauḍah-e-Anwar

Question 25: How an immature child be taken in front of the Golden Grille?

Answer: As for this purpose, he will have to be taken to the Masjid. We have just discussed the rulings. Therefore, make him behold the Great Green Dome from outside the Masjid.

Question 26: Are the rulings for a child girl about Hajj and 'Umraĥ the same as mentioned earlier?

Answer: Yes.

Glossary

Note: This glossary consists of only an introductory explanation to Islamic terms. For thorough understanding, please consult some Sunnī scholar.

'Arafaĥ [عَرَفَہ]: 9th day of Żul-Ḥijjaĥ (last Islamic month)

Du'ā [دُعَا]: Supplication

Farḍ [فَرْض]: It is an obligation without performing which one cannot be freed from duty and if some act is Farḍ in worship, the worship will not be accomplished without performing that act. Not performing a Farḍ deliberately is a grave sin.

Ghusl [غُسْل]: Ritual bath

Ḥājī [حَاجِی]: One who has performed Hajj

Ḥalāl [حَلَال]: Lawful (by Sharī'aĥ)

Ḥarām [حَرَام]: It is opposite of Farḍ; committing it deliberately even once is a grave sin.

Ḥujjāj [حُجَّاج]: Plural of Ḥājī, i.e. pilgrims of Hajj

Imām [اِمَام]: A Muslim who leads others in congregational Ṣalāĥ.

Īṣāl-e-Šawāb [اِیْصَالِ ثَوَاب]: Īṣāl-e-Šawāb refers to the act of spiritually donating the reward of virtuous deeds to the Muslims. Īṣāl-e-Šawāb may be made to all deceased and living male and female Muslims including even Muslim jinns. See its detailed method in the booklet '*Method of Fātiḥaĥ*' published by Maktaba-tul-Madīnaĥ.

Jabal [جَبَل]: Mountain

Kanz-ul-Īmān [كَنْزُالْاِيْمَان]: Name of the Urdu translation of the Holy Quran by Imām-e-Aĥl-e-Sunnat, Al-Ḥāj, Al-Ḥāfiẓ, Al-Qārī Imām Aḥmad Razā Khan عَلَيْهِ رَحْمَةُ الرَّحْمٰن.

Kawšar [كَوْثَر]: The pond of Paradise

Maḥram [مَحْرَم]: One with whom marriage is Ḥarām forever.

Makrūĥ [مَكْرُوْه]: Disliked

Makrūĥ Taḥrīmī [مَكْرُوْه تَحْرِيْمِى]: It is in comparison with Wājib; if it occurs in worship, the worship gets defective and the committer of Makrūĥ Taḥrīmī is considered a sinner. Although its gravity is lesser than that of Ḥarām, committing it a few times is a grave sin.

Makrūĥ Tanzīĥī [مَكْرُوْه تَنْزِيْهِى]: It is in comparison with Sunan-e-Ghayr Muakkadaĥ. It is an act which Sharī'aĥ dislikes to be committed, although there is no punishment for the one who commits it.

Mimbar [مِنْبَر]: Pulpit

Miskīn [مِسْكِيْن]: A Miskīn is the one who possesses nothing and has to beg others for food to satisfy hunger and clothes to cover the body. Begging is Ḥalāl (allowed) for him.

Miswāk [مِسْوَاك]: Natural tooth-stick made from a twig of a tree, typically made from peelu, olive or walnut tree

Mu'allim [مُعَلِّم]: Guide

Muftī [مُفْتِى]: An authorized scholar who is expert in Islamic jurisprudence to answer religious queries.

Muḥrim [مُحْرِم]: One in the state of Iḥrām

Mustaḥab [مُسْتَحَب]: An act which Sharī'aĥ likes to be performed but its abandonment is not disliked.

Na'at [نَعْت]: Poetic eulogy in praise of the Prophet of mankind, the Peace of our heart and mind, the most Generous and Kind صَلَّى اللهُ تَعَالٰى عَلَيْهِ وَاٰلِهٖ وَسَلَّم

Nafl [نَفْل]: Supererogatory act / worship

Nafs [نَفْس]: Centre of sensual desires in human body, psyche

Qaḍā [قَضَا]: To make up or compensate for any missed worship

Qiblaĥ [قِبْلَه]: The direction which Muslims face during Ṣalāĥ etc.

Qurbānī [قُرْبَانِی]: Ritual animal sacrifice called Naḥr in Arabic

Rak'at [رَكْعَت]: Unit/cycle of Ṣalāĥ

Ṣadaqaĥ [صَدَقَه]: Charity or alms

Ṣalāt/Ṣalāt-'Alan-Nabī ﷺ [صَلَاة عَلَى النَّبِی]: Supplication for asking blessings for the Holy Prophet صَلَّى اللهُ تَعَالٰى عَلَيْهِ وَاٰلِهٖ وَسَلَّم

Shar'ī [شَرْعِی]: According to Sharī'aĥ

Sharī'at/Sharī'aĥ [شَرِيْعَة]: Commandments of Allah عَزَّوَجَلَّ and His Noble Prophet صَلَّى اللهُ تَعَالٰى عَلَيْهِ وَاٰلِهٖ وَسَلَّم

Ṣubḥ-e-Ṣādiq [صُبْح صَادِق]: The true dawn

Sunnat-ul-Muakkadaĥ [سُنَّةُ الْمُؤَكَّدَه]: An act which the Beloved and Blessed Prophet صَلَّى اللهُ تَعَالٰى عَلَيْهِ وَاٰلِهٖ وَسَلَّم practiced continually but at times, also forsook it to show permissibility of its abandonment.

Sūraĥ [سُوْرَة]: Chapter of the Holy Quran

Taĥajjud [تَہَجُّد]: A supererogatory Ṣalāĥ offered at night after awakening, having offered Ṣalāt-ul-'Ishā

Ṭawāf [طَوَاف]: Moving around the Holy Ka'baĥ

Ummaĥ [اُمَّة]: Believers of the Holy Prophet صَلَّى اللهُ تَعَالٰى عَلَيْهِ وَاٰلِهٖ وَسَلَّم as a whole

Veil within veil [پردے میں پردہ]: Veil within veil is the translation of the Urdu term 'Parday mayn Pardaĥ' used in the Madanī environment of Dawat-e-Islami. It refers to the act of wrapping an extra shawl around dress from navel to knees.

Wājib [وَاجِب]: It is an obligation without performing which one will not be freed from obligation and if a Wājib act is missed in worship, that worship will be considered defective; however the worship will be considered performed. Not performing a Wājib once deliberately is a minor sin and leaving it a few times is a grave sin.

Witr [وِتْر]: Wājib Ṣalāĥ comprising three cycles offered with Ṣalāt-ul-'Ishā

Wuḍū [وُضُو]: Ritual ablution which is a pre-requisite for Ṣalāĥ, Ṭawāf and for touching the Holy Quran etc.

Wuqūf [وُقُوْف]: Ritual stay as a part of worship

Żikr [ذِكْر]: The remembrance of Allah عَزَّوَجَلَّ

Ziyāraĥ [زِيَارَة]: Holy places

Żul-Ḥijjaĥ [ذُوالْحِجَّة]: Name of the 12th month of the Islamic calendar

Bibliography

Sunan Abū Dāwūd, Dār Iḥyā-ut-Turāš Al-'Arabī, Beirut

Akhbār-ul-Akhyār, Fārūqī Academy Gambat, Pakistan

Al-Baḥr-ul-'Amīq fil-Manāsik, Muassasa-tur-Rayyān, Beirut

Al-Baḥr-ur-Rāiq, Quetta, Pakistan

Al-Īḍāḥ fi Manāsik Al-Hajj, Al-Maktaba-tul-Imdādiyaĥ, Makkaĥ

Al-Mabsūṭ, Dār-ul-Kutub 'Ilmiyyaĥ, Beirut

Al-Manāmāt, Al-Maktaba-tul-'Aṣriyyaĥ, Beirut

Al-Maslak-ul-Mutaqassiṭ, Karachi, Pakistan

Al-Mawāĥib-ul-Ladunniyyaĥ, Dār-ul-Kutub 'Ilmiyyaĥ, Beirut

Al-Mu'jam-ul-Awsaṭ, Dār-ul-Kutub 'Ilmiyyaĥ, Beirut

Al-Mu'jam-ul-Kabīr, Dār Iḥyā-ut-Turāš Al-'Arabī, Beirut

Al-Qaul-ul-Badī', Muassasa-tur-Rayyān, Beirut

Ash-Shifā, Markaz Aĥl-e-Sunnat, Barakāt Razā, Hind

Attarghīb Wattarĥīb, Dār-ul-Kutub 'Ilmiyyaĥ, Beirut

Baĥār-e-Sharī'at, Maktaba-tul-Madīnaĥ, Karachi, Pakistan

Balad-ul-Amīn, Maktabaĥ Farīdiyaĥ, Sahiwal, Pakistan

Bistān-ul-Muḥaddišīn, Karachi, Pakistan

Dār Quṭnī, Multan, Pakistan

Durra-tun-Nāṣiḥīn, Dār-ul-Fikr, Beirut

Durr-e-Mukhtār, Dār-ul-Ma'rifaĥ, Beirut

Fatāwā 'Ālamgīrī, Dār-ul-Fikr, Beirut

Fatāwā Razawiyyaĥ, Razā Foundation, Lahore, Pakistan

Fatḥ-ul-Bārī, Dār-ul-Kutub 'Ilmiyyaĥ, Beirut

Ĥidāyaĥ, Dār Iḥyā-ut-Turāš Al-'Arabī, Beirut

Ḥiṣn Ḥaṣīn, Al-Maktaba-tul-'Aṣriyyaĥ, Beirut

Ibn 'Asākir, Dār-ul-Fikr, Beirut

Ibn Mājaĥ, Dār-ul-Ma'rifaĥ, Beirut

Iḥrām and Fragrant Soap, Maktaba-tul-Madīnaĥ, Karachi, Pakistan

Iḥyā-ul-'Ulūm, Dār Ṣādir, Beirut

Irshād-us-Sārī, Karachi, Pakistan

Itḥāf-us-Sādaĥ, Dār-ul-Kutub 'Ilmiyyaĥ, Beirut

Jāmi' Tirmiżī, Dār-ul-Fikr, Beirut

Jāmi'-ul-'Ulūm wal-Ḥukm, Al-Fayṣaliyaĥ, Makka-tul-Mukarramaĥ

Jażb-ul-Qulūb, An-Nūriyaĥ Ar-Razawiyyaĥ Publishing Company, Lahore

Kashf-ul-Maḥjūb, Nawā-e-Waqt Printer, Lahore, Pakistan

Kitāb-ul-Hajj, Maktabaĥ Nu'māniyaĥ, Sialkot

Lubāb-ul-Manāsik, Karachi, Pakistan

Majma'-uz-Zawāid, Dār-ul-Fikr, Beirut

Malfūẓāt A'lā Haḍrat, Maktaba-tul-Madīnaĥ, Karachi, Pakistan

Mašnawī Maulānā Rūm, An-Nūriyaĥ Ar-Razawiyyaĥ Publishing Company

Mirāt-ul-Manājīḥ, Ziyā-ul-Quran, Lahore, Pakistan

Musnad Abū Dāwūd Ṭayālsī, Dār-ul-Ma'rifaĥ, Beirut

Musnad Bazzār, Maktaba-tul-'Ulūm wal-Ḥukm Madīna-tul-Munawwaraĥ

Musnad Imām Aḥmad, Dār-ul-Fikr, Beirut

Musnad Imām Shafi'ī, Dār-ul-Kutub 'Ilmiyyaĥ, Beirut

Muwaṭṭā Imām Mālik, Dār-ul-Ma'rifaĥ, Beirut

Qūt-ul-Qulūb, Dār-ul-Kutub 'Ilmiyyaĥ, Beirut

Rad-dul-Muḥtār, Dār-ul-Ma'rifaĥ, Beirut

Rauḍ-ur-Riyāḥīn, Dār-ul-Kutub 'Ilmiyyaĥ, Beirut

Ṣaḥīḥ Bukhārī, Dār-ul-Kutub 'Ilmiyyaĥ, Beirut

Ṣaḥīḥ Muslim, Dār Ibn Ḥazm, Beirut

Shu'ab-ul-Īmān, Dār-ul-Kutub 'Ilmiyyaĥ, Beirut

Ṭabaqāt-ul-Kubrā, Dār-ul-Kutub 'Ilmiyyaĥ, Beirut

Tafsīr Khazāin-ul-'Irfān, Maktaba-tul-Madīnaĥ, Karachi, Pakistan

Tafsīr Na'īmī, Maktaba Islāmiyaĥ

Tanbīĥ-ul-Mughtarrīn, Dār-ul-Ma'rifaĥ, Beirut

Tārīkh Baghdad, Dār-ul-Kutub 'Ilmiyyaĥ, Beirut

Wafā-ul-Wafā, Dār Iḥyā-ut-Turāš Al-'Arabī, Beirut

Wasāil-e-Bakhshish, Maktaba-tul-Madīnaĥ, Karachi, Pakistan

Index

'Arafaĥ 106, 117
'Arafāt 5, 9, 10, 18, 34
  Du'ās 110
  entering 105
  ritual stay in 107
'Arsh 154
'Umraĥ
  Qaṣr for 225
  reward of 177

A

Āfāqī 27, 32, 33, 142, 192, 193
Al-Amīn 169
Al-Madīna-tul-'Ilmiyyaĥ xix
Amrad 200
Arabia 132
Aṣḥāb-ul-Fīl 34
Ashĥur-ul-Hajj 26

B

Bāb-ul-Ka'baĥ 29
Bāb-uṣ-Ṣafā 31, 82
Bāb-us-Salām 29, 56, 136
Bařā 'Umraĥ 174
Baṭn 'Uranaĥ 35
Bayt-ul-Muqaddas 20

C

cave
  Ḥirā 171
  Jabal Šaur 171
compass 5, 101
cutting nails
  questions & answers 204

D

Dam 8, 49, 53, 124, 129, 133
  definition of 8, 181
  leniency in 181
Dār-ul-Iftā Aĥl-e-Sunnat xix
departure 122, 193
  from Madīnaĥ 167
Du'ā
  for reading the book iii
  from Ṣafā 88
  green marks 89
  safety from harms 14
  travelling 13

F

fragrant kohl 49

G

Ghusl 39, 107, 153

H

Ḥajar-ul-Aswad 28, 29, 35, 43
Ḥājī 21, 143
  forgiveness 18
  free from sins 18
Hajj 152, 170, 226
  Farḍ 146
  Ifrād 38
  Nafl 145
  Qirān 38
  ritual sacrifice 130
  Tamattu' 38
Hajj Badal
  Madanī pearls 149
  pre-conditions 145
Ḥalāl 26, 33, 45, 56, 72, 74, 119, 138
Ḥalq 28, 38
  Madanī pearls 133
  questions & answers 225
Ḥaram 28, 33, 34, 35, 109, 182
  explanation of 55
Ḥarām 10, 26, 33
  exposing thigh or Satr 53
Ḥaṭīm 30, 96, 161, 176

health certificate 5
Madanī pearls 7
Ḥil 33
house
Khadīja-tul-Kubrā 170
Ḥujrah 177

I

I'tikāf 79
Iḍṭibā' 26, 58, 81, 91, 100
questions & answers 198
Iḥrām 5, 8, 26, 33, 38, 42
Makrūĥ acts 46
man and woman 50
meaning of 45
method of putting on 39
permissible acts 48
precautions 52
prohibitions 45
impermissible
musical ringtone 198
Indo-Pak 32, 38
intention
'Umraĥ 40
Hajj 41
Hajj Qirān 41
important ruling 44
I'tikāf 56
Sa'ī 87
Ṭawāf 58
intercourse
questions & answers 202
Īṣāl-e-Šawāb 145, 174
Istilām 28, 43, 64, 66
definition of 60

J

Jabal-ur-Raḥmaĥ 34
Jamarāt 28, 34, 126
Jamra-tul-'Aqabaĥ 44
Jannat-ul-Baqī' 168
Jannat-ul-Ma'lā 172, 173
Ji'irrānaĥ 33
Juḥfaĥ 32

K

Ka'baĥ 27, 28, 29, 30, 51, 57
door 29
first glance 57
house of Allah 29
Karāmaĥ 20
Kawšar 10, 70
Khiṭmī 215
Kufr 118, 184
Kursī 154

L

Labbayk 42
Luqṭaĥ 95

M

Ma'żūr Shar'ī 195
Mad'ā 35
Madīna-tul-Munawwaraĥ 152, 153
Maḥram 10
Makka-tul-Mukarramaĥ 152, 170
Makrūĥ 11, 12, 14, 15, 40, 47, 48
Makrūĥ Tanzīĥī 49
Maktaba-tul-Madīnaĥ 52, 96, 154, 180
Maqām-u-Ibrāĥīm . 30, 31, 35, 75, 79, 93
Mas'ā 31
Masfalaĥ 171, 172
Mashāĥid-e-Mubārakaĥ
definition of 37
Masjid 'Āishaĥ 175, 243
Masjid Bilāl 170
Masjid Ḥilāl 170
Masjid Ji'irrāṇaĥ 174
Masjid Jinn 173
Masjid Khayf 173, 174
Masjid Qubā 177
Masjidayn Karīmayn 95
Masjid-ul-Ḥarām .. 28, 29, 31, 33, 55, 191
Du'ā of exiting 82
Du'ā of entering 56
Masjid-ur-Rāyaĥ 173
Maṭāf 27, 35, 176
Mīlayn-e-Akhḍarayn 31, 35

Mimbar 36, 160
an orchard of Paradise 177
Minā 5, 18, 34
Du'ā 101
leaving 101
Mīqāt 32, 33, 191, 193
Miskīn
definition of 182
Miswāk 5, 39, 48, 153, 242
Mīzāb-ur-Raḥmaĥ 30, 35, 176
mount Marwaĥ 31, 169, 171
mount Ṣafā 31, 82
Mu'allim 9, 10, 101, 102, 127
Muḥassir 34
Muḥrim 45, 49, 50, 53, 134
Multazam 30, 35, 79, 93, 138
definition of 77
Mustaḥab 35, 43, 80, 90, 99, 104, 130
Mustajāb 30, 63
Mustajār 30, 35, 172, 176
Muwājaĥaĥ 36, 162, 167
visit 155
Muzdalifaĥ 34
departure 122
stay 124
mysterious Ḥājī 20

N

Na'at 98, 151
Nafs 81
Najd 32
Nawāriyaĥ 175

P

Pakistan 237
parable 11, 164
Pilu
salvadora persica 242

Q

Qarn-ul-Manāzil 32
Qaṣr 28, 38, 133
Qiblaĥ 5, 79, 80, 134, 138

R

Ramī 28, 126, 127, 129, 138
10th Żul-Ḥijja-til-Ḥarām 228
11th and 12th Żul-Ḥijjaĥ 138
by the ill 129
first rite of 10th Żul-Ḥijjaĥ 126
Islamic sisters 129
Makrūĥ acts 141
Qaḍā 140
question & answer 223
Raml 27, 61, 67, 100, 137
questions & answers 198
Rauḍaĥ 154
removal of hair
questions & answers 205
ritual sacrifice 226, 228
questions & answers 224
Riyadh 32, 234
Rukn 'Irāqī 29, 30, 176
Rukn Aswad 29, 30, 63
Rukn Shāmī 29, 30
Rukn Yamānī 29, 30, 35, 63, 65, 176

S

Sa'ī 28, 31, 81, 90, 92
Makrūĥ acts 98
permissible acts 97
questions & answers 199
rulings 99
Ṣadaqaĥ 8, 49, 53, 143, 182
definition of 181
Ṣalāh 8, 10, 12, 40, 54
at Mas'ā 90
Farḍ 16
Madanī pearls 76
Qaṣr 16
Ṭawāf 75
Salām
buried in Jannat-ul-Baqī' 166
Fārūq A'ẓam 158
Holy Prophet 157
martyrs of Uḥud 179
Sayyidunā Ḥamzaĥ 178
Shaykhayn together 159
Ṣiddīq Akbar 158

Satr 53
Shajarah 5
Shar'ī Faqīr 214
Sharī'ah 57, 237
Shirk 118
Ṣubḥ-e-Ṣādiq 27, 34, 97, 123, 124, 129
Sunnah 5, 11, 14, 34
  of Iḥrām 53
Sunnat-ul-Muakkadah..27, 107, 124, 197
supplication
  fifth round 70
  first round 62
  fourth round 68
  Maqām-u-Ibrāhīm 76
  second round 64
  seventh round 73
  sixth round 72
  third round 66
Sūrah
  Al-'Alaq 171
  Al-Baqarah .... vi, 19, 83, 235
  Āl-e-'Imrān vii
  Al-Fātiḥah 11, 40, 75, 155
  Al-Ḥujurāt xvi
  Al-Ikhlāṣ 11, 40, 75, 110, 155
  Al-Kāfirūn 12, 40, 75, 155
  Al-Qaṣaṣ 12
  An-Naḥl 109
  An-Nās 12
  An-Nisā xv
  At-Taubah 171, 233
  Lahab 12
  Quraysh 14
  Ṭāḥā 153
  Zukhruf 14
Sutrah
  definition of 90

T

Ta'wīż 50
Tahband 54, 221, 222
Talbiyah 26, 43, 101, 104, 115
Tan'īm 33
Taqṣīr
  definition of 91
  Islamic sisters 91
  Madanī pearls 133
Ṭawāf 27, 29
  Ḥarām acts 96
  Makrūh acts 96
  method of 58
  permissible acts 97
  questions & answers 193
  Ṣalāh 75
Ṭawāf-ul-'Umrah 28
Ṭawāf-ul-Qudūm 27, 90, 91, 137
  penalty 197
Ṭawāf-ul-Wadā' 27
Ṭawāf-ur-Rukhṣat
  Madanī pearls 142
  questions & answers 192
Ṭawāf-uz-Ziyārah 27, 79, 91, 100
  Madanī pearls 136
  questions & answers 187
tomb
  Sayyidatunā Maymūnah 175

U

use of perfume
  questions & answers 208

W

Wājib 8, 10, 27, 34, 53, 75, 124
wearing stitched clothes
  questions & answers 217
Wuḍū 43, 97, 98, 99, 153, 163
Wuqūf 34, 35

Y

Yalamlam 32

Z

Zakāh 10, 122, 145, 232
Zam Zam well 31, 35, 79
Żāt 'Irq 32
Żikr 96, 160
Żul-Ḥulayfah 32

Table of Contents

Du'ā for Reading the Book iii
Transliteration Chart iv
Translator's Notes v
56 Intentions for Pilgrims of Hajj and 'Umrah vi
Congratulations for Your Intention of Visiting Madīna-tul-Munawwarah! xix

RAFIQ-UL-HARAMAYN 1

Travellers of Madīnah and help from Mustafa ﷺ 1
16 Useful Madanī pearls for Ḥujjāj 2
List of items for pilgrims 5
5 Madanī pearls for luggage 6
Madanī pearls about health certificate 7
When should pilgrims travelling by air put on Iḥrām? 7
Fragrant tissue paper in an aircraft 8
Jeddah to Makkah 9
Iḥrām of those flying to Madīnah 9
Transport organized by Mu'allim 9
Twenty eight (28) Madanī pearls regarding travelling 10
 A parable 11
 Du'ā for the protection of aeroplane from falling and burning 12
6 Madanī pearls of offering Ṣalāh during journey 16
3 Sayings of the Holy Prophet ﷺ 18
70 Million virtues on every step 18
The angels embrace those going for Hajj on foot 19
Commandment of Holy Quran during Hajj 19

Treasure of devotion is essential for Ḥājī 20
Adopt affiliation with true devotee 20
1. Mysterious Ḥājī 20
2. Ḥājī who slaughtered himself 21
How is it to call oneself Ḥājī? 21
An anecdote 22
How is it to display a 'Hajj congratulations board'? 22
Hajj-pilgrimage on foot 23
Even unable to perform Ṭawāf 23
Attack of 'ostentation' and 'desire for respect' on Ḥājī 24
Two examples of ostentation of Ḥujjāj 25
55 Terms 26
Names of 4 corners of Ka'baĥ 29
There are 5 Mīqāt 32
29 Places where one's Du'ā is accepted 35
Types of Hajj 38
1. Qirān 38
2. Tamattu' 38
3. Ifrād 38
Method of putting on Iḥrām 39
Iḥrām of Islamic sisters 39
Nafl Ṣalāĥ of Iḥrām 40
Intention for 'Umraĥ 40
Intention for Hajj 41
Intention for Hajj Qirān 41
Labbayk 42
Recite Labbayk considering its meaning 42
One Sunnaĥ after reciting Labbayk 43
9 Madanī pearls of Labbayk 43

Important ruling regarding intention....44
Meaning of Iḥrām....45
Ḥarām acts in Iḥrām....45
Makrūĥ acts in Iḥrām....46
Permissible acts in Iḥrām....48
Difference in Iḥrām of man and woman....50
9 Useful cautions in Iḥrām....52
An important caution....54
Explanation of Ḥaram....55
Entering Makkaĥ....55
Make intention of I'tikāf....56
First glance at Holy Ka'baĥ....57
Most virtuous supplication....57
Halting for supplication during Ṭawāf is forbidden....58

METHOD OF 'UMRAH....58

Method of Ṭawāf....58
Supplication of first round....62
Supplication of second round....64
Supplication of third round....66
Supplication of fourth round....68
Supplication of fifth round....70
Supplication of sixth round....72
Supplication of seventh round....73
Maqām-u-Ibrāĥīm....75
Ṣalāĥ for Ṭawāf....75
Supplication of Maqām-u-Ibrāĥīm....76
4 Madanī pearls about offering Ṣalāĥ at Maqām-u-Ibrāĥīm....76
Now come at Multazam....77
Du'ā to be made at Multazam....78

An important ruling 79
Come at Zam Zam well 79
Recite this Du'ā after drinking Zam Zam water 80
How to make Du'ā whilst drinking Zam Zam water 80
Do not drink very cold water 81
Eyesight improves 81
Sa'ī of Ṣafā and Marwaĥ 81
Wrong way 83
Du'ā of mount Ṣafā 83
Intention of Sa'ī 87
Du'ā when descending from Ṣafā/Marwaĥ 88
Du'ā to be recited between green marks 89
A precaution to be taken during Sa'ī 90
Ṣalāĥ of Sa'ī is Mustaḥab 90
Ṭawāf-ul-Qudūm 90
Ḥalq or Taqṣīr 91
Definition of Taqṣīr 91
Taqṣīr for Islamic sisters 91
Advice for those performing Ṭawāf-ul-Qudūm 91
Advice for Mutamatte' 92
Advice for all Ḥujjāj 92
What to do during stay in Makkaĥ? 93
Very important caution 94
Ruling on taking others shoes unlawfully 95
Advice for Islamic sisters 95
Seven Ḥarām acts during Ṭawāf 96
Eleven Makrūĥ acts during Ṭawāf 96
Seven permissible acts during Sa'ī and Ṭawāf 97
Ten Makrūĥ acts in Sa'ī 98
Four miscellaneous rulings regarding Sa'ī 99

Important advice for Islamic sisters 99
Rain and Mīzāb-ur-Raḥmaĥ 99
Put on the Iḥrām of Hajj 100
A Madanī advice 100
Leaving for Minā 101
Quarrels over staying place in Minā first day 102
Du'ā of night of 'Arafaĥ 103
Spending night of 9th Żul-Ḥijjaĥ in Minā is Sunnat-ul-Muakkadaĥ ... 104
Leaving for 'Arafāt 104
Du'ā of pathway to 'Arafāt 105
Entering 'Arafāt 105
Two great virtues of the day of 'Arafaĥ 106
Seeing women on 'Arafaĥ 106
Making stones witness in plains of 'Arafāt 106
Fortunate Hajj pilgrims 107
9 Madanī pearls regarding ritual stay in 'Arafāt 107
Emphatic advice of Imām Aḥmad Razā Khān رَحْمَةُ اللهِ عَلَيْه 109
Du'ās of 'Arafāt 110
Madanī pearl 114
It is Sunnaĥ to make Du'ā in 'Arafāt whilst standing 115
Du'ā of 'Arafāt (English) 116
Continue to make Du'ā even after sunset 121
Freed from sins 122
Departure for Muzdalifaĥ 122
Method of offering Maghrib and 'Ishā Ṣalāĥ in combination 123
Collect stones 123
An important caution 123
Ritual stay in Muzdalifaĥ 124
Du'ā to be recited on the way from Muzdalifaĥ to Minā 125
Recite this Du'ā on seeing Minā 125

Ramī; first rite of 10th Żul-Ḥijjaĥ 126
5 Madanī pearls of precautions about Ramī 126
Eight Madanī pearls regarding Ramī 128
Ramī by Islamic sisters 129
Ramī by the ill 129
Ramī on behalf of the ill Hajj pilgrims 129
Seven Madanī pearls of ritual sacrifice of Hajj 130
Ḥājī and the ritual sacrifice of Eid-ul-Aḍḥā 132
Tokens for animal sacrifice 132
17 Madanī pearls regarding Ḥalq and Taqṣīr 133
10 Madanī pearls regarding Ṭawāf-uz-Ziyāraĥ 136
18 Madanī pearls regarding Ramī of 11th and 12th Żul-Ḥijjaĥ 138
12 Makrūĥ acts in Ramī 141
19 Madanī pearls about Ṭawāf-ur-Rukhṣat 142

Hajj Badal 145

17 Pre-conditions of Hajj Badal 146
9 Miscellaneous Madanī pearls regarding Hajj Badal 149

Journey to Madīna-tul-Munawwaraĥ 151

Method of enhancing fervour 151
How long will it take to get to Madīnaĥ? 152
Quranic proof for remaining barefoot 152
Preparation for the visit 153
Grand Green Dome appears 153
Enter via Bāb-ul-Baqī’ 154
Ṣalāĥ in gratitude 155
Appearing before Golden Grille 155
Presence at the sacred Muwājaĥaĥ 156
Make Salām to Holy Prophet ﷺ 157

Make Salām to Ṣiddīq Akbar رَضِیَ اللهُ عَنْهُ 158
Make Salām to Fārūq A'ẓam رَضِیَ اللهُ عَنْهُ 158
Make Salām to Shaykhayn رَضِیَ اللهُ عَنْهُمَا together 159
Make following Du'ās 160
12 Madanī pearls....................160
Recite near Golden Grille....................162
Don't turn your back towards Golden Grille for Du'ā 162
Reward of fifty thousand I'tikāf....................162
Reward of five Hajj daily....................163
Say Salām orally 163
Old woman blessed with grand vision....................164
Await expectantly! 164
A Memon Ḥājī blessed with seeing the Holy Prophet ﷺ 165
Do not spit in sacred streets....................165
Jannat-ul-Baqī' 165
Salām to those buried in Jannat-ul-Baqī' 166
Broken heart....................166
Farewell visit....................167
Al-Wada' Yā Rasūlallāĥ ﷺ 167
Al-Wadā' Tājdār-e-Madīnaĥ....................168
Ziyārāt (holy sites) in Makka-tul-Mukarramaĥ 169
Birthplace of Holy Prophet ﷺ 169
Jabal Abū Qubays....................169
House of Khadīja-tul-Kubrā رَضِیَ اللهُ عَنْهَا 170
Cave of Jabal Šaur....................171
Cave of Ḥirā....................171
Dār-ul-Arqam....................172
Masfalaĥ 172
Jannat-ul-Ma'lā....................172

Masjid Jinn 173
Masjid-ur-Rāyaĥ 173
Masjid Khayf 173
Masjid Ji'irrānaĥ 174
Tomb of Sayyidatunā Maymūnaĥ رَضِیَ اللهُ عَنۡهَا 175
11 places in Masjid-ul-Ḥarām where Holy Prophet ﷺ offered Ṣalāĥ . 175

Ziyārāt [holy sites] in Madīna-tul-Munawwaraĥ 177
Orchard of Jannaĥ 177
Masjid Qubā 177
Reward of 'Umraĥ 177
Grave of Sayyidunā Ḥamzaĥ رَضِیَ اللهُ عَنۡهُ 178
Excellence of making Salām to martyrs of Uḥud 178
Salām in court of Sayyidunā Ḥamzaĥ رَضِیَ اللهُ عَنۡهُ 178
Collective Salām to martyrs of Uḥud 179
How to visit these holy sites? 180

Offences and their Expiations 181

Definition of Dam etc. 181
Leniency in Dam etc 181
Important rulings regarding *Dam*, Ṣadaqaĥ and fasts 182
Rulings for sacrifice of Hajj and meat of animal of Dam 182
Fear Allah عَزَّوَجَلَّ 183
Double expiation for Qārin 184
Details of double expiation for Qārin 184
Questions and answers about Ṭawāf-uz-Ziyāraĥ 187
Ṭawāf-uz-Ziyāraĥ of menses-experiencing woman whose flight is booked 189
Very important point about intention of Ṭawāf 191

Questions and answers about Ṭawāf-ur-Rukhṣat 192
Important ruling of Ṭawāf-ur-Rukhṣat 192
Miscellaneous questions and answers about Ṭawāf 193
Raising hands when uttering Takbīr of Ṭawāf 194
What if one forgets the rounds during Ṭawāf? 194
What if the Wuḍū invalidates during Ṭawāf? 194
Important ruling of Ṭawāf for Ma'żūr Shar'ī 195
Ruling for Nafl Ṭawāf performed by woman experiencing menses. 196
Ruling of performing Ṭawāf on the first or second floor of Masjid-ul-Ḥarām 197
How is it to recite Munājāt aloud during Ṭawāf 197
Questions and answers about Iḍṭibā' and Raml 198
Questions and answers about Sa'ī 199
Questions and answers about kissing and caressing 200
An important question 201
Walking hand in hand with wife 202
Questions and answers about intercourse 202
Questions and answers about cutting nails 204
Questions and answers about removal of hair 205
Questions and answers about use of perfume 208
Use of fragrant soap in the state of Iḥrām 213
Muḥrim and rose-garlands 214
Questions and answers about wearing stitched clothes etc. 217
Questions and answers about using tissue paper in the state of Iḥrām. 219
Question and answer about ritual stay in 'Arafāt 223
Question and answer about ritual stay in Muzdalifaĥ 223
Question and answer about Ramī 223
Questions and answers about ritual sacrifice 224

Questions and answers about Ḥalq and Taqṣīr 225
Miscellaneous questions and answers....................226
How is it to put on Iḥrām after the sunset of 13th Żul-Ḥijja-til-Ḥarām 229

HAJJ AKBAR....................233

Guidance for those working in Arab 233
Ḥīlaĥ for not putting on Iḥrām....................234
How is it to ask for financial help for Hajj or 'Umraĥ?....................235
How is it to overstay for Hajj on 'Umraĥ-Visa?....................236
Ruling for the Ṣalāĥ of illegal stayer....................237
To cause discomfort to pigeons and locusts in Ḥaram....................238
Cutting trees of Ḥaram 241
Question and answer about passing Mīqāt without Iḥrām....................243

HAJJ OF CHILDREN....................244

Excellence of Ṣalāt-'Alan-Nabī ﷺ 244
Method of immature child's Hajj....................246
Method of intention and Labbayk on behalf of an immature child. 248
Method of Istilām of Ḥajar-ul-Aswad and intention of Ṭawāf on behalf of an immature child....................249
Method of a child's 'Umraĥ....................251
Child and Nafli Ṭawāf 251
Child and paying visit to the Rauḍah-e-Anwar 253

♦♦♦

Glossary....................254
Bibliography 258
Index....................261